Self-Determination Movement in Manipur

About the Centre

Conflict and Human Rights Studies Network, Manipur is a network of academicians and scholars dedicated to the study of conflict originating from armed struggle and others, and related human rights issues in the Northeast India. The network strives to fill up the gap between academicians and human rights activists to bring about peaceful resolution to the ongoing armed-conflict in the region.

Activities of the Network

A. Publication

(i) Annexation of Manipur 1949, Forwards Books: New Delhi 2014.

(ii) United Nations and The Human Rights in Manipur, Forwards Books: New Delhi (2013).

B. Seminar

Two Days National Seminar on "Singularity of India: Integration, Homogenization and Racism" held at Classic Hotel, Imphal on January 28–29, 2013.

C. Exhibition

International Photo Exhibition, Women and Armed Conflict in Manipur, at Second International Conference on Human Rights and Peace and Conflict in Southeast Asia held at the Millennium Hotel Sirih at Jakarta, Indonesia on 17-18 October, 2012.

Upcoming Activities:

(i) Publication of Horizon: A Journal of Cross Disciplinary Studies (Bi-Annual International Journal).

(ii) Publication of working papers.

Secretariat:
Centre for Manipur Studies, Manipur University
Canchipur, Imphal-795008, INDIA

About the Editors

Aheibam Koireng Singh is Assistant Professor, Centre for Manipur Studies, Manipur University. He received his doctoral degree from Manipur University, Canchipur and specializes on the studies of ethnicity and inter-community conflicts. He can be reached at <akoireng@gmail.com>.

Shukhdeba Sharma Hanjabam is Assistant Professor of Social Work, the Indira Gandhi National Tribal University, Regional-Campus, Manipur. He received his doctoral degree from the Tata Institute of Social Sciences, Mumbai and specializes in human rights and conflict transformation especially in the context of the North East India. He can be reached at <hanjabam@gmail.com>.

Homen Thangjam is Assistant Professor of Political Science, the Maharaja Bodhchandra College, Imphal. He received his doctoral degree from the Jawaharlal Nehru University, New Delhi and specializes in democratization theories and conflict transformation. He can be reached at <homenth@gmail.com>.

Self-Determination Movement in Manipur

Edited By

Aheibam Koireng Singh
Shukhdeba Sharma Hanjabam
Homen Thangjam

Published for

Conflict and Human Rights Studies Network, Manipur

by

CONCEPT PUBLISHING COMPANY PVT. LTD.
NEW DELHI-110059

ISBN-13: 978-93-5125-097-5 (HB)

First Published 2015

Published and Printed by

Concept Since 1974

Concept Publishing Company Pvt. Ltd.
A/15-16, Commercial Block, Mohan Garden
New Delhi-110059 (India)
T : 25351460, 25351794, *F* : 091-11-25357109
E: publishing@conceptpub.com, W: www.conceptpub.com
Editorial Office: H-13, Bali Nagar, New Delhi-110 015, India.

Cataloging in Publication Data—*Courtesy:* D.K. Agencies (P) Ltd. <docinfo@dkagencies.com>

Self-determination movement in Manipur / edited by Aheibam Koireng Singh, Shukhdeba Sharma Hanjabam, Homen Thangjam.
pages cm
Includes bibliographical references and index.
ISBN 9789351250975 (H.B)
ISBN 9789351251248 (P.B)

1. Manipur (India)—History—Autonomy and independence movements. 2. Self-determination, National—India—Manipur. 3. Manipur (India)—Politics and government. I. Singh, Aheibam Koireng, editor. II. Hanjabam, Shukhdeba Sharma, 1983-, editor. III. Thangjam, Homen, editor. IV. Conflict and Human Rights Studies Network (Manipur, India)issuing body.

DDC 954.17 23

Preface

The concern for right to self-determination is primarily embedded in the issue of human rights. Human rights are universal in content. The right to self-determination, a fundamental principle of human rights law, is an individual and collective right to "freely determine... political status and [to] freely pursue... economic, social and cultural development". The International Court of Justice (ICJ) refers to the right to self-determination as a right held by people rather than a right held by governments alone. The right to self-determination is a right which reflects the importance given to communities, collectives and families in many societies and the general inherent communal quality of humans. The purpose of the protection of this right is to enable these communities as communities to prosper and transmit their culture as well as participate fully in the political, economic and social processes, thus allowing the distinct character of a community "to have this character reflected in the institutions of government under which it lives". It also forms part of the empowering process of human rights. The right to self-determination is indisputably the highest rules of international law and they must be strictly obeyed at all times. Both the International Court of Justice and the Inter-America Commission on Human Rights of Organisation of American States have ruled on cases in a way that supports the view that the principle of self-determination also has the legal status of obligations of a State owed to the international community as a whole, the international community is under a mandatory duty to respect it in all circumstances in their relations with each other. But despite notable recognition of the right to self-determination, there is still a great deal of disagreement among states, and among international scholars, as to the scope and parameters of the right to self-determination, as well as *who*, exactly, is entitled to such a right.

At a time when India had just become independent after long British colonial rule, there were only three principalities in the Northeast—Assam, Tripura and Manipur. Much before the first general election to be held in India in the year 1952, elections on the basis of secret ballot and universal adult franchise for the 53-member assembly was held in Manipur in 1948 for the first time in the history of Indian subcontinent. And an elected assembly took oath of office in September of the same year which set into motion a historic tryst with democratic governance. However, Manipur's right to self-determination was violated and sabotaged with the merger of Manipur to India following the signing of Merger agreement under contentious circumstances. Consequent upon signing the Merger Agreement, the administration of Manipur was taken over by the Dominion of the Government of India. Much to the misfortune of Manipur, instead of allowing its elected legislature and newly borne democracy to grow, it was unceremoniously replaced by bureaucratic rule under a non-local, Chief Commissioner handpicked by New Delhi, who exercised both executive and legislative powers. The contentious merger was resisted through an armed movement led by legendary leader Hijam Irabot. His idea of an independent Manipur was endorsed by the people of Manipur at a public meeting on 3rd August, 1949. After Irabot's death in 1951, the legacy of the movement for exercising right to self-determination was kept alive and continues to sustain till date. Since the late sixties of the passing twentieth century, Manipur had witnessed the sprouting of armed self-determination movements.

Two important studies of the United Nations on the right to self-determination set out—a history of Independence or self-rule in an identifiable territory; a distinct culture; and a will and capacity to regain self-governance as factors that give rise to possession of right to self-determination by a group. This present volume examines whether Manipur fulfils the criteria of possessing the right to self-determination set out by United Nations and other internationally accepted benchmark. It also dwelt on the erstwhile sovereign and pre-merger (to India) times of Manipur and the changes in her political status after becoming an integral part of India.

The opening chapter titled ***Revisiting the Idea of Right of the People to Self-Determination*** by Homen Thangjam traces the historical evolution of self-determination and argues that it remains an inviolable and most fundamental right of the people even in the contemporary times. Further, it argues that it cannot be misplaced as an idea that should be totally accommodated within the liberal republican discourse of rights, nationalism, and the European nation-state system. Such an understanding can throw new perspective on various self-determination movements witnessed today across the globe by a subjugated nation or colonized population to establish a sovereign, independent state—to secede from a multinational state or to dissolve colonial ties of dependency to an imperial "mother country". Perceived cognizance given to the fact that imperialism and colonialism has ended by the 1970s, and thus, the need for reconceptualising term stands under scrutiny given the fact that many nations continue to exist as colonies. Reconceptualization of the term has sidelined the issue of secession. This is witnessed in the invocation of the term in support of demands for local autonomy or self-government at the sub-state level as a means to preserve the culture or safeguard the security of national or aboriginal minorities. And even, many social movement activists (particularly proponents of a post-modernist "politics of identity") that seeks to invest the principle with a much looser meaning furthermore, dilutes the cause of the subjugated nation or colonized (including neo-colonialism as a corollary of globalization) population.

The second chapter titled ***Problem of 1949 Annexation of Manipur***, by *Naorem Sanajaoba* attempts to address the significant questions and other collaborative issues surrounding the merger of Manipur which remains an inevitable and crucial issue of the land. The questions relate with the political status of Manipur before it became an integral part of India on 15 October, 1949; the legality of Manipur's merger to India as per the existing norms and standards of international law; and any likelihood of Manipur regaining its pre-merger political status. It also examines the appropriateness of the Government of India's stand that the issue of Manipur falls within the sovereignty of India, and that any individual or country have no right to interfere in its internal affairs. It consistently maintains that Manipur enjoyed a sovereign status by 15 August, 1945 and became a sovereign people's republic before being eventually annexed by India. As regards the legality of the merger, the chapter construes it to be illegal and void as no reasons could be found to say that a treaty/instrument signed by a mere titular monarch as valid and binding. So, that is a wrong, illegal document. Concerning the regaining of the lost pre-merger political status of Manipur, it testifies that UN system does not allow and permit 'aggression' and 'annexation' and even resorts to power to stop aggression and annexation if it becomes inevitable

The third chapter titled ***Integration or Annexation? Manipur's Relations with India 1947-1949*** by John Parratt and Arambam Saroj Nalini Paratt which constitutes the second chapter of this volume re-examine the circumstances and implications of absorption into the Indian Union. It premises that a number of the factors which were advanced half a century ago to justify the takeover of Manipur, now look increasingly unconvincing. Sardar Patel's theory of a common Aryan blood as a uniting bond for the Indian subcontinent simply does not apply in much of the north-east, which is ethnically, linguistically, and culturally quite distinct. The supposed Communist threat in Manipur was grossly (and possibly deliberately) exaggerated, and the other insurgency movements were in the main a direct result of Indian annexation. The claim by the Union Government that Manipur suffered from underdevelopment was probably true, though most Manipuris would argue that since 1949 it has remained neglected and grossly underfunded, with much of its resources being used to fund the wholly counterproductive presence of Indian security forces. But more important has been the questioning on the part of Manipuri intellectuals of the whole legality of the merger. The chapter exhorts that independent India, which proclaimed its dedication to democracy, wilfully refused to recognize the democratically elected government of Manipur, and instead persisted in dealing with the former feudal ruler, who himself repeatedly protested that he had surrendered his power to the elected Assembly. Furthermore, Manipur was not a petty state surrounded by Indian territory, but a border state more akin to Sikkim and Kashmir. It is difficult to deny the force of these arguments, and to resist the conclusion that the Union Government, in its desperation to expand its borders, simply annexed Manipur.

The fourth chapter titled ***Narratives of Self-Determination Struggles in Manipur*** by Lokendra Arambam concludes by drawing the attention of the international community as well as lovers of peace and humanity, with a sense of urgency, to consider the issues of *'armed conflict'* that is prevailing in Manipur and the Northeast and deeply ponder over the resistance by minority nationalities for over four decades, in spite of the unequal balance of forces and departures by the state from the international principles of proportion. It also emphasizes the inevitable necessity for the Government of India to accept that there is *'armed conflict'* in the region under international paradigms of understanding the phenomenon. That the dissident forces are well organized groups with capabilities and commitments to international codes and conducts of war and are still holding on to precious unreported areas in the territory of conflict, withstanding the armed might of one of the strongest military powers of Asia. That since the conflict has been on for the last forty years, one should take first steps for minimization of violence, especially over the bodies of civilians and non-combatants through the humanitarian intervention of the International Committee of the Red Cross and Red Crescent in Northeast India. International intervention under the *'Responsibility to Protect'* on issues of human security should be given more teeth, rather than leaving it as wishful thinking since respect for state sovereignty seems to be the abiding principle of international relations. But when the principles of state sovereignty is challenged and questioned on its basic foundations, other paradigms of conflict study and analysis are called forth for understanding and resolving problems of dignity and distributive justice, it concluded.

The fifth chapter titled ***Manipuri People's Right to Self-Determination*** by Shukhdeba S. Hanjabam, focuses on armed conflict demanding right to self-determination (RSD) that has developed in Manipur since 1949. It analyses the legitimacy of the claims for demanding right to self-determination by the Manipuri people in the light of the guidelines of the United Nations for exercising the right to self-determination. The guidelines being—(i) a history of Independence or self-rule in an identifiable territory, (ii) a distinct culture, and (iii) a will and capacity to regain self-governance. It concludes that Manipuri people fulfil all the three criteria for exercising RSD.

The seventh and concluding chapter titled ***The Manipur Nation: A Position*** by Centre for Organisation Research and Education (CORE) is a compilation based on various sources— government, non-government, media, official and people's archival materials, etc. It comes with a rider that views and opinions expressed in this chapter are not necessarily those of the CORE or any of its members. The chapter starts with Leishemba's quotation, "*We had our independence for thousands of years, but our sovereignty was forcibly removed in 1949. So, our people are very eager to have their sovereignty again. It is our genuine demand and one day, I hope, we will be successful. Armed struggle is not the best way, but it is one of the ways.*" The chapter in its final concluding words writes, "*if Leisemba's words* *are to come true, the future of the Manipur Nation itself may need to be viewed through a more enlightened framework that would include the current perceptions of its peoples and the international community, and not just base itself on narrow orthodox legalist model that may be already soon in disuse.*"

Annexures are also incorporated to enrich the present volume with reliable material source.

Contents

Acknowledgements

We are thankful to

(i) Editor, Gandhi Marg, Gandhi Peace Foundation, for the permission to reproduce, "Right to Self-Determination and the People of Manipur", Gandhi Marg, New Delhi, Vol. 32, No. 4, January-March, 2011.

(ii) CORE for the permission to reproduce "The Manipur Nation: A Position".

(iii) Kanglaonline for the permission to reproduce, "Integration or Annexation? Manipur's Relations with India 1947-1949".

List of Tables and Figures

List of Tables

List of Figures

Acronyms

ADC	=	Aide de Camp
AFSPA	=	Armed Forces Special Powers Act
AM	=	Ante Meredian
CATS	=	Covert Apprehension Technique
COIN	=	Counter-insurgency operations
CIDCM	=	Centre for International Development and Conflict Management
CPI	=	Communist Party of India
DSCO	=	Doctrine of Sub Conventional Operations
HH	=	His Highness
ICC	=	International Criminal Court
ICCPR	=	International Covenant for Civil and Political Rights
ICJ	=	International Court of Justice
KCSI	=	Knight Commander Star of India
KIA	=	Kachin Independence Army
MAR	=	Minority at Risk
MLA	=	Member Legislative Assembly
MSA	=	Manipur State Assembly
NE	=	North East

NGO	=	Non Governmental Organisation
NIA	=	National Investigation Agency
NSCN (IM)	=	National Socialist Council of Nagaland (Isaac Muivah)
NSCN (K)	=	National Socialist Council of Nagaland (Khaplang)
PLA	=	People's Liberation Army
PM	=	Prime Meredian
PREPAK	=	People's Revolutionary Party of Kangleipak
RPF	=	Revolutionary People's Front
UK	=	United Kingdom
UN	=	United Nations
UNPO	=	Unrepresented Nations and Peoples Organisation
UNLF	=	United National Liberation Front
WHAM	=	Winning the Hearts and Minds of People

Notes on Contributors

Centre for Organisation Research and Education (CORE) is in Special Consultative Status with the Economic and Social Council of the United Nations since 2005. CORE's main focus is documentation of human rights abuses and advocacy for indigenous peoples' rights in the North East region of India cantered in Imphal the capital of Manipur. Our work revolves around instances of trauma and torture, summary or extrajudicial execution, violations of indigenous rights, land rights, development rights, right to self- determination, as well as unjust evictions and environmental and cultural destruction. We also operate the the Human to Humane Transcultural Centre for Torture and Trauma (H2H), an independent health and humanitarian service that provides counselling and support for survivors of Torture in Manipur, India.

Mission of CORE: "Working towards the recognition and respect for the right to a self-determined future in partnership with the Indigenous Peoples of the North Eastern Region of India, with respect for our ancient inheritance, building on our faith in humanity's role of trusteeship of our natural resources, in peace with all other peoples."

It can be contacted at http://coremanipur.org/

Homen Thangjam, See about the editors.

John Parratt, was previously Professor of Third World Theologies at the University of Birmingham. He has taught and researched extensively in Africa and the Pacific, and also in Manipur. He is the author of numerous books on the interaction of religion, culture and politics in the developing world. He has also edited *Notes on Meithei (Manipuri) Customs and Beliefs* by J.C. Higgins (Ministry of Arts and Culture, Imphal 1998) and published *Wounded Land: Politics and Identity in Modern Manipur* (Delhi, 2005). and ***Arambam Saroj Nalini Parratt*** (1933-2009), wife of John Parratt, was born in Imphal, Manipur, and studied at the Universities of Calcutta and London. She obtained her doctorate from the Australian National University. From 1975-90 she taught at institutions in southern Africa, including the universities of Malawi and Botswana. She lectured at several universities in Africa and was an honorary professor of Manipur University in 2001. At the time of her death she was an honorary research fellow of the Institute for Textual Scholarship and Electronic Editing at the University of Birmingham. Her books include *The Religion of Manipur* (Calcutta, 1980), and *The Court Chronicle of the Kings of Manipur*, original text, translation and notes, Vol. 1 (London and Delhi, 2005), Vol. 2 (Delhi, 2009). *John Parratt and Arambam Saroj Nalini Parratt* has jointly co-authored *Queen Empress vs. Tikendrajit, the Anglo-Manipur Conflict of 1891* (Delhi, 1992) and *The Pleasing of the Gods, Meitei Lai Haraoba* (Delhi, 1997).

Lokendra Arambam, noted scholar and eminent theatre Director, is formerly Director of Audio Visual Research Centre (AVRC), Manipur University. He was awarded his doctoral degree in 1996 on the Cultural History of the Meiteis of Manipur. He was a visiting Professional Fellow at the School of Arts and Aesthetics J.N.U. in 2005, 2013, and also a visiting faculty at the Department of History at Manipur in 2007. He led the Manipur delegations to the International Festivals in Italy in 1988 and 1990, in India and China in 1994. He did workshops on Manipur Martial Arts at London and Dusseldorf in 1988. He took dance scholars to Southeast Asia (Yogyakarta, Bali, Bangkok, and Chiangmai) for studies of use of performing arts for deepening democracy under the Ford Foundation sponsorship in 2008. He was the Artistic Director of Ford Foundation project entitled "50 Years of Celebrations in Northeast India organizing performances on the Brahmaputra River in 2002. These also included international production staging Manipur Macbeth on the Thames River of London in 1997, the production of the International Fusion Dance Workshop and Symposium on Inter-cultural Dialogue between Northeast India, and Southeast Asia at Guwahati and New Delhi in 2010, and the staging of the India Indigenous Theatre Festival at Guwahati and New Delhi in 2011. Aside from his being a theatre person, Dr. Lokendra is also a scholar.

He wrote articles for national seminar on aspects of Manipur theatre, culture, and folklore. He contributed a chapter in the Oxford Companion to Indian Theatre 2004 (ed. Dr. Anand Lal), and also in the Padatik publication of Indian Performing Arts RASA under Dr. Anand Lal in 1995. Presented papers on Manipur Dances at the World Dance Alliance International Dance Conference organized by the University of Malaya at Kuala Lumpur 2011. But aside from his being an academic, a scholar and his being a theatre actor, playwright and director, Dr. Lokendra Arambam is also a human rights and a peace advocate.

He can be contacted at lokendra.arambam@gmail.com

Naorem Sanajaoba (1945-2009), born in Manipur, formerly a Dean and Head, School of Law, Gauhati University is a human-rights defender since early 1960s, active campaigner against colonialism of all forms, racism, fascism and virulent casteism. He taught Human Rights, International Humanitarian Laws, Legal Philosophy and Jurisprudence, Administrative Law in the PG Department of Law as a founder-teacher since 1976 in the University of Gauhati, India. He subscribes to critical theory and critical movements in legal philosophy. Some of his important works are: *Manipur: Past and Present: History, Polity and Law (Vol. I); Manipur: Past and Present: Philosophy, Culture and Literature (Vol. II); Manipur: Past and Present: Naga and Kuki Chin (Vol. III); Manipur: Past and Present: The Ordeals and Heritage of a Civilization Volume Pan Manipuris (Vol. IV); Rights of Oppressed Nation (1996); Human Rights Principles and Abuses (1994); Human Rights in the New Millennium* (2000); *Industrial Tribunal Working, Procedure, Judicial Trends; Socio-legal Problems and Developing Society; Law and Society: Strategy for Policy Choice 2001; Current Legal Essays: Humanitarian and Federal Issues, International Human Rights (Set of 3 Vols); Manipur: A British Anthology: State and Country (2 Vols-Set); A Manual of International Humanitarian Laws, Manual of International Humanitarian Laws.*

Shukhdeba S. Hanjabam, See about the editors.

CHAPTER – 1

Revisiting the Idea of Right of the People to Self-Determination

Homen Thangjam

Introduction

Self-determination, in the most general sense, refers to the capacity to control one's own destiny, free of interference by others. The ideological or philosophical roots are often traced back to the American and French revolutions.[1] This chapter while tracing the historical evolution of the idea of the term, argues that it remains an inviolable and most fundamental rights of the people even in the contemporary times and cannot be totally misplaced as an idea that should be accommodated within the republican understanding of the term. Such an understanding can throw new perspective on various self-determination movements witnessed today across the globe by subjugated nations or colonized population to establish a sovereign, independent state – to secede from a multinational state or to dissolve colonial ties of dependency to an imperial "mother country". Perceived cognizance given to the fact that imperialism and colonialism has ended by the 1970s, and thus, the need for reconceptualizing term stands under scrutiny given the fact that many nations continue to exist as colonies. Reconceptualization of the term has sidelined the issue of secession or liberation. This is witnessed in the invocation of the term in the most minimal sense as support of demands for local autonomy or self-government at the sub-state level as a means to preserve the culture or safeguard the security of national or aboriginal minorities. And even, many social movement activists (particularly proponents of a post-modernist "politics of identity") that seeks to invest the principle with a much looser meaning furthermore, dilutes the cause of the subjugated nation or colonized (including neo-colonialism as a corollary of globalization) population.

Liberal Theses on Right to Self-determination

Woodrow Wilson, in his Self-determination Speech delivered on February 11, 1918, consequent to announcement of Fourteen Points on January 8, 1918, remarked, "National aspirations must be respected; people may now be dominated and governed only by their own consent. Self-determination is not a mere phrase; it is an imperative principle of action." Jan Klabbers remarks that in spite of the enthusiasm expressed by Wilson there was already countervailing opinions, for example as provided by Robert Lansing, Wilson's own secretary of state. If Wilson's Fourteen Points marked the birth of a new doctrine in international law, then Lansing's critique already ensured that the delivery was not without complications.[2]

This observation reveals two interesting yet opposite sides of self-determination current in the liberal discourse. First aspect is that it appeals to our senses of democracy and subsidiary: government by and for the people. As Isaiah Berlin stated people would rather be ruled by a dictator from their midst than "by some cautious, just, gentle, well-meaning administrator from outside."[3] And this finds its source, so Berlin suggested, in our desire to be recognized as free and, somehow, authentic humans, being governed from the outside would imply being less than fully free and, therewith, being less than fully human. This is the democratic appeal and main attraction of the right to self-determination.

The second aspect is the problem associated with self-determination. It tends to stimulate instability and disorder. Self-determination, while a beacon of hope to oppressed people, becomes subversive when regarded from other perspectives, eventually favouring a breakup of states over other modes of settlement and coexistence. This difficulty or rather fear emanates from the security and integrity of the modern nation states, whose advent was predicated on the prior emergence of such defining features of capitalist modernity as the discourse on rights, the ideology of nationalism, and the European nation-state system.

The nation-building projects of modern European states were undertaken to strengthen their positions relative to major rivals and often involved attempts to unify and homogenize the population within the borders of the nation-state, usually through coerced assimilation or "ethnic cleansing" (including forced population transfers and genocide in some circumstances). For several of the major European powers, it also involved the conquest and colonial subjugation of other, far-flung territories and peoples with the aim of consolidating empires whose purpose was to enrich and empower the imperial nation-state or "mother country". Political domination, military subjugation, and economic exploitation of colonies stimulated the emergence of anti-imperialist movements and nationalist projects within colonized populations otherwise divided along tribal, religious, and linguistic lines.

Self-Determination Movements

Independence struggles by the colonial possessions of the major imperial powers began long before the term self-determination came into use. The first such struggle was waged against Britain by several of its "settler colonies" in North America, and its success resulted in the founding of the United States of America in 1776. Encouraged by revolutionary events in France, the people of Haiti rose up against French rule in the 1790s, eventually establishing an independent republic in 1804. By the late nineteenth century, Spain had lost most of its colonial possessions in the Americas. The success of these New World independence struggles heightened the nationalist aspirations of subjugated nationalities in the multinational states—the Austro-Hungarian, Ottoman, and Russian empires—that dominated much of Eurasia and the Middle East prior to World War I.

Within the imperial nations themselves, few supported the right to self-determination of national minorities at home or colonized peoples abroad. The major exception before 1914 was the international socialist movement. Thus, Karl Marx argued that English wage workers could never achieve their emancipation as a class so long as they remained complicit in the national oppression of the Irish. At its 1896 Congress, the Marxist Second International adopted a resolution affirming the right of all nations to self-determination.

In Russia, Vladimir Lenin saw the aspirations of the oppressed nationalities of what he called the czarist "prison house of peoples" as integral to the broader struggle for democracy, insisting that the only way to forge working-class unity across national lines was to combat "great Russian chauvinism" and recognize the right of Ukrainians, Georgians, and other nationalities to establish their own independent states. However, Lenin distinguished between recognizing the right to self-determination and actually advocating independence. The right to self-determination, he wrote, is similar to the right to divorce; one can affirm the right without advising the action. After the victory of the Bolshevik Revolution in 1917, Lenin established the right of nations to self-determination as a fundamental programmatic plank of the Third (Communist) International, advocating national liberation struggles in the colonial world and waging an unsuccessful, deathbed struggle against the Russian chauvinist policies of Joseph Stalin and his acolytes in 1923. The subsequent consolidation of bureaucratic rule under Stalin transformed the Soviet Union into a Russian-dominated multinational state in which the right of the constituent, nationally based republics to secede was extinguished.

At the end of World War I, the principle of national self-determination found a new ostensible champion in the American president Woodrow Wilson, acquiring currency, for the first time, in liberal political discourse. "'Self-determination' is not a mere phrase," Wilson declared in 1918, "it is an imperative principle of action which statesmen will henceforth ignore at their peril".[4] But Wilson soon qualified his support for the idea, recognizing the dangers that the principle could pose to European stability. Subsequently, U.S. advocacy of the right of national self-determination proved inconsistent. After World War II, the United Nations, under American leadership, upheld a principle of international law that affirmed the right of colonies to independence from overseas empires but that recognized no right of secession for national minorities within established states.

In the post-World War II era, formal political independence was achieved by the great majority of former colonies in Africa, Asia, and the Western Hemisphere, opening the way, in most cases, to their neocolonial economic and political subjugation by the great powers. However, the demand for self-determination continued to be vigorously asserted by Northern Irish Republicans and Scots in the United Kingdom, Québécois in Canada, Basques in Spain, Tamils in Sri Lanka, and by many would-be nationalist movements operating within the hundreds and perhaps thousands of "imagined communities" that had defined themselves as nations. Under the watchword of self-determination, the 1990s saw the rapid breakup of the Soviet Union and the Yugoslav federation and the emergence of a plethora of new nation-states in Europe and Asia. The dispossessed status of the Palestinian people, resulting from the creation of the state of Israel in 1948 and the consolidation of a Hebrew-speaking nation on territory claimed by both Jews and Palestinians as a homeland, remains an intractable national problem at the beginning of the twenty-first century. Here the question arises: Under what conditions can two "interpenetrated peoples" reconcile their mutually conflicting claims to self-determination?

The UN Charter

In 1941 Allies of World War II signed the Atlantic Charter and accepted the principle of self-determination. In January 1942 twenty-six states signed the Declaration by United Nations, which accepted those principles. The ratification of the United Nations Charter in 1945 at the end of World War II placed the right of self-determination into the framework of international law and diplomacy.

Chapter 1, Article 1, part 2 states that purpose of the UN Charter is: "To develop friendly relations among nations based on respect for the principle of equal rights and self-determination of peoples, and to take other appropriate measures to strengthen universal peace."

Article 1 in both the International Covenant on Civil and Political Rights (ICCPR) and the International Covenant on Economic, Social and Cultural Rights (ICESCR). Both read: "All peoples have the right of self-determination. By virtue of that right they freely determine their political status and freely pursue their economic, social and cultural development."

The United Nations Universal Declaration of Human Rights article 15 states that everyone has the right to a nationality and that no one should be arbitrarily deprived of a nationality or denied the right to change nationality.

However, the charter and other resolutions did not insist on full independence as the best way of obtaining self-government, nor did they include an enforcement mechanism. Moreover, new states were recognized by the legal doctrine of *uti possidetis juris*, meaning that old administrative boundaries would become international boundaries upon independence even if they had little relevance to linguistic, ethnic, and cultural boundaries. Nevertheless, justified by the language of self-determination, between 1946 and 1960, the peoples of thirty-seven new nations freed themselves from colonial status in Asia, Africa, and the Middle East. The territoriality issue inevitably would lead to more conflicts and independence movements within many states and challenges to the assumption that territorial integrity is as important as self-determination.

Self-Determination and the Politics of Identity

The radical ferment of the 1960s inspired a much looser definition of the concept of self-determination, such that it was often used to describe the aspirations of any group confronting putatively oppressive treatment. The original impetus to this redefinition was provided by the 1960s Black Power movement in the United States. Reacting against the liberal, integrationist perspective of the mainstream Civil Rights movement, many African American activists (notably Malcolm X, Stokely Carmichael, and the Black Panthers) embraced black nationalism. Having defined African Americans as an "oppressed nation" or as an "internal colony" (however problematically), these activists proclaimed the right of the black population to various forms of "self-determination"—sometimes through proposals for "separation" from "White America" but more commonly through demands for "black control of the black community." It is notable that few of these schemes were implemented—their most enduring legacy probably being black studies programmes in higher education.

The stage was thus set for the emergence of a decidedly amorphous notion of self-determination, one with which other marginalized or oppressed sectors could easily identify. The concept was also extended to notions of "empowering" individual victims of abuse or poverty through community organizing. Self-determination merged with the broader notion of "liberation" and was invoked by activists who championed not only the rights but also the unique identities of racial and ethnic minorities, women,mp: gays, and the disabled. Indeed, for many advocates of a post-modern "politics of identity," self-determination became virtually synonymous with unfettered expression of sectoral identity based not only on nationality but on gender, race, or sexual orientation as well.

NOTES

1. For a brief standard overview, see David Raic, *Statehood and the Law of Self-Determination* (2002), pp. 172-77.
2. Jan Klabbers, "The Right to Be Taken Seriously: Self-Determination in International Law", *Human Rights Quarterly*, Vol. 28, No. 1, February, 2006), pp. 186-87, (pp. 186-206). Robert Lansing observed that it is an evil thing to permit the principle of self-determination to continue to have the apparent sanction of the nations when it has been in fact thoroughly discredited and will always be cast aside whenever it comes in conflict with national safety, with historic political rights, or with national economic interests affecting the prosperity of a nation.
3. Isaiah Berlin, "Two Concepts of Liberty", in Isaiah Berlin (ed.), *Four Essays on Liberty*, 1969, pp. 157-58.
4. Moynihan, D.P. *Pandaemonium: Ethnicity in International Politics*. Oxford: Oxford University Press. 1994, pp.78-79.

BIBLIOGRAPHY

Anderson, Benedict. 2006. *Imagined Communities: Reflections on the Origin and Spread of Nationalism*. Rev. ed. London and New York: Verso.

Hobsbawm, Eric J. 1992. *Nations and Nationalism since 1780*. 2nd ed. Cambridge, U.K. and New York: Cambridge University Press.

Lenin, V.I. [1914] 1977. *The Right of Nations to Self-Determination: Selected Writings*. Westport, CT: Greenwood Press.

Löwy, Michael. 1998. *Fatherland or Mother Earth?: Essays on the National Question*. London and Sterling, VA: Pluto Press.

Moynihan, D.P. 1994. *Pandaemonium: Ethnicity in International Politics*. Oxford: Oxford University Press.

CHAPTER – 2

Problem of 1949 Annexation of Manipur*

Naorem Sanajaoba

In these recent few years, the intelligentsias have started giving their attention, and discussing on the issue that Manipur had forcibly been merged in the year 1949. In addition to it, there has been uninterrupted public curfew on 15 October every year since 1991. According to the official press release issued by the state, Manipur had been merged to India with the willingness of the masses.[1] However, according to the newspapers which reflect the voice of the people, bandh had been organized with the overwhelming participation of the masses. *Hindustan Times*, a leading national English newspaper, dated 19 April 1993 had on its featured news item titled, "Tact needed to assuage anger in Manipur" stated—"And according to report, it (*bandh*) was such a success that not a single soul stirred out of the houses." It further added, "The immediate Post-Independence euphoria soon gave way to widespread resentment over the Merger issue." Because of all these reasons, the question surrounding the merger of Manipur remains an inevitable and crucial issue of the land.

On this very issue, three very important and significant questions emerge very clearly. They are:

First Question

What is the political status before Manipur became an integral part of India on 15 October, 1949?

---

* Translated by Dr. Aheibam Koireng Singh.

Second Question

Whether the integration or merger of Manipur to India is right or wrong as per the existing norms and standards of International Law?

Third Question

After the merger of Manipur to India, whether there doesn't have any scope for Manipur of regaining its pre-merger political status?

Keeping these three questions in imperative and prime consideration, other corresponding and collaborative issue also emerges. To cite an example—

> How far, the stand taken by the Government of India that, the issue of Manipur falls within the sovereignty of India, any individuals or country have no right to interfere in the internal affairs of the country, is true?

Let me give my understanding in brief on this very big historical and people's question from the perspective of Manipur nation.

Parameters used in this discussion are briefly mentioned because solution, responses, and stances are taken depending on the appropriateness, and rightness and wrongness of the parameter. Let the first pick be from the wrong stance. It is not possible to unearth the truth if the history of Manipur is perceived from the viewpoint/ perspective of British imperialism and *inter alia* legacy. Why? Because, if the parameter and yardstick set by imperialism are used, possibility of having a perspective that transcends beyond imperialism is very remote and almost ruled out. The case of merger of Manipur should be viewed and perceived from the base that the state of Manipur has historically evolved (continuity of state).

Since 1,100 AD (*Sic.* 429 AD, Bogeshwar), both the residents of hills and plains have been cohesively under the political constitution in early state (Manipur) except for some brief spell of trying and testing difficult times.

Writings of L. Oppenheim[2], Max Sorensen[3], J.G. Starke[4], James Crawford[5], Lauterpacht[6], G.I. Tunkin[7] and other UN documents, *Transfer of Power*[8] Vol. I-XII edited by Nicholas Mansergh, E.W.R Lumby, *Accession of States* by V.P. Menon, *The Great Divide: Britain, India, Pakistan*[9] by H.V. Hodson, Philps and Doreen (ed)'s *The*

Partition of India, Nehru's *Discovery of India*, Lapierre's *Freedom at Midnight*, Durga Das' *From Curzon to Nehru*, Philip Ziegler's *Mountbatten* are referred and taken into account of such authoritative and well known sources while discussing the issues of Manipur in the light of ending international law and paramountcy. In addition to it, Maulana Azad's *India wins Freedom*, D.R. Manekar's *Accession to Extinction*, H.M. Seervai's *Partition of India: Legend and Reality*, Wavell's *The Viceroy's Journal*, Bipan Chandra, *et al.* (ed)'s *India's Struggle for Independence*, Stanley Wonpert's *Jinnah of Pakistan*; and from the perspective of Manipur, British Reports, N. Sanajaoba (ed)'s *Manipur: Past and Present* (Vols. I-III), Manipur University publications of contemporary times have been source materials. Let me discuss the issue of Manipur in entirety using the historical documents and various analytical tools. Inevitably, some foreign vocabularies and nomenclatures will be used as it is so as to avoid the controversy surrounding and arising out of the people.

First Issue

In between two world wars (Inter-war period, 1919-1945), the political status of the states was very dynamic and characterised by fluidity. Its stature and level changes and doesn't have a definable static character. To categorise the political status would be next to impossible. The state system that existed before the First World War does not match with the present times as the former was colonial times. A long historical past of imperialism and colonialism has made the matter more complicated and obscured.

British paramountcy is neither colony, it infringes upon the independence of the states under monarchy, terminology which is not recognised by the international law. Because of it, the unfeasibility and impracticality of appropriately categorising the states' status of sovereign and semi-sovereign occurred during the time of paramountcy (Table 2.1).

The political status of Manipur starting from pre-1947 to the year 1972 has been given above in the form of a chart. Firstly, the political status of Manipur in the pre-1947 was not included in the purview of colonialism. This has been treated as true by various colonial sources, Manipuri sources, and other independent sources. Philips Ziegler in his work, *Mountbatten: The Official Biography (1985)* writes, "As the boundaries of British India has gradually extended in the first half of the nineteenth century, an increasing number of princely states had entered into treaty arrangements with the new power, under which they accepted the presence of a British residents in their capitals and a degree of subordination to the Raj, but were not absorbed into the colonial bloc".[10]

Table 2.1: Transformation of Manipur State

Period	*Status of State*	*Order*
Pre 1947*	International Protectorate	1
26 July, 1947	Autonomous State (Constitution adopted)	2
11 August, 1947	Associate state (sovereign within Indian Constitution)	3
15 August, 1947	Sovereign state	4
18 October, 1948	Sovereign People's Republic (Assembly functions)	5
15 October, 1949	Annexed state (Continuous state with suspended sovereignty)	6
January 21, 1972	Constituent state of India (Susp. Sovereignty)	7

Source: Political status of states during the inter-war period (1914-1945) and varied in the comity of nations. Categories altered.

James Crawford, while mentioning about the princely state stated that the native states in the Indian subcontinent are included in the purview of neither the protectorate state nor the colonial protectorate. Their status is same as international protectorate.[11] I, myself, have earlier dwelt sufficiently enough on the issues of Manipur during those days of paramountcy.[12] When the paramountcy came to an end, the state can exercise the option of joining either of the two dominions or remaining independent under particular political arrangement. Congress had persistently tried hard and made all possible efforts to substitute and replace the British paramountcy but the British have firmly taken the stance that it was beyond their jurisdiction.

The issue that needs to be clarified at the first instant is the interpretation of the native state by the Congress did not match and synchronise with interpretation of the British. From the viewpoint of the Congress leadership, states of Moghul, Maratha, and Sikh were very often found to be mentioned as native states. Manipur was never a part of it. Manipur in its historical past and contemporary times also was not mentioned in the "*Blood relation*" state of Sardar Patel. It is viewed from the perspective of the Congress' native state. Manipur belongs to the same category of separate state like Burma, Ceylon (Sri Lanka). Congress has falsely deemed the Indian subcontinent as a continuous state.

Manipur had its own political constitution in the year 1947. By virtue of it, despite being under international protectorate, Manipur became an autonomous state. Since the said constitution was given neither by the British nor by the Congress, the Manipur constitution stands unique and independent outside their political authority. V.P. Menon himself writes that the status of the Manipur state was outside the purview of British India. And in August 1947 also, it was a part of neither India nor Pakistan.[13]

On 11 August, 1947, Manipur after signing the Standstill and Accession Act which accordingly had agreed to hand over the three subjects to the (soon to be realised) Indian confederation remained as Associate State. Granville Austin, while describing the status of the states writes, "Somewhat later (*sic*. after the Cabinet Mission) most of them (states) become loosely attached to the Union Government in a relationship more closely resembling confederation than federalism—although several threatened to remain independent".[14] In the case of independence of the associate state, there has been widespread agreement.

James Crawford writes, "even if foreign affairs, defence and other subjects are handed over to another state, associate state remained independent as it happened to Western Samoa."[15] He further mentioned that associate state can cease to be so basing on the principle of self-determination exercised through the free and genuine expression of the will of the people.[16] In the case of Manipur becoming a case of associate state, the free and genuine expression of the people were bypassed. And also Manipur cannot ceased to be associate state, as no visible initiative is forthcoming from the metropolitan state (India) which would pave way for solutions of issues as Metropolitan state is day by day becoming more and more imperialist.

Keeping this aside, even after accession, the state doesn't lose its independence. It has been very categorically mentioned in the Clauses 7 and 8 of Accession Treaty.

Clause 7 of the Instrument of Accession states:

> "Nothing in this instrument shall be deemed to commit me (Manipur King) in any way to acceptance of any future Constitution of India or to fetter my discretion to enter into arrangements with Government of India under any such future constitution."

Clause 8 states:

> "Nothing in this instrument affects the continuance of my sovereignty in and over this state, or save as provided by or under this instrument, the exercise of any powers, authority and rights now enjoyed by me as ruler of this state."

On 15 August, 1947, the political status was elevated with Manipur becoming a sovereign status. Manipur in actuality became a sovereign peoples' republic when its assembly with its members elected through adult franchise had its session on 18 October, 1948. When an independent Manipur became a part of India, there was a harsh change in the political status of Manipur. India annexed Manipur. The said annexation had been denounced and opposed altogether by the duly elected government of that contemporary time, hills and valley brethren, different parties, leftist movement. Today, it is being continued by organisations spearheading the liberation movement through resistance. During that time, only a fragment of Congressman pleaded for merger of Manipur.[17]

Second Issue

Whether the annexation of Manipur is right or wrong in the benchmark and practices of universally accepted jurisprudence has become a very crucial issue.[18] Instrument of accession, Standstill Agreement, Indian Independence Bill, 1947 did not infringe upon the independence and sovereignty of the state. The Indian Independence Bill, 1947 neither prohibited the state from accession to either of the dominion nor issued any mandate for accession. Instrument of accession also neither leads to devolution or suspension of state continuity. Viceroy Mountbatten took great responsibility in facilitating the accession—it is cited below.

Firstly E.W.F. Lumby writes that the people of London took the acts of Mountbatten concerning accession as very arbitrary and excessive.[19] H.V. Hodson writes that Mountbatten illegally bypasses the Secretary of State and seeks Plenipotentiary Powers.[20] In fact, Mountbatten never gave consideration to the interest of the state.

Secondly, as per laws and norms, when the political department worked for the sovereignty of the state, Mountbatten worked for the accession.[21] As per Sir Conrad Corfield's arrangement, a treaty relation between the state and as the paramountcy is very clear. So, accession before the end of paramountcy was considered as a "Breach of Faith".[22] It is because of this reason that Sir Conrad Cornfield, who holds the Charge of Political Department left his department and fled on 23 July without attending a meeting of kings he called on 25 July, 1947.

Thirdly, concerted effort by Mountbatten to chart out a strategy to thwart and obstruct Communist movement, and to bring in India to the Commonwealth.[23] The strategic importance of Indian ocean charted out by Clement Atlee and the determined effort to fill the void created out of Pakistan with the state's territory. In short, he left no stones unturned and tried his level best for accession so as to serve the long term British interest. In addition to it, Mountbatten had the personal ambition of becoming the first Sea Lord or Governor General of Dominion of India. In fact, it can be said that the personal ambition nursed by Mountbatten falls in the Nehru-Patel-Gandhi's trap of abolishing the independence of the states. Altogether about 20 states deserve to continue its existence as independent states, remaining others were of miniscule village size only.

All the attempted annexation by India were not given consent and sanction by the United Nations:

The Security Council of the United Nations after accepting the complaints on the invasion of Hyderabad put forward by Nizam on September 1948 was no longer pursued after the Nizam accepted defeat.[24] India's relation with Bhutan, as per Treaty of Friendship signed on 8th August, 1949, India gave guidance to Bhutan's relation with other countries. Why the dispute is still continuing today—the instruction by the Security Council to conduct Plebiscite in Kashmir could not be conducted by India. Article 2A and 10th Schedule were incorporated by the 35th Constitution Amendment regarding Sikkim which accordingly took over the Defence, Communications, External Affairs and Social Welfare. The 35th Amendment says, "Sikkim will not be a part of territory of India, but an associate state. But in the 36th Amendment Sikkim was annexed by India. The Indian empire is expanding exactly the same like the British did in earlier times—this imperial expansion is likely to doom one day.

Though, the complaint regarding the annexation of Manipur was not put up to the UN Security Council, UN had in very categorically made it known from the above mentioned that annexation is illegal. Though the dispute comes to a standstill as there was no longer alteration, in Manipur, there is a history of continued resistance in various forms by the people. Next, what can be contemplated is whether the Maharaja of Manipur has the power to integrate or merge Manipur to its neighbouring state.

In addition to the agreement to the treaty relation of Manipur by Akbar Hydari, Debeshwar Sharma, Katju, there have been many documents stating that British Paramountcy allows and gives sanction to the independence of the state.[25] Article 8 of the Vienna Convention also says that an act relating to the conclusion of a treaty performed by a person who does not have full power as authorized to represent a State for that purpose is without legal effect.[26] The treaty is invalid if it is signed without any capacity.[27] Max Sorensen in his work stated that the treaty which was made to sign or act under duress or coercion is invalid.[28] This very position was also shared and agreed by G.I. Tunkin.[29] He writes that treaty which was signed violating the law and internal sovereignty of the country should be challenged.[30] 'Unequal treaties' which derogate one party are treated as *Jus Cogens* by James Crawford.[31]

The constitution of Manipur rather than authorising and giving Treaty making power only accorded a mere figurehead to the Maharaja of Manipur. In addition to it, Maharaja no longer holds any power after Manipur had a representative, republican and popular government. Maharaja himself also had written so many times to Shri Prakash Menon. That is why Maharaja would have signed the Merger agreement without any treaty-making power, capacity. The first article of the Merger Agreement reads: "His Highness, the Maharaja of Manipur hereby cedes to the Dominion Government full and exclusive authority, jurisdictions and powers for and in relation to the governance of the state." The Maharaja no longer has the power of cession. Lastly, one Shri Prakasha without any mention of the post and portfolio he holds was a signatory to the treaty.

There are many internationally agreed documents on rules governing the treaty in the world. Either in one reason or another, it would be hard to find the rationality that a just treaty had been signed. In Oppenheim's word, such cases are subjugation.[32] V.P. Menon who is a signatory along with the Maharaja in that illegal treaty himself proclaimed that the case of Manipur was that of taking over. He writes: "In view of its position as a border state and its undeveloped character, it was decided to take over Manipur as a Chief Commissioners Province"[33]. The reason, that this scheming and crafty imperial had given in justification of taking over the state, are, firstly, Border state; and secondly, underdevelopment. If it goes by the shrewd logic of this imperialist, then there will be no country in the world which would not be annexed by the USA—because when a new state is annexed, one new state is bound to become a border state. But if we go by the prevailing UN system and the international laws governing territories of the state(s), the annexation of Manipur is not right. A very recent case of liberating Kuwait from Iraq by the United Nations Security Council Resolution 660 using force is still fresh in people's memory. Whereas since all small states being not oil rich, they could not get benefit out of international politics of oil. In India's view, her southern boundary is protected by sea, northern boundary by the Himalayan Mountain range, and its Hindustan heartland will be safe only if the North-eastern states serve as its outpost in her eastern boundary.

Maharaja was made to sign the treaty under duress and coercion by house arresting using full military might. The people of this land of Manipur had not forgotten it till this day. The Telegram send by Shri Prakash to Sardar Patel on 18 September, 1949 illustrates how the Maharaja was detained under duress – "HH must not under any circumstances be allowed to return to Manipur with his advisers and I have accordingly instructed police to detain here his party if they attempt to return before signing of agreement.

> "Please telegraph immediately repeat immediately authority for detention of HH and advisers under Regulation III or by *whatever other means you consider might be appropriate*. (Italics added).
> Have already warned sub-area to be prepared for any eventuality in Manipur."[34]

No reasons could be found to say that a treaty/instrument signed by a mere titular monarch who was already a prisoner with no power to sign again encircled by the military is right. So, that is a wrong, illegal document. That is why, the Maharaja of Manipur concealed and kept the merger agreement in secret from the people. One thing which the learned Pandits of India should not forget is – it is legal to withdraw a sum of money from a bank cashier using valid note, but it would be certainly wrong if that sum of money is forcefully robbed at gunpoint wearing black mask. Nobody will say it is right to annex

Manipur at gunpoint. People never accept and approve the Manipur annexation.

Third Issue

A question has always been asked whether a state after its annexation could regain its lost political status or has lost all its status. Possible ways and already applied benchmark are given below. In addition to it, the UN's Committee of 24 had been looking after to de-colonise the colonised states, and if need arises, reports were submitted to the Security Council. This issue can also be mentioned in relation to the case of Manipur.

State Retained

An independently existing state may ceases to exist as a state when the state no longer maintains to do so. Even after being illegally annexed, Ethiopia, Austria, Poland, Czechoslovakia, Albania could regain and save its state from losing its entity.[35] In the recent past, three Baltic States integrated under Nazi-Soviet Secret Pact could regain its state as earlier in the form of Estonia, Lithuania and Libya. James Crawford writes: A state can continue to exist for example even if its government is reduced to relative impotence or even if its territory is wholly occupied".[36] The trend that is observable in today's world is decolonisation. Paul Kennedy in his "*Rise and fall of Great Powers* (1988)". "*Preparing for the twenty first century* (1993)" writes about the great political fragmentation and emerging economic globalisation of the world. The sovereignty of the annexed state can also be treated as a case of suspended sovereignty.[37] Wrongfully annexed state can also again be created.[38] Why because annexation of that state could also be due to the inability to resist annexation. Retrocession of treaty is also accepted benchmark.[39]

In addition to it, according to universally accepted benchmark, as in the Western Sahara Case, state can recognize and follow self-determination benchmark. The benchmark of the self-determination unit shall always override the 'Territorial Integrity Rule' of the state which perpetrate annexation.[40] Moreover, when a new state is created, it is always followed by two ways of devolution and secession. As in the case of Greece seceding from the Ottoman Empire, and Netherland from Belgium, it was on the basis of secession benchmark that

Indonesia, North Korea, North Vietnam, Bangladesh, Guinea-Bissau was created and came into existence.[41] Today, International law, after so many changes, has created many new laws concerning the creation and resurrection of state on the basis of historical legality. Jawaharlal Nehru writes that States shall have the right to secede after 10 years.[42] Any of the international laws and benchmarks does not approve, allow or support annexation of state irrespective of whether the state is member of the United Nations or not. It even furthermore threatens and violates world peace and security. The prime objective and responsibility of the UN is to maintain world peace and security. UN system does not allow and permit 'aggression' and 'annexation'. It even resorts to power to stop aggression and annexation if it becomes inevitable.

Table 2.2: Countdown Annexation 1947 AD

1.	19 April	- Nehru ultimatum to states – threats with hostility
2.	15 May	- Manipur Draft Constitution ready
3.	20 May	- British Cabinet resolution – states to be fully independent
3a.	2 June	- Nehru-Mountbatten's Secret Revised Plan
4.	3 June	- Mountbatten's negative attitude to the states
5.	15 June	- AICC stand: State's sovereignty lies with state people
6.	17 June	- Jinnah categorical: state to be independent sovereign
7.	25 June	- Interim cabinet accepts states department creation
8.	1 July	- Manipur king (Maharaja) becomes nominal figurehead
9.	2 July	- Assam-Manipur Agreement: Indian agent to stay in Imphal
10.	2 July	- Secretary of State, Listowell: States not subject to British parliamentary Legislation
11.	5 July	- Patel on Blood theory, 'all knit by bond of blood'— possibly Aryan-Dravidan blood theory (?) of state.
12.	5 July	- Gandhi to Mountbatten: States should not be independent Gandhi possibly wants Indian empire not British
13.	10 July	- Indian Independence Act, 1947: British suzerainty over states in Indian subcontinent lapses
14.	25 July	- Mountbatten officially declares states independence
15.	26 July	- Manipur Constitution adopted
16.	28 July	- Mountbatten reception to Rulers (Lunch on August 1) – Diplomatically pressurises for Indian Dominion (His ambition to be India's Governor General)
17.	31 July	- State Negotiating Committee approves 2 agreement drafts

(*Contd.*)

Table 2.2 (*Contd.*)

18.	8 August	- Mountbatten reports to Listowell: states remain independent save three subjects – States not committed to Indian Constitution or GI Act. 1935 etc.
19.	9 August	- Listowell approves Mountbatten's 25 July proclamation
20.	10 August	- Manipur King directly takes over hill administration
21.	11 August	- king signs treaty of Accession: under Cl. 7 and 8 – Manip[ur's independence retained in the escape clause (cf. 5 April, 1946 meeting of Nikhil Manipur Mahasabha and MPM, Res 6 Part II- Manipur to be independent – R.K. Bhubon in chair)
22.	14 August	- King swears in the Interim Council
23.	15 August	- King hoists PAKHANGBA FLAG in Council Hall. Paramountcy cleared of Manipur
24.	28 August	- King announces – Manipur is sovereign
25.	6 November	- Indian Congress agent Debeshwar Sharma admits that Manipur is sovereign: Sovereignty lies with Manipur people (Categorical)
1948 AD		
26.	2 January	- Manipur King attends Ruler's meeting at Shillong attended by Sardar Patel and State's Ministry – Later announced that Manipur becomes independent.
27.	28 February	- Hijam Irabot attends Calcutt Communist Conference with Asian Revolutionaries – adopts militant Chinese Revolutionary line (later on practised too)
28.	25 May	- Congress Election Manifesto: To abide by Manipur Constitution (Congress members majority in the Constitution Drafting Committee)
	26 May	- Assam Prime Minister Gopinath Bordorloi pleads autonomy of Manipur
29.	11 June – 27 July	- Manipur Assembly election-popular government
30.	23 June – 3 July	- Akbar Hyadari's reconnaissance to annex Manipur
31.	2 August	- Akbar Hydari's letter to the King: Dewan simply watches "Treaty Relation" between two countries—Manipur and India. He is very categorical about the word Treaty like Katju
32.	22 August	- Akbar Hydari abolished Dominion agency
33.	22 August	- P.C. Ghose preaches Purbanchal theory in meeting
34.	18 September	- Manipur Hills and Plains meeting opposes Ghose proporsal
35.	20 September	- Tomal Congress writes to Indian Constituent Assembly: Manipur independent unit of India (probably in the sense of continent)
36.	21 September	- Manipur State Council declares Krishak Sabha and Praja Sangha unlawful organisations
37.	21 September	- Hijam Irabot goes underground.
38.	18 October	- Manipur Legislative Assembly opened: popular sovereign government operates

(*Contd.*)

Table 2.2 (*Contd.*)

39.	26 November	- Prajashanti Led Government (Non-Congress) sworn in: Insignificant Congress minority propagates for Indian annexation of Manipur: Annexation would nullify unlawfully the Manipur Constitution, they themselves drafted in the Committee
1949 AD		
40.	10 March	- Assembly Q. No. 21 L. Achou about Governments knowledge of the information about Manipur's merger with India
41.	22 March	- Assam Governor Shri Prakash discusses with king about Manipur Communist insurgency. Rustomji Chatterjee at Imphal
42.	14 April	- India Government asks King to transfer all powers to Dewan (an unconstitutional parallel centre of power)
43.	16 April	- King appointed Major General Amar Singh as Dewan
44.	5 June	- Manipur Socialist Party meeting urges for referendum on Manipur-India Relation
45.	25 June	- Prakash secret memo, to King – India does not recognise Manipur State Council and the elected assembly (Popular Sovereign)
46.	26 July	- Congress Bulletin 4: Indian Congress backs Manipur Congress – Slogan to dethrone the Constitutional figurehead—King
47.	29 July	- Hill MLAs against annexation of Manipur by India
48.	3 August	- Public meeting resolution to India's Prime Minister. Manipur cannot be merged with India
49.	15 August	- 4000 Congressmen celebrate Independence and day and Students' Federation hoists Black Flag, Ex-Minister Dr. Leiren hoists Black Flag
50.	25 August	- Ruling Manipur MLAs against annexation of Manipur—Meeting resolution to Deputy Prime Minister. India not to annex Manipur to his country
51.	7 September	- Shri Prakash telegrammes King to discuss "Affairs of State" at Shillong
52.	8 September	- Young Socialist League meeting opposes annexation
53.	17 September	- King reaches Shillong
54.	18, 19 September	- King communicates to Indian agent at Shillong that he lacks capacity to enter into treaty as all political powers have been lawfully transferred to people
55.	18 September	- Shri Prakash telegrammes to Patel and V.P. Menon: Manipur Maharaja detained under Regulation III and 'ANY OTHER MEANS' (Code language of House arrest of king under military seize). – King as captive and mental torture
56.	18 September	- PS to King writes to Shillong SP to withdraw forces encircling Manipur King. Seize continues. Maharajah's

(*Contd.*)

Table 2.2 (*Contd.*)

		all communication lines snapped. Literally, he is a captive
57. 20 September	-	Psychic oppression and seize continues on the king
58. 21 September	-	King coerced under duress to sign annexation treaty
59. 21 September	-	Bhagyabati Patrika Manipur Public opinion: Manipur cannot be subjugated and made subservient to a foreign nation (India)
60. 15 October	-	Mr. Velodi, State Minister. India occupies Manipur
61. 15 October	-	Major General Amar Singh takes over Manipur against people's will
62. 15 October	-	Gazette of India, Ministry of State Notification No. 219-p, Dated 15 October 1949-order to dissolve popular Ministry and the elected Manipur Legislative Assembly (Suspended Sovereignty)

NOTES AND REFERENCES

1. *Poknafam,* Vernacular Manipuri Daily, Imphal, 15 October 1991; *Manipur Mail,* Popular English Daily, Imphal, 15 October 1991.
2. Lassa Francis Lawrence Oppenheim (1858–1919), was a renowned German jurist. He is the author of the internationally renowned *International Law: A Treatise*, the first edition of which was published in 1905-1906.
3. Max Sorensen (1913–1981) was a Danish diplomat and professor of international law. In 1949 he was a member of the Danish delegation to the London Conference on the Treaty of London, which established the Council of Europe. Between 1949 and 1951, he represented Denmark in the United Nations Commission on Human Rights. From 1954, he sat on the Sub-Commission on Prevention of Discrimination and Protection of Minorities for two years, and he also sat on a committee that deals with the application of the International Labour Organization addressed conventions until 1964. In 1955 he was appointed to the European Commission on Human Rights where he sat until 1973. He served as president of that commission from 1967 to 1972. From 1956 to 1972, he also served as a legal adviser to the Danish Foreign Ministry. He headed the Danish delegation for the first and second United Nations Law of the Sea Conferences in 1958 and 1960, respectively. He was appointed to sit as judge *ad hoc* on the International Court of Justice by the governments of Denmark and The Netherlands for North Sea Continental Shelf cases (1968-1969). He retired from the University of Arhus in 1972. From 1973 to 1979,

Sorensen sat as a judge on the European Court of Justice. From 1980 to 1981, he sat as a judge of the European Court of Human Rights. He was the first of four lawyers who spoke at both institutions. He died in 1981 at the age of 68 years.

4. Joseph Gabriel Starke (1911-2006), Principal works include An Introduction to International Law (1947; by Shearer *sub nom*. Starke's International Law (11th ed. 1994); Studies in International Law (1965); The ANZUS Treaty Alliance (1966).
5. James Crawford, S.C., FBA is Whewell Professor of International Law, and concurrently Research Professor of Law, Latrobe University. He was the first Australian member of the United Nations International Law Commission and in that capacity was responsible for the ILC's work on the International Criminal Court (1994) and for the second reading of the ILC Articles on State Responsibility (2001). In addition to scholarly work on statehood, collective rights, investment law and international responsibility, he has appeared in more than 40 cases before the International Court of Justice and other international tribunals, and is engaged as expert, counsel and arbitrator in international arbitration. In 2012, he was awarded the Hudson Medal by the American Society of International Law. Recent work includes *The International Law of Responsibility* (co-edited, OUP, 2010), *The Cambridge Companion to International Law* (co-edited, CUP, 2012) and *Brownlie's Principles of Public International Law* (editor, OUP, 2012).
6. The Lauterpacht Centre is part of the Faculty of Law and the scholarly home of international law at the University of Cambridge. In this role, it seeks to provide both a framework and forum for critical and constructive thought about the function, content and working of law in the international community as well as to develop an appreciation of international law as an applied body of rules and principles.
7. GI Tunkin also served as the president of the Soviet Association of International Law from its founding in 1957 until his death. Tunkin is the author of nine leading books on international law and general theory of state and law. Tunkin's textbooks on international law formed the core of the international law curriculum in the USSR for over forty years. Following the dissolution of the USSR, his works have had lasting influence.
8. Published by HMSO, London, 1970-1983.
9. The Great Divide: Britain, India, Pakistan by H.V. Hodson offers an authoritative account of the dramatic step of the birth of the new nation of Pakistan in the retreat of the British imperialism. The book first describes the historical events that paved the way for The Great Divide.

Hodson then goes on to chronicle, in fascinating detail, the hectic five months of the last viceroyalty of India and the aftermath of the transfer of power, which saw dreadful massacres and migrations in Punjab and sharp struggles over Kashmir and other regions. The epilogue summarizes events since partition and assesses their effect on the fragile stability of nations in the subcontinent.

10. Philips Ziegler, *Mountbatten: The Official Biography,* 1985, p. 404.
11. James Crawford, *The Creation of States in International Law,* pp. 210-211.
12. N. Sanajaoba, Post Paramountcy Sovereign Status of Viable States and other two papers, Manipur Seminar, Johnostone School, 1991).
13. V.P. Menon, *Integration of States*, pp.11, 97.
14. Granville Austin, *The Indian Constitution: Cornerstone of a Nation*, p. 243. This book provides a history of the Indian Constituent Assembly. It discusses how and why the members of the Assembly wrote their constitution as they did.
15. James Crawford, N. 11, p. 295.
16. *Ibid.*, pp. 376-377.
17. *Please see Countdown Annexation Diary.*
18. *Please see Countdown Annexation Diary.*
19. Philips, C.H. and Wainwright, M.D., eds. *The Partition of India: Policies and Perspectives 1935-47*, Allen and Unwin, London, 1970, p. 96.
20. H.V. Hodson, *The Great Divide: Britain, India, Pakistan*, p.119.
21. *Ibid.,* pp.123-124.
22. *Ibid.,* pp. 530, 534.
23. Larry Collins, Dominique Lapierre, *Mountbatten and Partition of India*, pp. 166-171.
24. Scor 3rd yr. No. 109, 357th Meeting, 16th September 1948, See Crawford, p. 112.
25. Nicholas Mansergh, E.W., R. Lumby, *Transfer of Power,* Vol. I-XII.
26. J.G. Starke, ed, *International Law*, p. 426.
27. *Ibid.*, p. 448. See 6 Reasons of invalidity of Treaty.
28. Max Sorensen, *Manual of Public International Law*, St. Martin's Press, 1968, p. 202.
29. G.I. Tunkin, *International Law*, p. 169.
30. *Ibid.*, p. 169.
31. James Crawford, N. 11, p. 81.
32. Lassa Francis Lawrence Oppenheim, *International Law. A Treatise*, pp.566-577.
33. The Story of the Integration of the Indian States, p. 289.
34. N. Sanajaoba, ed., *Manipur: Past and Present*, Vol. I, p. 354.

35. James Crawford, N. 11, p. 148.
36. *Ibid.*, p. 411.
37. *Ibid.*, p. 310.
38. *Ibid.*, p. 412, 414.
39. *Ibid.*, p. 380.
40. *Ibid.*, p. 379.
41. *Ibid.*, p. 247.
42. Jawahar Lal Nehru, *Discovery of India*, p. 534.

CHAPTER – 3

Manipuri People's Right to Self-Determination

Shukhdeba S. Hanjabam

Introduction

Manipur is located in India's Northeast with a population of 2.3 million (0.21% of India's population) and a geographical area of 22,327 sq. km. It comprises of mainly three major ethnic groups belonging to Mongoloid and Tibeto-Burman linguistic group, namely, (1) the Meitei, (2) the Manipuri Nagas and (3) the Manipuri Kuki-Chins-Mizo. Besides, a small Muslim-Manipuri segment locally known as Meitei-Pangal have settled in Manipur since the reign of King Khagemba (1597–1652). It is to be noted that the aforementioned ethnic groups have over a long period of time intermingled culturally, linguistically and in most other fronts too. The Meiteis who are numerically the most predominant community mainly inhabit the valley. The Meitei-Pangal, whose origin had connections with the Meiteis, are also mainly found in the Imphal valley. The tribes comprising Naga and Kuki-Chin-Mizo mainly inhabit the hills though a good number of their villages are spread over the valley. Thus the state of Manipur comprises Meiteis, Meitei-Pangal, 33 Scheduled Tribes, and 7 Scheduled Castes. Besides there are many tribes demanding recognition as ST.

As per the Royal Chronicle, "Cheitharol Kumbaba", Manipuris had established a sophisticated kingdom at a time when state formation was unknown to most parts of Asia. There was a Constitutional Government since 1947. The British administered the State of Manipur directly from 1891 till 1907 after Manipur ceased to be an independent Kingdom. However, the Crown did not annex the state of Manipur as a part of British territory. When the British prepared to depart, the Cabinet Mission suggested on 12th May, 1946 that when India achieved independence, British paramountcy over other princely states would lapse. Thus Manipur regained her independence after the British left.

The King proposed to surrender power to the people through a Constitution and on 15th May, 1947 Manipur Draft Constitution was ready and on 26th July, 1947, Manipur State Constitution Act was adopted. After the adoption of the Constitution, Manipur became an "autonomous state". Since the constitution was not provided by the British or the Dominion of India, Manipur did not come under their purview.

The relation between sovereign Manipur and the Dominion of India was guided by the Instrument of Accession and the Standstill Agreement signed by Maharaja of Manipur on 11th August, 1947 ceding Currency, Defence, External Affairs and Communication to Dominion of India. But Manipur remained as an "Associate State" with complete internal independence. Whether the Governor General consented to the Agreement is still shrouded in mystery. On 28th August, 1947, the King announced the sovereign status of Manipur. Dominion of India agent admitted that Manipur is Sovereign.[1] The clauses of the Instrument of Accession clearly stated the sovereignty status of Manipur.

> Clause 7, "Nothing in this Instrument shall be deemed to commit me in any way to acceptance of any future constitution of India or to fetter my discretion to enter into arrangements with Government of India under any such future condition."
>
> Clause 8, " Nothing in this Instrument affects the continuance of my sovereignty in and over this State, or save as provided by or under this Instrument, the exercise of any powers, authority and rights now enjoyed by me as Ruler of this State."

The Constitution provided for a 53 member Assembly of which 18 were reserved for the hills. The remaining seats were for the valley. Elections were held on 11th and 30th June for the valley and 26th and 27th July, 1948 for the hills. It was based on universal adult franchise (both male and female)—the first of its kind in Asia. The first meeting of the first Manipur State Assembly was held on 18th October, 1948 at the Durbar Hall. A popular Ministry also started functioning.[2] But the Sovereignty of Manipur was short-lived as Manipur was merged with India under threat of use of force on 21st September, 1949.

The circumstance under which Manipur merged into India completely bypassing the elected representatives still remains contentious.[3] This is why the New Delhi rule is considered as alien or a sort of foreign domination in Manipur.

Resourceful Kabaw Valley was given away to Burma in appeasement without consulting the people in 1953. The merger was rejected by many as it was not discussed and ratified by the Manipur Legislative Assembly. The National Convention on Manipur Merger Issue held at Imphal (28 and 29, 1993) resolved that the Agreement, signed by and between the Maharaja of Manipur and the representatives of the Dominion of India on the 21st September, 1949 did not have any legal and constitutional validity. People generally term it as "annexation" rather than merger.

The Indian dominion being a member of the United Nation since 1945 have failed to comply with the United Nations Charter Article 2(4) which reads as "All members shall refrain in their international relations from the threat or use of force against the territorial integrity or political independence of any state, or in any manner inconsistent with the purpose of the United Nations", by committing aggression

Table 3.1: Transformation of Manipur State

Period	*Status of State*
AD 33-early 20 century	Sovereign State
1891-1946	International Protectorate
26 July, 1947 (Constitution adopted)	Autonomous State
11 August, 1947	Associate State (Sovereign within Indian confederation)
14 August, 1947	Sovereign State
18 October, 1948	Sovereign State (Assembly functions)
15 October, 1949	Annexed State (Continuous State with suspended sovereignty)
21 January, 1972	Constituent State of India (suspended sovereignty)

Source: Political status of State during the inter-war period (1919-1945) had varied in the comity of nations (Sanajaoba 2006).

on Manipur and thereby becoming culpable of breach of peace. Further, UN General Assembly Resolutions 2625 (XXV), 1970 and 2734 (1970) provide that no territorial acquisition resulting from the threat or use of force shall be recognized as legal.

The officials of India made attempts to dilute the independence of Manipur referring to it as one of the 560 native-states.[4] Manipur, which was having the same status of Sri Lanka and Burma of that time could not be placed within the fold of native-states, which had been signatories to India's Standstill Agreement of 1947.[5]

Self-Determination Movement

The people of Manipur enjoyed a phase of self-governance through the Manipur State Assembly after the King surrendered power to the elected representatives. But the government of India dissolved it through its military might and the Indian army was deployed in Imphal to prevent any possible trouble arising from this development on 15th October, 1949.[6] Since then the military deployment continues in Manipur. The contentious merger was resisted through an armed movement led by legendary leader Hijam Irabot. His idea of an independent Manipur was endorsed by the people of Manipur at a public meeting on 3rd August, 1949. Under the banner of Manipur Students' Federation a protest was registered by hoisting 'Black Flag' and holding a meeting at Porompat, Imphal-East, on 15th August 1949. All political parties except the Manipur Congress, which itself was a divided on merger issue, passed resolutions against the merger. Media reported on the possible bad consequences of the merger.[7]

There have been a number of accounts about the forced conquest of Manipur by the Indian government.[8] The Kangla fort in Imphal, from where the kings of Manipur used to rule, was brought under military control in 1949 and remained so till 2004. As a result of exploitation, denial of right to self-determination and decades of uneven development, movements for Manipuri national liberation emerged. All shades of mainstream parties in India have flatly rejected the right of the people of Manipur to self-determination. Historian Gangumei Kabui observed that occupying Kangla—capital of Manipur Kingdom by the Indian armed forces since the forceful merger is a symbol of subjugation of Manipur by government of India. Earlier, it was "British subjugation" and now it is "Indian subjugation".

Unfortunately Irabot died at his head quarters in Kabaw Valley on 26 September, 1951 without realizing his dream of an "Independent Socialist Republic of Manipur". The movement was later suppressed by the state, but many educated youth have continued the movement since then. The Manipur National Union proclaimed Manipur's independence in 1953; The Meitei State Committee took to armed struggle in 1960. The United National Liberation Front was formed in 1964. In 1968, Revolutionary Government of Manipur (RGM) established a government-in-exile with its headquarters in Sylhet in erstwhile East-Pakistan (now Bangladesh) but later merged it with PLA. In September 1978, the People's Liberation Army (PLA), with a leftist ideology and alleged training in guerrilla warfare in China, was founded. The PLA started armed struggle since 1979 against the State forces. The Revolutionary People's Front (RPF) and its military wing PLA unilaterally signed Article 3 of the Fourth Geneva Convention in 1997 and also submitted a memorandum to the UN Decolonization Committee.[9] Begum Khaleda Zia had acknowledged the armed struggle of Manipur as a liberation struggle in the parliament". RPF and its armed wing PLA reaffirmed its stand not to have a political dialogue with the Indian government except on the issue of independence and sovereignty of Manipur after their second congress (July 14 to December 4, 2008).[10] V.V. Rao recorded that the PLA had a broad vision encompassing the interest of all the colonized, subjugated people everywhere, beyond the borders of Manipur.[11]

Subsequently, Manipur also witnessed the growth of a number of other organizations since 1970s. The armed groups have boycotted the Independence Day and Republic Day for many decades stating that this day reminds subjugation and suspension of Manipur's sovereign status. In order to tackle the situation, Manipur was declared a disturbed area and the Armed Forces Special Powers Act, (AFSPA) 1958, was imposed in September 1980 by a notification of the Home Department, Government of Manipur, under instruction from the Government of India. Even before the notification, various parts of Manipur had been declared disturbed from time to time—with the enactment of the Act in 1958.[12] It is an invocation of un-proclaimed emergency. Once the area is declared disturbed, anyone in the central armed forces may arrest, search, or even kill a person on mere suspicion and no prosecution, suit or other legal proceeding shall be instituted, except with the previous sanction of the Central Government, a situation that people term as granting 'licence to kill' with impunity.

The roots of the AFSPA can be traced to the infamous Rowlett Act 1919. People who protested against the Act on 13 April, 1919 at Jallianwallah Bagh were massacred by the British forces under General Dyer.[13] The AFSPA's predecessor—the Armed Forces Special Powers Ordinance, 1942, had been enacted in order to neutralize Quit India movement. It was a colonial instrument, used for legitimization of British regime and continuation of its colonialism. In its AFSPA 1958, India not only inherited the same powerful political potency of AFSPO, 1942 but also added that anyone can be killed only on suspicion which was not encompassed even by the previous one in colonial rule.

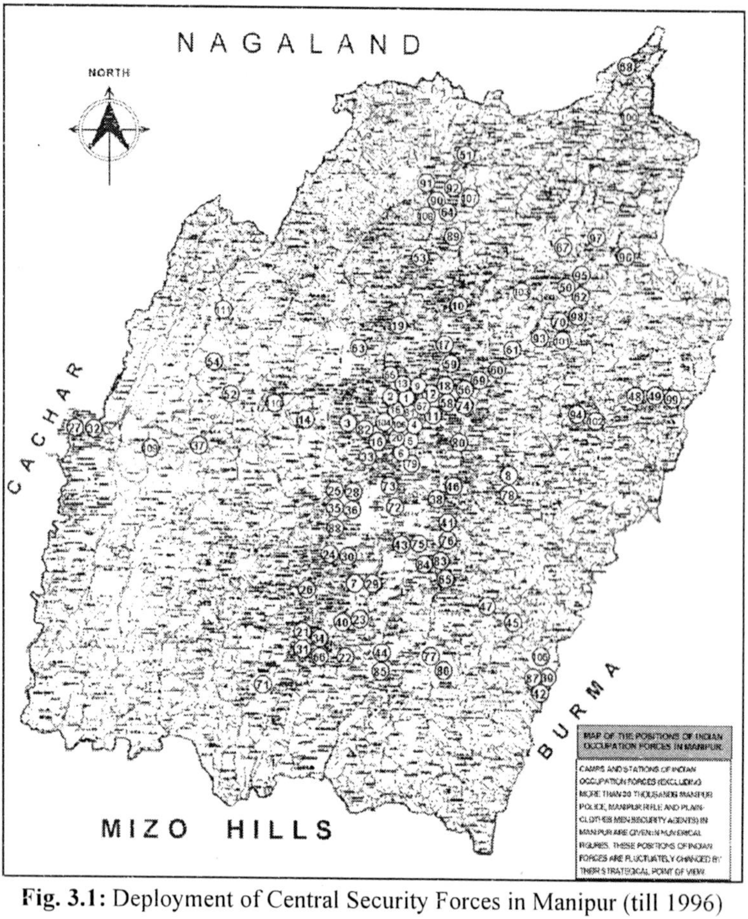

Fig. 3.1: Deployment of Central Security Forces in Manipur (till 1996)

Map showing the location of Indian military forces in Manipur—each number represents the location of a base or a battalion. Notice the concentration in the centre of the state rather than on the border.[14]

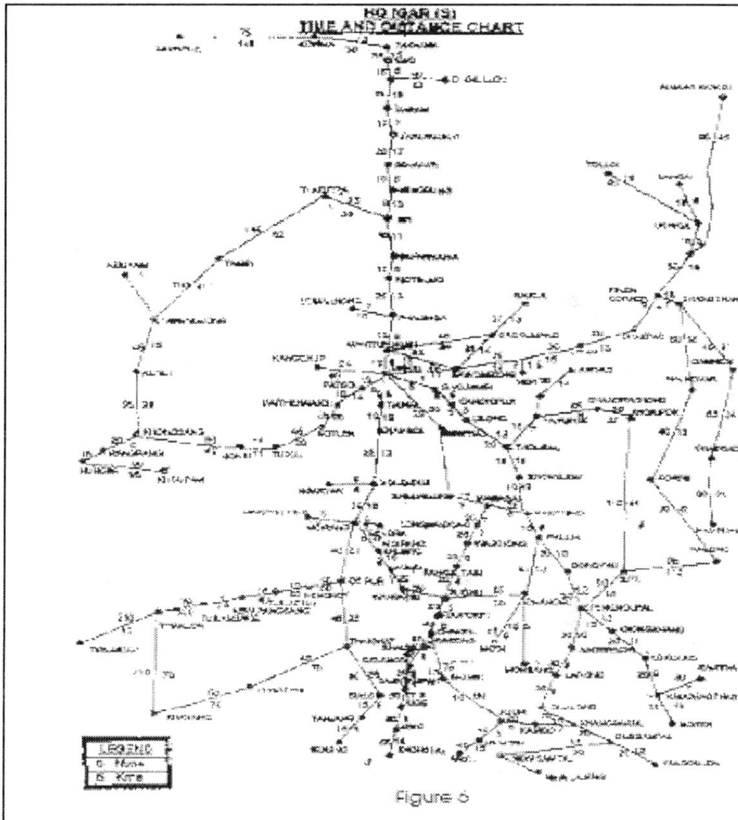

Justice First, December 2008 Vol. I No. 1

Fig. 3.2: Military Installations of Inspector General Assam Rifles (IGAR)—South in Manipur

Manipuri People's Right to Self-Determination

The International Court of Justice refers to the right to self-determination as a right held by the people rather than a right held by the government alone. The right to self-determination is indisputably a norm of *jus cogens*. *Jus cogens* norms are the highest rules of international law and they must be strictly obeyed at all times. The International Court of Justice and the Inter-American Commission on Human Rights of the Organization of Americans States have ruled on cases in a way that support the view that the principle of self-determination also has the legal status of *erga omnes*. The term "*erga omnes*" means "flowing to all". Accordingly, erga omnes obligations of a State are owed to the international community as a whole: when a principle achieves the status of *erga omnes* the rest of the international community is under mandatory duty to respect it in all circumstances in their relation with one another.[15]

Two important United Nations studies on the right to self-determination set out factors that give rise to possession of right to self-determination by a group. The factors are as follows: [16]

(i) a history of Independence or self-rule in an identifiable territory;
(ii) a distinct culture; and
(iii) a will and capacity to regain self-governance. These factors of self-determination are being examined below with particular reference to Manipur.

(i) History of Independence or Self-Rule in an Identifiable Territory

Manipur—an ancient Asian state was known by different names to different peoples—'Poirei-Meitei-Leipak' or 'Kangleipak' to the indigenous people of Manipur; 'Kathe' or 'Ponnas' to the Burmese; 'Hsiao-Po-lo-Mein' to the Chinese; 'Cassay' to the Shans; 'Moglai' to the Cacharis and Bengalis and 'Mekle' to the Assamese (as well as to the British in the 18th Century) in the pre-Christian period. The Manipuri's themselves knew the State by as many as 22 names in different ages and at different times. The name Manipur was first officially introduced in the early eighteen century during the reign of King Garnibniwaz (1709–48 AD). Professor Acharya of Guwahati University observed that Manipur was known to the Arabic, Persian, Greek, Romans, Chinese, Burmese, Shan and other historians, as international trade route of the past passed through the country. The early state of Pragjyotishpur or Kamrup, or, present Indian state of Assam has been for millennia a buffer between the state of Manipur and State of India known as Bharat for Millennia.[17] All the available maps beginning from 1500 AD by Henry Yule indicate an identifiable territory of Manipur.

The Kingdom of Manipur had been ruled by 76 indigenous kings from AD 33 to 1955. The Kingdom was governed based on the written constitution "Loyumba Shinyen". This decree was issued by King Loiyumba in 1110 AD and was based on the earlier codes and conventions. Oinam Bogeshwar, the renowned Meitei scholar observed that there was a centralized constitutional government since AD 429.[18] All the events in Manipur are recorded in the Kingdom Chronicle "Cheitharol Kumpaba" which is available in the Royal Palace of Manipur, Local custodians as well as the Indian Library Office London and archives around the world especially in United Kingdom.

The historical capital and focal centre of the state was Kangla, the control of which lay at the roots of all political and religious power. The legendary 'Kangla' complex had been the capital of Manipur from the very ancient times down to 1891. There were three Courts of Justice in the Kingdom. The Highest Court of Justice was the 'Cheirap Court'. Traditional customary laws were the basis of judgments. The Cheirap tried all cases except murder and high treason and could inflict all punishment except death sentence, which was exclusively within the power of the king. The king was the highest appellate authority in the state. There is another Court called Pacha Loisang (women's court) in which all cases of disputes involving women were dealt with. The Chief Queen was the head of the Court. These two courts were in existence since AD 33. The Military Court tried all offenders who belong to the Army. 18 outposts were opened in Manipur during the reign of Meidingu Kiyamba (AD 1467-1508). Modification and developments were made by the preceding kings.[19]

Manipur was recognized by foreign nations, especially by the Shan with the 1470 Agreement between the King Kiyamba of Manipur and Khekhomba of Pong in upper Burma. It was followed by the Anglo-Manipur Friendship Treaty in 1762, Anglo-Manipuri Defence Protocol of 1763, Treaty of Yandaboo, 1826 between the British government and the Burmese government after the Burmese occupied Manipur (1819-1826 remembered as "Seven Year Devastation").[20] Britain and Manipur continued their friendship by mutually opening offices of political agents in each other's territory. In 1835, the British decided to retain a Political Agent in Manipur with a view to preserving friendly relations, and preventing border feuds and disturbance. The Political Agent acted like an ambassador in the country. Manipur also had its Political Agent in the British Territory in Lakhimpur (Cachar) as well as Calcutta.[21]

When the British Viceroy had a summit meeting with Maharaja Chandrakiti of Manipur in August 1874, a mutually beneficial agreement was reached. By this arrangement, both the contracting parties had agreed to assist each other to protect their respective interests. The relationship broke down in March 1891which resulted in the Anglo-Manipur War. The British army was initially defeated on 24 March, 1891 but finally Manipur army was defeated on 25th April, 1891. The heroic resistance of the Manipuris against the mightiest Super Power of the world of that period in two major battles was acknowledged by Queen Victoria in her proclamation to forgo her right to annex Manipur. The Queen sent a telegram on 1st August 1891 to the then British Government of India, which reads as "Trust Senapati will not be executed. He was not guilty of murder". Lord Lansdowne thought that the humiliation, his mighty government suffered at the hands of Manipur heroes could be neutralized only by the execution of the Manipuri heroes and by transportation of the King and his thirteen officials.[22]

Barrister Ghose's petition to the British Government "Did the Manipur Princes obtain a Fair Trial, argued Manipur was an independent Kingdom in alliance with the British power, which was recognized by the British Government. So the British government did not have the necessary jurisdiction to try the Manipuri Princes and the argument was based on International Law prevailing at that time. Therefore, Manipur was not annexed to the British territory, but remained as an international protectorate. It is supported by the statement of Philip Zieglers who wrote to Mountbatten that, "As the Boundary of British India has gradually extended in the first half of the nineteenth century, an increasing number of Princely States had entered into treaty arrangements with the new power, under which they accepted the presence of a British Resident in their capitals and a degree of subordination to the Raj, but were not absorbed into the colonial bloc".[23]

The present boundary of Manipur with an area of 22,327 sq. km. more or less remained fixed since the controversial transfer of Kabaw Valley to Burma (now Myanmar) in 1834.[24] Sanajaoba observed that, in historical times, the boundary of Manipur fluctuated across the

Table 3.2: The establishment of Police (Civil and Armed Battalions) in Manipur (AD 33-1826)

Sl. No.		*Civil Police*	*Year*	*Reigning King*	*Armed Battalion*
1.	Establishment of Lallup, Patcha Pheida, Panchayat		33	Pakhangba	
2	Leikai Lakpas and NingolLakpas		2nd Century	Khuyai Tompok	
3.	Establishment of jail		664	Naothingkhong	
4.	Laws Codified		1074-1112	Loyumba	
5.	Establishment of 18 Police Outposts		1467-1508	Kiyamba	
6.	(i)	Establishment of Doliapas (Civil Police)	1596	Khagemba	
	(ii)	Dolaipas replaced Loishanglois			
7.	(i)	Changes in the functioning of Patcha Pheida	1709-1740	Garib Niwas	

existing national and international boundaries, as Manipur happened to be a force to be reckoned with in South East Asia.[25] Henry Yule's map indicates Manipur of AD 1500 and AD 1580—with a larger territory to the south and eastern frontier beyond the Chindwin deep in Burmese territory. In spite of the periodic fluctuations, the territory and boundary of Manipur remained considerably stable and nearly unaltered for at least half a millennium in the recent past. This stability deserved notice in the context of significant territorial re-alignments that took place in Asia, especially in South East Asia. The parameter stipulated by the Montevido Convention, 1933 of an independent state, viz, (a) territory, (b) population, (c) government, and (d) capacity to maintain external relation, has been found in the State of Manipur. Manipur had, therefore, been recognized as sovereign state in as early as 1762. Manipur thus meets the first criterion of history of independence or self-rule in an identifiable territory.

(ii) A Distinct Culture

The people of Manipur are mongoloids unlike the majority Indo-Aryans-Dravidians who control the Indian system. It was admitted in 'Kirata Jana Krti' by Dr. Sunitkumar Chatterjee, the most renowned Indologist. Dr. Grierson (1967) in his most authoritatively volumes of the Linguistic Survey of India recorded that the Manipuri people

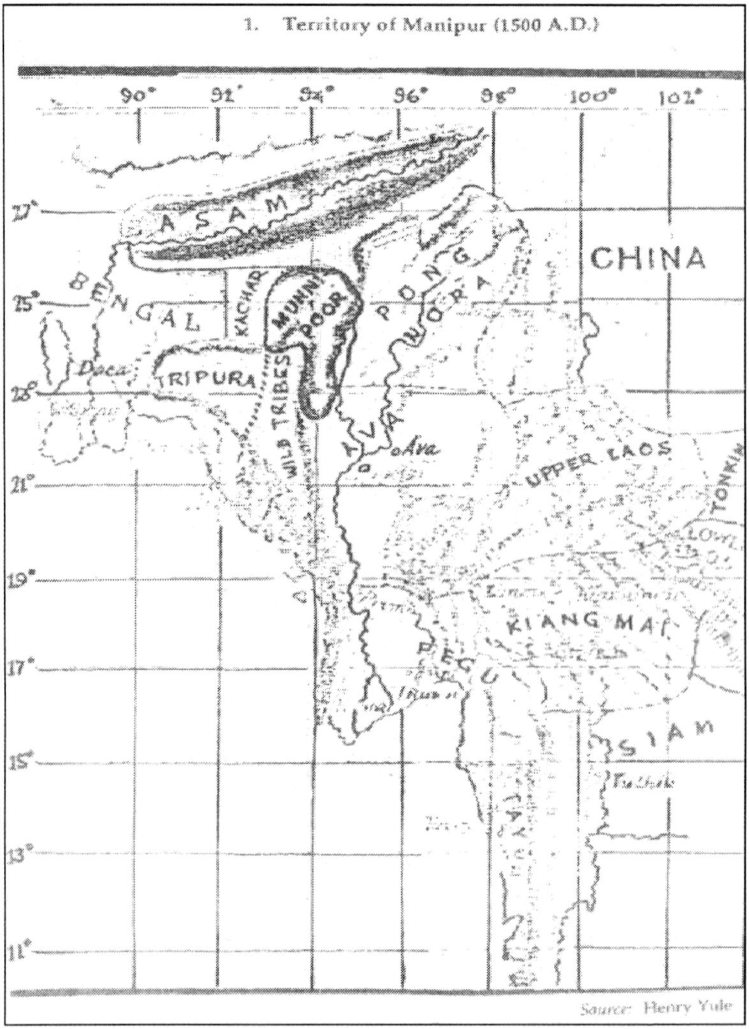

Source: Sanajaoba (1995).

Fig. 3.3: Manipur Territory in Henry Yule Map AD 150

are speakers of Tibeto-Burman language which is different from the present day India. The people of Manipur follow the indigenous religions. Some have converted to Christianity. Some scholars have tried to project the religion of Manipur as Hindu after the King adopted Hinduism in the 18 century, but the reality is different. Historian

Arambam prefers to use the term "Meiteinisation of Hinduism" rather than "Hindunisation of Meitei". He used the Meiteinisation of Hinduism as a concept on the strength of the indigenous culture itself, which did not indicate total surrender of the society to the 'higher religion', but used the higher culture for indigenous needs of the day.[26] Dr Sunitkumar Chatterjee estimated the age of the Meitei language and literature: 'The beginning of this old Manipuri literature (as in case of Newari) may go back to 1,500 years, or even 2,000 years, from now.[27]

Since Manipur maintained her independence till the British interference in 1891, the people of the British India were alien or foreign to the people of Manipur. Manipur State as well as the Manipur Constitution Act precedes the Indian State which was created in 1947 as well as the Constitution of India. There was no India before 1947, but British India, Mughal India, and Ashokan Empire etc.[28] It is also supported by the fact that the publications of the first Prime Minister of India do not mention anything about Manipur and her people.[29] Manipur thus qualifies the second criterion of a distinct culture.

Table 3.3: Fee received annually (1901-02 to 1907-08) from Foreign Nationals

Year	*Receipt*
1901-02	Rs. 4,428
1902-03	Rs. 4,281
1903-04	Rs. 5,730
1904-05	Rs. 5,794
1905-06	Rs. 5,939
1906-07	Rs. 8,964
1907-08	Rs. 9,256

Source: UCM (2005).[30]

(iii) A Will and Capacity to Regain Self-Governance

It is no doubt that the resistance groups in Manipur are evidence of willingness to defend the right to self-determination and thus self-governance. They have defended it since the forceful merger of Manipur on 15th October, 1949. They managed to carve out a 'liberated zone' where they ran their civil administration.[31] It was reported during the visit of the media team including a national media-CNN/IBN to the general headquarters of a resistance group—the UNLF/MPA at the Chandel district of Manipur. It was reported again when the RPF/PLA interacted with the visiting media team in their training command headquarter located in the Ukhrul district in Manipur near the Indo-Myanmar border.[32] The liberated zone in Manipur is administered by the political wings of the resistance groups.

The first organized group that supports the movement of right to self-determination was the student groups. All Manipur Students Union (AMSU) was formed in 1965 as a reaction to the artificially created famine in Manipur under New Delhi rule. Initially the idea of self-determination was not in vogue, but by 1968 the students started campaigning for self-governance. The idea of self-determination was supported by the Union as many of them have seen the independence status of Manipur in their own eyes before the forceful merger with India. It was hardly 15-20 years away. In the year 1994-95, AMSU developed a platform for discussion on right to self-determination in Manipur. The leader of AMSU was pulled up by the government, but released after the clarification on why the AMSU organized the platform for right to self-determination.[33]

The people of Manipur particularly the Meiteis contested the identities brought by the adoption of Hinduism. This contestation is a part of a general Meitei renaissance, a movement to resist the political, religious and cultural dominance of India in Manipur.[34] The highly developed Manipur language was denied recognition by the Government of India. The movement for recognition of Meitei language was initiated since the late 1960s. The non-violent aspects of the agenda of these groups have been adopted by several grassroots Meitei organizations such as the Pan Manipuri Youth League which was established in 1968. Their activities include efforts to reestablish pre-Hindu temples and religious ceremonies. The effects of the revivalist movement can be seen in the increase in the number of native priests and story tellers who performed at major ceremonies and in the resurrection of native games, folk songs, and martial arts. A negative yearly remembering of the burning of pre-Hindu scriptures by Pamheiba (*Garibniwaz*) has also been instituted. The increase in the number of participants at this ceremony indicates a growing support for the revivalist movement: while two to three thousands people participated in 1979, the number swelled to more than eight thousand in 1990.[35] The general interest in the early Meitei literature is evidenced by the many study groups, workshops and courses at Manipur University focused on pre-twentieth-century Meitei Manuscripts.[36]

The people's movement for right to life which is suspended by AFSPA began in 1974 raised by Kanglei League—a regional political party during elections to the Manipur State Legislative Assembly. Later it merged with the Manipur People's Party. In the early part of 1980, Amnesty International took note of the Act and a letter was sent to Mr. Yamben Laba—a human right activist of Manipur. After the imposition of AFSPA to whole of Manipur on October 10, 1980, the Manipur Human Rights group led by Mr. Laba moved the Supreme Court of India contending that the AFSPA is *ultra vires* of the provisions of the Constitution of India. In 1982, a letter from the Naga Peoples Movement for Human Rights addressed to the Chief Justice of the Supreme Court of India was also converted into a writ petition challenging the AFSPA. In 1984 the Delhi based Peoples Union for Democratic Rights also filed a writ petition contending that Parliament lacks the legitimacy to pass such draconian laws. In 1988, the student organizations of Manipur and Nagaland and political parties joined hands to fight for the cause of human rights. National Human Rights Commission visited Manipur in 1996 and it was followed by the Supreme Court judgment upholding the Act (Laba Not Dated). The Meira Paibis movement was born out of the movement against AFSPA in the late 80s. The movement is now institutionalized and continues even today. Mention can be made of Irom Sharmila's fast-unto-death agitation since November 2, 2000 and the violent incident of the killing and rape of Ms. Manorama Thangjam that led to the historic self-immolation of Manipur Students Federation leader Chittaranjan and a nude protest by the women of Manipur in 2004.

The civil society responded very actively since the early 1990s. The National Convention on Manipur Merger Issue was held on 28-29 October, 1993 at Imphal which deliberated upon the forceful merger and resolved that it did not have any legality and constitutional validity. It was closely followed by the National Seminar on Human Rights held on 8-9 December, 1994 at Imphal which resolved that "The Union Government of India be strongly urged upon to allow the 'people of Manipur to exercise their legitimate Right to Self-Determination". Similarly, the Seminar organized by the Committee on Advancement of the Fourth World People held on 12 August, 1998 resolved that "That the people of Manipur, who have been subjected to...different forms of colonialism under the Indian state for the last half a century, should be lawfully empowered to freely determine their own political destiny and to use their natural and human resources by their own free will." The People of Manipur while celebrating the United Nations Day on 24th October, 1999 at Imphal reaffirmed its solidarity to the United Nations and two important points were declared: (I). That the UN and its organs be urged upon to enlist Manipur as after-acquired Non-Self-Governing-Territory in regard to Chapter XI of the UN Charter, and (II). That the Union Government of India, in the capacity of Administering Power be entrusted with the international responsibility of fulfilling her obligations in regard to Manipur as a Non-Self-Governing-Territory.

In the last decade the civil society in Manipur has been campaigning to resolve the Manipur issue through a plebiscite. It is interesting to note that the current campaign in Manipur for a plebiscite on the issue of Manipur's independence by the civil society organizations was initially proposed by the RPF in the 90s and UNLF in 2005. Among those who addressed such a plebiscite meeting in Imphal on June 6 was the heir of the former king of Manipur, apart from other dignitaries such as a former Lok Sabha member, a former Human Rights Commissioner, the president of the Manipur Working Journalists' Union, leaders of political parties and several women leaders—always a potent force in Manipur.[37] It is to be noted that the participants in discussions on self-governance included those who had served the Government of India. The above discussions reflect the strong national will to govern their territory through their people.

Conclusion

Manipur had been ruled by the British from 1891 to 1947 and has been ruled by Government of India for 23 years from 1949 to 1972. In this period, the composition of the population of Manipur was altered; the backbone of economy as well as the self-governance was destroyed through the New Delhi-appointed rulers. Considering the changes in socio-political-economic situations during the rule of New Delhi, Manipur should qualify as a Non-Self-Governing-Territory. Jorris Duursman, in his "Fragmentation and the international relations of Micro States" observes that "People who find themselves in similar circumstances as colonies will enjoy a complete right of self-determination even if they are not specifically mentioned in the list of the Non-Self-Governing-Territories.[38]

As per the UN study guidelines, the Manipuri people possess the right to self-determination. The Manipuri people who have not exercised their inalienable right to self-determination since 1949 have not abdicated this right in any sense of the term. The Government of India is suppressing the right through military might. The right of the people of Manipur has to be exercised for a respectable and peaceful solution to Manipur issue. The national liberation movement is exercising its right to self-defence and self-preservation, without any prejudice to the genuine self-integrity of India.[39] It has also been observed that when we review situations invoking the principle of self-determination, we encounter what we must call the politics of avoidance: the principle of self-determination has been reduced to a weapon of political rhetoric.[40] The international community, therefore, has abandoned people who have the claim to the principle of self-determination. But fortunately the right to self-determination has been continuously evolving conceptually and experientially in response to the pressure of events, geopolitical priorities, and the prevailing moral and political climate.[41]

NOTES AND REFERENCES

1. Naorem Sanajaoba, *Manipur Past and Present volume III, Manipuri Nagas and Kuki-Chins*, Mittal Publications, New Delhi, 1995.
2. Rajkumar Maipaksana, "Constitutional Development in a Nutshell" in, *Annexation of Manipur 1949*, Peoples Democratic Movement, Imphal, 1995.
3. Neera Chandhoke, *A State of One's Own: Secessionism and Federalism in India*. Working Paper No. 80 Crisis State Programme, LSE, London, 2006.
4. Naorem Sanajaoba, "Key Note address to the National Convention on Manipur Merger Issue" in, *Annexation of Manipur 1949*, Peoples Democratic Movement, Imphal, 1995.
5. S. Bhubol, "Governance Deviate Peace-Path-Now Ripe for Resolution", *The Orient Vision*, 6, 1 and 2 (2009).
6. Sanjib Baruah, *Durable Disorder: Understanding the Politics of Northeast India*, Oxford University Press, New Delhi, 2005.
7. Sajal Nag, *Contesting Marginality: Ethnicity, Insurgency and Subnationalism in North-East India*, Manohar Publications, New Delhi, 2002.
8. Kunal, Chattopadhyay, *et al.*, *The Permanent Revolution and Results and Prospects—Leon Trotsky*, Aakar Books, New Delhi, 2005.

9. Naorem Sanajaoba, Armed Forces Special Power Act, 1958– a Law for extra judicial execution in perpetuity. Paper at *AASU- Apunba Lup, One Day Convention*, Guwahati, 2006.
10. Sobhapati Samom, 'Talks only on the issue of sovereignty of Manipur', *North East Sun*, 31 May, 2009.
11. Centre for Organization Research and Education (CORE), "The Manipur Nation: A Position" in Laifungbam Debabrata Roy, *et al.*, *Contour of Conflict: Pathway of Peace*, ICTCP-North East Zone, Guwahati, 2007. Hereafter CORE.
12. Core, Manipur*: A Report on Impunity of Human Rights Violations under the AFSPA 1958, Amended-1972*. Submitted to the Special Rapporteur on the Human Rights and Fundamental Freedoms of Indigenous People, 2002.
13. Soyam Lokendrajit Singh, *Why AFSPA Should be Repealed*. Manipur University Students Union, Imphal, 2004.
14. Andrew Robinson, *The Rhizomes of Manipur*. Seminar Paper, Institute of Asia Pacific Studies, University of Nottingham, 2005.
15. Karen Parker, "Understanding Self-Determination: The Basics", paper presented to *First International Conference on the Right to Self-determination*, United Nation, (August 2000).
16. *Ibid*. The said two important studies are: *A Critescu, The Right to Self-Determination*, U.N. Doc. E/CN.4/Sub.2/404/Rev. 1, U.N. Sales No. E.80. XIV. 3 (1980); and, H. Gros Espiell, *The Right to Self-Determination*, U.N. Doc. E/CN.4/Sub.2/405/Rev.1, U.N. Sales No. E.79.XIV.5 (1980).
17. Core 2007, N. 11.
18. *Ibid*.
19. Soibam Ibomcha Singh, *Community Policing: Principles, Practices and Perspectives in the Context of Manipur*. Akansha Publication, New Delhi, 2007.
20. Shukhdeba S. Hanjabam, "The Meitei Upsurge in Manipur", *Asia-Europe Journal*, 6, 1, 2008.
21. N. Sanajaoba, *Manipur Past and Present, Vol. 1, History, Policy and Law*, Mittal, New Delhi, 1988.
22. *Ibid*.
23. Cited in Sanajaoba, *Manipur: Past and Present*, Vol. III, 1995, N.1.
24. AMCTA, Manipur: Fact File, (Imphal 2001).
25. Sanajaoba, N. 23.
26. Lokendro Arambam, "Puya Meithaba: Indianisation and its Predicaments—A Contemporary Re-Interpretation", *The Orient Vision*, 5, 1 (January-March 2008).
27. Cited in Sanajaoba, N. 21.

28. J.J. Roy Burman, Contour of Naga Upsurge, *Asia Europe Journal*, 6,1 (2008).
29. Core, 2007, N. 11.
30. United Committee Manipur, Influx of Migrants into Manipur: A threat to the Indigenous Ethnic People, Imphal, 2005.
31. Sagolsem Hemanta, Khenjoi, *Chingsangda* tr., In the Hill Ranges of Khengjoy, Imphal, 2006.
32. Shoma Chaudhury, "Life In A Shadow Land". *Tehelka Magazine*. 6, 15 August, 2009.
33. This information is based on interview with AMSU leaders.
34. E Nilakanta Singh, *Fragmentation of Manipur Culture,* Omsons Publications, New Delhi, 1993.
35. W. Ibemu Devi, *Meitei Revivalism*, unpublished M.A. Thesis, Manipur University, 1991.
36. Cited in S. Chelliah "Asserting Nationhood through Personal Name Choice: The case of the Meitei of Northeast India", *Anthropological Linguistics*, 47: 2, 2005.
37. M.S. Prabhakara, The States: Degree of Separatism, *The Frontline*, 23, 18 September, 2006, pp. 9-22.
38. Duursman Jorris, Fragmentation and the international relations of Micro States, Cambridge University Press, Cambridge, 1996.
39. Core 2007, N. 11.
40. Parker, N. 15.
41. Richard A. Falk, *Human Rights Horizons: The Pursuit of Justice in a Globalizing World*. Routledge, London, 2000.

CHAPTER – 4

Integration or Annexation? Manipur's Relations with India 1947-1949

John Parratt and Arambam Saroj Nalini Paratt

Introduction

The manner and legality of what Menon euphemistically called the integration of the Princely States into India after 1947[1] has still not yet received the scholarly attention it deserves. Apart from the high profile cases of Hyderabad and Kashmir, and Vanja Rangaswami's study of the southern states of Mysore, Travencore and Cochin, little in depth analysis of the fate of individual Princely States has been attempted.[2] The two north-eastern states of Tripura and Manipur were among the very last to be absorbed, and Menon and his master Sardar Patel seem to have regarded them merely as a small mopping up operation. However the case of Manipur raises particularly large issues both as to the manner and the validity under international law of its absorption. Menon's own semi-official account reveals Patel's and his own agenda. Specifically with regard to Manipur, which is dismissed in Menon's account in less than page, he reveals not only a serious lack of factual knowledge about the state (which is all the more surprising given Manipur's critical role in the events of World War II), but even more extraordinarily he fails even to get the date of merger correct.[3] His bland comment that 'the merger was signed by the Maharajah? masks—whether deliberately or through ignorance—a situation which was far more complex and controversial. Manipuri written traditions trace its existence as an independent state back to the first century.[4] It established diplomatic relations with the British through a resident Political Agent in 1835. In 1890 a dispute over succession arose, which gave the British an opportunity to intervene in the internal affairs of the state, and the following year Manipur suffered a military defeat at their hands.[5]

However, the state was not annexed to the Crown, though it did lose some of its autonomy. A boy Raja, Chura Chand, was appointed by the British, and the colonial power ruled through the Political Agent until he attained his majority. After Chura Chand's coronation in 1908 the administration of the state was handed back to him, and he ruled with the assistance of an appointed Durbar of which the Assistant Political Agent was the President. The British retained direct control over the Hills and over the 'Reserve' in the heart of the capital Imphal. The Political Agent, acting for the Governor of Assam, had some degree of veto over the rajah's rule, though this was seldom used.[6]

Manipur's Internal Politics to 15th August, 1947

Towards the end of the 1930s popular movements for democratic reform began to emerge.[7] Partly in response to British calls for more responsible government, but much more as a result of continual lobbying from within the state itself the Maharajah Bodh Chandra[8], reluctantly agreed to the setting up of a 'Constitution Making Committee' in March 1947.[9] The Committee completed its work quite swiftly and the new constitution was adopted by royal decree in July 1947. Perhaps surprisingly, the recommendation was for elections to a Legislative Assembly by full adult franchise, with no required qualification for voting in terms either of education or land ownership.[10] Due largely to the procrastination of the Maharajah elections were not held until June and July the following year. In the meantime an Interim Council was set up, largely made up of appointees of the Maharajah and Assistant Political Agent Frank Pearson, which took office the day before Indian independence was declared.[11]

Manipur's celebration of Indian independence proved a curious affair, neither the Maharajah nor the Governor of Assam, Sir Akbar Hydari, seeming to be clear as to what status it conveyed upon the relation between India and Manipur, or how the event should rightly be observed. The Manipuri leaders, whatever their views on the integration issue, seem to have taken at face value British assertions[12] that the end of British paramountcy would mean sovereign independence and the freedom for Manipur to negotiate its relationship with the new India. As it turned out the events of 15th August, 1947 in Manipur bordered on the farcical, and neither of the two British officers most intimately involved, Political Agent G.P. Stewart[13] and Frank Pearson seemed particularly competent or well briefed. Stewart initially rejected the Maharajah's proposal for a flag hoisting ceremony on 14th August, and instead requested Bodh Chandra to come to the residency at midnight, which after some demur the Maharajah agreed to do.[14] Eventually Hydari tactfully indicated to the Maharajah that he would consider it a courtesy if the Union flag might be hoisted on that day along with the Manipur national flag[15] in the area of the old capital (the Kangla) situated in the Reserve.[16] Stewart, taking an over zealous stand on his new (but very temporary position) as 'Dominion Agent', vehemently rejected this idea, since in his opinion neither the Reserve nor the other former British enclaves in Manipur were to be formally retroceded to Manipur on 15th August. Eventually only the Pakhangba flag was raised, first in the Kangla and subsequently in the Palace compound. Pro-Congress supporters, however, made a show of[17] unofficially displaying the Union flag in public places in Imphal. Stewart's brief speech expressed the wish that the agreements (the details of which he did not specify) would be carried out for the peace and prosperity of Manipur.[18]

Pearson meanwhile had been desperately trying to finalise the acceptance of his nominees for the Interim Council only five days before the hand over of power, in the face of the procrastination of the Maharajah and the latter's suspicion of the motives of his brother, Maharajkumar Priyabrata, Pearson's proposed Chief Minister. Pearson was clearly quite naive as to the motives and qualities of the pro-Congress candidates. While his nominees were eventually pushed through, Pearson himself lost face, failed to put in an appearance at the swearing in of the Interim Council, and departed Manipur hurriedly leaving only a farewell note.[19]

Manipur's Relations with India Before 15th August, 1947

Manipur's relationship to the Government of India, effected through the Governor of Assam, had been since 1891 fraught with tension and inconsistencies, and, as we have noted, the Maharajah's rule since 1908 had been subject to certain reins of control. In this respect Indian independence left numerous loose ends to disentangle. There had been a certain degree of lassitude and case by case decisions in interpreting the various rules for the governing of Manipur.[20] However, that may be, on 15th August, 1947 these agreements fell away. According to the Indian Independence Act (1947, paragraph 7b) on that date 'the suzerainity of His Majesty over the States lapsed and with it all treatises and agreements.' Indian independence had been announced on 10th July, 1947, and on 25th of the same month Mountbatten had declared that suzerainity over the States also lapsed and they were, therefore, independent. Against this background it is important to examine those agreements made during this period between Manipur and the Government of India (whether or not through the Governor of Assam). Three such agreements stand out as especially important:

1. the written memoranda between the Governor of Assam and the Maharajah dated 1st and 2nd of July, 1947;[21]
2. the Instrument of Accession, signed by on 11th August, 1947;
3. the Merger Agreement signed on 21st September, 1949.

The first two of these agreements were signed during the period of agitation leading up to responsible government, the last, of course, well after the democratically elected government had taken power in Manipur.

The memorandum of 1st July, 1947, which was signed by the Maharajah and the Manipuri members of the then ruling Durbar, covered a number of heads including Manipur's representation on the Constituent Assembly, the setting up of the Interim Council, and the need for a new constitution within one year. With specific regard to the relationship between Manipur and India the main points of agreement were:

1. that Manipur would need assistance from India 'both in external defence and internal security;[22]
2. the Union would retain control of Posts and Telegraphs facilities, and that the arrangements regarding import and export, currency, and provincial taxation on goods would continue;

3. the Union would appoint an officer; 'to represent the Government in these matters in Manipur';
4. that there would be the minimum of interference in the internal affairs of the State;
5. that the retrocession of the British Reserve should be expedited, but that for the time being the Union Government would retain control of the cantonment, the Residency and Political Agent's office, and the area known as Barapura (*sic* Babupara); and
6. the matter of future rental payment for the alienated territory of the Kabaw Valley would be taken up with the Union.[23]

The 2nd of July agreement[24] was also signed by the Maharajah and members of the Durbar (this time including Pearson in his capacity as President). This allowed rather more in the way of interference in Manipur's internal affairs, including a provision that the Maharajah would accept an officer appointed by the Union Government to carry out the Governor's functions as regards the agreement, and that this official (the Dominion Agent) could call for papers relating to the Hill tribes and issue advice, and further that no orders regarding the Hill tribes could be issued without his advice.[25] However (and somewhat contradictorily), it further stipulated that in the application of the power vested in him under this section the Dominion Agent shall avoid interference in the day-to-day administration of the Hills. Precisely what the status and practical meaning of this latter clause was is unclear, but in point of fact the Maharajah did officially assume full control over the Hills on 10th August, 1947. The Legislative Assembly made provision for Hill members in proportion to the population and also for two Hill members to sit on the Council of Ministers. Whatever reservations the British and their successors might have had about the possible neglect of the Hill tracts by the government in Imphal thus were clearly unfounded.

Even though these agreements were signed before the elected government assumed power in Manipur, there is nothing in them which would contradict the sovereign powers of that Legislature, save in those specific areas set out in paragraphs 1 and 2 of the memo of July 1st, 1947. These areas were broadly those covered by the Act of Accession, which was signed by the Maharajah on 11th August, 1947. The essence of this Act is really contained in the attachment, the Schedule. This acceeded (as far as was relevent to Manipur) Union control over defence, external affairs, and communications. At the same time it explicitly guaranteed to the ruler his continued sovereignty over the State.[26]

Continuing Indian-Manipur Relations After 15th August, 1947

On the day of India's independence there were demonstrations in Imphal, organised largely by left wing groups, agitating for the replacement of the pro-Congress Interim Council by an elected Assembly. These were well attended but were also marked by a certain amount of pro-Union activity, including the waving of Indian flags. As we have seen, largely due to the procrastination of Bodh Chandra and the desire of the Interim Council to hang on to power, the elections for the Legislature were not held until June and July 1948.

The results of these elections were inconclusive, and a coalition government took office made up of the majority of the Praja Santi (a broad pro-royalist party), supported by the Peasant Party (the Krishak Sabha), and the Hill members.[27] The expectations of the Manipur State Congress that it would control the state were disappointed. As the second largest party the Manipur State Congress became the official opposition, and this was to have repercussions in their attempts to seize power with the support of the All India Congress later on. However, the new Legislature was not scheduled to take office until 18th October, 1948, and in the meantime the pro-Congress Interim Council continued to hold power, and did what it could to disadvantage its opponents.[28]

Stewart left Manipur on 17th August, and his place as Dominion Agent was taken by Debeswar Sharma. Sharma did not arrive until November and seems to have been a quite disastrous choice. The Manipuri leaders regarded him as too smooth to be trusted, and it was not long before he was plunged headlong into a baptism of fire which cruelly exposed his deviousness and inadequacies.[29] The Congress in Manipur had been rent into two factions for some time, and both were dominated by men whose main aim seems to have been to seize political power and all its material benefits. Boycotts and strikes became commonplace, and were often hijacked by one or other Congress group for their own ends. Sharma was drawn into the mire of local politicking with disastrous consequences for his official position. He was dismissed by Hydari in May 1948.[30] The Governor decided that he would henceforth deal directly with Manipur himself, and went on to appoint MK. Priyabrata, who was still Chief Minister, to act on his behalf with the title of 'Dewan.'[31] The confusion of these two roles, with their different responsibilities, in the same person was to have unhelpful repercussions later on.

Sir Akbar Hydari died on a visit to Manipur in December 1948.[32] He was succeeded by Sri Prakasa, a very different character and a career diplomat with a very clear agenda for the swift and ruthless integration of the north eastern states of Manipur and Tripura. Fortuitously, and as it turned out unhappily for Manipur, Prakasa had already met Bodh Chandra some years before. In 1934, during the reign of his father Chura Chand, Bodh Chandra had been sent out of the state to Banares into virtual exile because his father had suspected he had been implicated in a plot to seize the throne. There he had been befriended by Prakasa, and lived with him for three years.[33] Whatever the exact relationship between the two, Bodh Chandra clearly felt obligated to Prakasa on a personal level and this seems to have clouded his judgement with regard to state affairs. Prakasa, for his part, lost no time in preparing the ground for a takeover of Manipur. He visited Manipur in March 1949. In a meeting with Bodh Chandra he continued to give the Maharajah the impression that the Union Government had no designs on the state, and later put in writing that the 'distinct identity of Manipur would be preserved, and that no merger with the Centre or any other territory would be effected, except military relations for the defence of India as a whole'.[34] This last comment was ominous (though no one in Manipur realised this at the time), and the following month Prakasa sent his military adviser with Rustomji (the special adviser for the northern states) to assess the suspected Communist threat.[35] Despite the evident public concern that these visits were harbingers of an Indian takeover, the Legislative Assembly failed to debate the darkening political situation. The Maharajah meanwhile began to realise that, since Prakasa intended to appoint a new dewan in place of Priyabrata, he would be well advised to clarify this official's role and authority. In a long memorandum to the Governor[36] he stipulated that if a dewan were appointed it should be a person acceptable to the Maharajah himself, that he should have the power to demand the dewan's removal, and that the dewan should 'have the minimum of interference in the administration of the state' and function only to safeguard the treaty obligations between Manipur and the Union. Bodh Chandra's memorandum was rudely ignored, and Prakasa proceeded to reinvent unilaterally the powers of the dewan. On 14th April, 1949 Rustomji came back to Imphal with the new dewan, Major-General Rawal Amar Singh.[37] Rustomji brought with him a letter setting out the powers which the Government of India had given to the dewan over the State of Manipur.[38] These were severe and wide ranging. Crucially the Indian Government demanded that 'the administration of Manipur State would be carried on under the general superintendence, guidance and control of the Dewan', who would have the right to call for any papers from any ministry and 'pass such orders as he might consider fit and proper on them, in consultation with the Minister concerned'. The Dewan would further have direct charge of the portfolios of Law and Order, Administration of the Hills, State Forces, and Relations with the Government of India, and would also have the ultimate say in the distribution of portfolios (such as remained) within the Council of Ministers.[39] Nothing in previous agreements warranted such sweeping powers for the representative of the Government of India, and these demands were thus without any legal basis. Prakasa, however, continued to feed the gullibility of the Maharajah with the myth that nothing in these requirements affected the dignity of the State. Rustomji demanded the Maharajah issue an order accepting the appointment of Rawal Singh and the conditions of his appointment within two days. No discussion was permitted, and Bodh Chandra weakly caved in to pressure.[40] Neither the Council of Ministers nor the Legislature questioned the sweeping powers given to the Dewan over the State, nor whether, since the Maharajah's authority had now passed to the elected Legislature, he actually had the power to make the proclamation appointing a dewan with such vastly enhanced powers. The way towards annexation had now been smoothed by a skilful combination of deviousness and bullying on Prakasa's part. The weakness of the Maharajah's response, and the lamentable failure to grasp political realities on the part of the Legislature, had made a takeover virtually certain.

Bodh Chandra subsequently began to have second thoughts. Two months later he wrote to Prakasa and belatedly pointed out that there was no provision in the State Constitution for a Dewan with these powers and that it was in any case up to the Assembly to approve the regulations.[41] Unsurprisingly Prakasa cursorily dismissed this protest with the comment that the Government of India did not recognise the Council of Ministers or the Assembly, and regarded the Maharajah as the sole ruler of the State. To add insult to injury he went on to instruct the Maharajah to make full use of the advice of the Dewan, with a veiled threat of the consequences if he did not.[42] This was indeed a cynical response: the Government of independent India, which proclaimed democracy as a major plank in its platform, was now declaring itself unwilling to recognise the democratically elected government of a state on its borders.

Meantime, as news of these events became public, reactions became polarised. The Socialist parties submitted a formal protest at the Dewan's assumption of powers which constitutionally belonged to the Legislature, but since their own agenda was for the merger of Manipur with other territories in Assam they secured little popular support. An attempt by the Manipur State Congress (which was by now largely in the pocket of the All-India Congress) to drum up support for full merger with India at a mass public meeting backfired badly when most of the crowd decamped to another venue. There they passed strong resolutions denouncing the Manipur Congress' deceitfulness, and insisting that the kingship must not be abolished nor the state be integrated into India.[43] The Hill MLAs convened and declared themselves firmly against any merger proposal, as did the Muslim members.[44] The Communists predictably denounced the Nehru government as inefficient and lackeys of the West. In August the MLAs belonging to the ruling coalition Praja Santi party, which favoured a separate state, authorised N. Ibomcha (a Meitei) and Lunneh (a Hill Member) to prepare a paper setting out coherent reasons why Manipur should not be merged with India. Copies of this paper were sent to the Prime Minister Nehru, to Deputy Prime Minister Sardar Patel (who was also of course in charge of the States), to the Governor of Assam, and to the Dewan.[45] But by this time of course the Government of India had long since determined on its course of action. Their plea fell on deaf ears and no opportunity was afforded the members to put their case orally.[46] The stage had been set for the final act.

'Is There No Brigadier in Shillong'

The main players on the Indian side, Rawal Amar Singh and Prakasa realised that the simplest way to attain their objective was to isolate the weak Maharajah from his advisers and the Council of Ministers, and subject him to pressure. Meanwhile Rustomji, aware of the antagonism between Bodh Chandra and his brother Priyabrata, who still retained his position as Chief Minister, continued to cultivate the latter's confidence.[47] Events conspired to lead Bodh Chandra to play into their hands.

Bodh Chandra was by now becoming more and more irritated at the Dewan's frequent and often tactless interference in the affairs of the state. This came to head in a sharp conflict over an issue concerning the legality of the election of a Muslim member to the Legislature. The Maharajah determined to address his complaint about the Dewan directly to the Governor, and on 29th August sent a telegram to Shillong asking for a meeting with Prakasa. In early September Prakasa, together with Rustomji, went to Delhi to meet Menon, who instructed the Governor to expedite the merger of Manipur. From there they were summoned to Bombay to receive further orders from Sardar Patel, who was by then seriously ill. When Prakasa ventured to suggest that the Maharajah might not agree to sign the merger document, Patel's reply left him in doubt as to the course of action he would need to take in such an eventuality: was there, he demanded, no brigadier in Shillong?[48] On his return Prakasa invited the Maharajah to discuss the situation in Manipur. Bodh Chandra was later to claim that he did not suspect that a proposal for a full merger with India would be on the agenda at this meeting. If this is so then it would indicate that the Maharajah was totally out of touch with events, for by early September the press both within and outside the state had been speculating about the matter. The speaker of the Assembly had also unsuccessfully requested that the issue of a possible merger should be debated in the House. At any rate Bodh Chandra, together with his advisers, servants, and an escort departed from Imphal in a fleet of cars on 15th September, and reached Redlands, his personal residence in Shillong, on 17th. He immediately sent his ADC to the Governor's residence to advise Prakasa of his arrival, only to be told that the latter was away from Shillong.[49] Meanwhile Redlands was surrounded by a strong contingent of the Indian army, who pitched their tents within the grounds. Plain clothes police also appeared and refused to allow anyone in or out. Attempts by the Maharajah's staff to send out telegrams were refused, and since there was no telephone in the building the Maharajah's party found themselves virtual prisoners. Requests to withdraw the security police were ignored.[50]

Prakasa arrived back late in the evening and it was arranged that he would meet Bodh Chandra at 9 a.m. on the 18th. The Maharajah's party, consisting of Bodh Chandra himself, his ADC Mayengbam Anandamohon, and his private secretary, Sanasam Gourahari, arrived shortly before the appointed hour but were then kept waiting for some time. Prakasa eventually appeared, and with him Rustomji and the secretary, Krishnamurthy. The latter now presented the merger document to the Maharajah, who read it through and commented that he could not sign it without first consulting his Council of Ministers. This position he maintained despite crude threats from Rustomji.[51] Prakasa's approach, perhaps because he knew Bodh Chandra, was more diplomatic. However, he argued that he was under orders from Menon, and could not accept the Maharajah's proposal to return to Imphal and consult his ministers. He stressed that the merger had to be signed within 'a few days'. A further meeting was agreed for the following morning.

According to Gourahari, Bodh Chandra was so deeply upset that he wept profusely on the way back to Redlands, and Gourhari feared that he would 'behave insanely'[52] Prakasa continued to pressurise Bodh Chandra by sending him a written message to the effect that he had now been instructed that the merger had to be signed by the 30th. The Maharajah, by now composed, again responded that it would be unconstitutional for him to sign the merger, since sovereignty in Manipur had been transferred to the elected Assembly.[53] Prakasa immediately cabled Patel that since the Maharajah was intending to return to Imphal for consultation he had instructed the police to detain him and his party if they attempted to leave Redlands. He requested the Deputy Prime Minister immediately to telegraph instructions for Bodh Chandra's detention under any orders whatsoever.[54] Both the police and army guards on Redlands were doubled.[55]

Next morning, September 19th, Bodh Chandra wrote to the Governor cancelling their appointment since in his view it would serve no purpose. A brisk exchange of notes continued throughout the day. Prakasa repeated that it was the Government of India's intention to deal only with the Maharajah as the sole ruler of the state, and then promised that the Government would take responsibility for any objections which might be raised within Manipur (though quite how they intended to do this was not specified). Bodh Chandra was mollified to some extent, but still not convinced, and repeated his view that under the Manipur constitution only the Council of Ministers could decide on the merger. He agreed to meet the Governor again and read, and even commented on the draft agreement (succeeding in the process in securing a substantial increase in his own privy purse) but continued to maintain that he could not sign the document alone.

Prakasa now decided on a more intimate approach, and sent a message to say that he would come unaccompanied to Redlands that afternoon. He arrived one hour early, while the Maharajah was taking a siesta. When he emerged, only half dressed. Prakasa spoke to him 'as a son' and told him that the Indian Government was quite prepared to use force. He went on to say that if this were about to happen he would have to resign as Governor of Assam, and his replacement would be likely to impose much harsher conditions on Manipur. Bodh Chandra gave in and agreed to sign that day. His ADC, Gourahari, had been confined to his room under guard while this conversation was going on. When he remonstrated with his ruler Bodh Chandra responded that they would try the merger for a few years, apparently under the impression that it could be reversed.[56] The final version of the agreement contained no indication of the way the state would be governed. Its main provisions concerned the Maharajah's Privy Purse, and the privileges he would retain, and the conditions of service for public servants.[57] Back in Manipur rumours about the signing began to circulate (including one that the Maharajah had been forced to sign at gun point). Though there was much talk, there was little action. No voice was raised in the Assembly, and the honourable members occupied their final days discussing the matter of liquour tax. Most MLAs seemed intent on preserving their privileged positions under the new regime, but in this almost all of them were to be disappointed. The focus of opposition now shifted to the underground armed resistance movements.

The handover ceremony took place on 15th October on the polo ground in a heavy rainstorm. The Governor of Assam was not present and attendance was sparse. Many of the Manipuri leaders (including MK. Priyabarta) stayed away. The same day Rawal Amar Singh became the first Indian Chief Commissioner of Manipur. His first act was to issue an order abolishing the Council of Ministers and the assembly, and appropriating all powers in his own hands. A few days earlier a battalion of the regular Indian army had been stationed in Imphal to discourage any possible riots against the merger and to neutralise the contingent of the Assam Rifles, whose loyalty to India was considered doubtful. Along with integration into the Indian Union an era of heavy military presence had begun.

Conclusion

Half a century on, Manipuri politicians and historians (in common with those elsewhere in the north-east) have begun to re-examine the circumstances and implications of absorption into the Indian Union. A number of the factors which, at the time, were advanced to justify the takeover of Manipur, now look increasingly unconvincing. Sardar Patel's theory of a common Aryan blood as a uniting bond for the Indian subcontinent simply does not apply in much of the north-east, which is ethnically, linguistically, and culturally quite distinct. The supposed Communist threat in Manipur was grossly (and possibly deliberately) exaggerated, and the other insurgency movements were in the main a direct result of Indian annexation. The claim by the Union Government that Manipur suffered from underdevelopment was probably true, though most Manipuris would argue that since 1949 it has remained neglected and grossly underfunded, with much of its resources being used to fund the wholly counter-productive presence of Indian security forces.

But more important has been the questioning on the part of Manipuri intellectuals of the whole legality of the merger. Aside from the now largely discredited remnants of the old Manipur Congress, most would argue that on 15th August, 1947 full independence returned to Manipur.[58] The State Constitution, adopted the previous month and brought to fruition with the convening of the Legislative Assembly in the October of the following year, was the first in the subcontinent to grant full adult franchise, with the Maharajah as a constitutional sovereign.[59] The bitter irony, as Manipuris see it, is that independent India, which proclaimed its dedication to democracy, wilfully refused to recognise the democratically elected government of its tiny neighbour, and instead persisted in dealing with the former feudal ruler, who himself repeatedly protested that he had surrendered his power to the elected Assembly. Furthermore, Manipur was not a petty state surrounded by Indian territory, but a border state more akin to Sikkim and Kashmir. It is difficult to deny the force of these arguments, and to resist the conclusion that the Union Government, in its eagerness to maximise its borders, simply annexed Manipur.

There would, of course, have been severe practical difficulties in the way of Manipur's preserving its independence. The Union Government controlled most of its finances and indeed froze all the State funds held by the Treasury. Furthermore, Menon's interpretation of the defence clause in the Standstill Agreement and the Act of Accession would have enabled Indian troops to enter the state, not only on the grounds of external threat, but also whenever internal security appeared to be threatened,[60] and one can well imagine that pretexts for such action would not have been hard to create. The inaction of the United Nations, which disapproved of the invasion of Hyderabad in 1948 and of Goa thirteen years later, gives no grounds for thinking that Manipur would have had practical support from the international community at the time. In the end, as Priyabrata asks,[61] to which court could Manipur have appealed? All that could have been done, he concludes, was 'to act like Mr. Phizo'.[62]

NOTES AND REFERENCES

1. V.P. Menon, *Integration of the Indian States*, Madras, 1956. References below are to the 1996 edition.
2. See Rangaswami, *The Story of Integration: A New Interpretation*, Madras, 1981; Ian Copland, *Revisionist the Princes of India in the Endgame of Empire 1917-1947*, Cambridge, 1997 unfortunately contains only three minor references to Manipur, all of them to one degree or another inaccurate. There are no indexed references to Manipur in T.P. Mansergh, *The Transfer of Power*. Apart from Kashmir, Manipur was in the last group of states to be integrated (along with Tripura, Bhopal and Cooch Behar).
3. *N.1*, p. 302. Menon gives it as 15th October, 1948, which a full year too early.
4. L. Ibungohal Singh and N. Khelachandra Singh, *Cheitharol Kumbaba* (Royal Chronicle), Manipuri Sahitya Parishad, Imphal 1987. While the first sections of the Chronicle are cast in mythological language it is substantially historically correct from about the 14th century. Apart from a brief period of Burmese domination between 1819-1825 Manipur functioned as an independent monarchy.
5. See John Parratt and Saroj Arambam Parratt, *Queen Empress vs. Tikendrajit: The Anglo-Manipur Conflict of 1891* (New Delhi, 1992).
6. For the situation during this period see J. Shakespear, *Manipur under British Management 1891-1907*, Shillong, 1907; and Lal Dena *British Policy towards Manipur 1891-1919,* Imphal, 1984.
7. See Saroj N. Arambam Parratt and John Parratt 'The Second Women's War and the Emergence of Democratic Government in Manipur' forthcoming in *Modern Asian Studies*. For general surveys of this

period see especially Karam Manimohan Singh, *Hijam Irabot Singh and Political Movements in Manipur*, New Delhi, 1989; and N. Lokendra Singh, *The Unquiet Valley: society, economy and politics in Manipur 1891-1950*, Mittal, New Delhi, 1998.

8. Bodh Chandra had succeeded his father Chura Chand in 1941. The first formal demand for a democratic constitution was made by the Nikhil Manipuri Mahasabha in 1938, though the socialist reformer Hijam Irabot had made public calls for reform earlier than this. See John Parratt And Saroj N. Arambam Parratt 'Hijam Irabot and the Radical Socialist Democratic Movement in Manipur' forthcoming in *Internationales Asienforum*.
9. This committee was composed partly of members nominated by the Maharajah and partly by election with limited franchise. Most of the nominated members were strong Manipur Congress supporters; the Durbar President, Frank Pearson, who made no secret of his support of Indian Congress and opposition to full franchise, was largely responsible for securing their appointment.
10. The constitution provided for the appointment of a Council of Ministers from the members of the Legislature, but the appointment of the Chief Minister remained in the gift of the Maharajah. This was the first election on the basis of full adult franchise on the Indian subcontinent, the rest of India had to wait until 1952.
11. Maharajkumar Priyabrata, the brother of the Maharajah, replaced Pearson as Chief Minister.
12. Menon himself gives some of the relevent statements by Attlee and Mountbatten (*op. cit.* p. 476) and also by Nehru and Patel (p. 276): though of course it is clear that neither Nehru nor Patel was inclined to consider full independence of any state as a realistic option.
13. Who actually knew Manipur quite well, having served as Durbar President in the reign of Chura Chand.
14. Lt. Col. (R.H. Bhuban Singh has a highly amusing account of this meeting based on eyewitness reports, see his *The Merger of Manipur*, Imphal, 1988, pp. 71-74.
15. Known as the Pakhangba flag, it consisted of an intricately coiled snake symbol, representing Pakhangba, the ancestral deity of the Meiteis.
16. This area, the Kangla, was the former palace compound, which was seized by the British in 1891
17. Bhuban, whose sympathies were for Indian integration, maintains both flags were raised (*op. cit.* p. 74), but the official programme, quoted by Karam Manimohan (*op. cit.* p. 250), and eyewitness accounts, do not support this. The raising of the Pakhngba flag in the Kangla can

only be regarded as a statement that full sovereignty had returned to 'Meiteileipak' (Manipur). This is confirmed by the entry in the Cheitharol Kumbaba for Friday 29th of the month Thawan (June/July), which states that 'at ten minutes past ten o'clock the maharajah and the maharani sat in the Kangla and performed a religious rite, saying that from that day onwards they had possessed the country. At ten forty a flag with the insignia of Pakhangba was flown in the state durbar in the Kangla. At eight o'clock in the presence of all the people the bara sahib, in the state durbar hall, handed over all the land of Manipur into the hands of Srijut Maraharajah. Asongshangbam Major fired an eighteen canon salute.'

18. Karam Manimohan, *op. cit.* p. 251.
19. Pearson's memoir confirms Manipuri reports of him as politically clumsy and naive, and clearly taken in by the Congress leaders (British Library, Oriental and India Office Collections (hereafter O&IOC) MS EUR F226/21). Most other sources, English as well as Manipuri, regard the Manipur Congress leaders as unprincipled power seekers. I can find no supporting evidence for Pearson's claim that Congress wanted him to stay on as Chief Minister, though this is not unlikely as they were obviously cleverly manipulating him for their own ends: as it turned out the Congress Party failed to dominate the Legislature.
20. The last British orders regarding the administration of Manipur were promulgated in 1935: during the Second World War Manipur was under military rule.
21. Manipur State Archives (hereafter MSA) Secret file C July 1947: the full texts are also given by Karam Manimohan, *op. cit.* pp. 223-24.
22. though the interpretation put on the latter phrase by Patel and Menon went far beyond what the Manipuris understood by it.
23. The Kabaw Valley, situated between Manipur and the Chindwin River, was in Manipuri possession until it was occupied by the Burmese during the first Burmese war. It was subsequently recaptured by Maharajah Gumbhir Singh in 1824-25. At the Treaty of Yandaboo the British agreed to allow the Burmese to occupy it for in exchange for an annual rental fee payable to the Maharajah.
24. This was actually a revision of an earlier draft which had been rejected a few days before.
25. This clause was presumably in deference to the fact that after 1891 the British had assumed direct control over the hills: this provision in fact limited the democratic representation of the hill peoples in contrast to the Manipur constitution.
26. 'Nothing in this Instrument affects the continuance of my sovereignty in and over this State, or, save as provided under this Instrument, the

exercise of any powers, authority and rights now enjoyed by me as Ruler of this State or the validity of any law at present in force in this State' (paragraph 8).

27. Besides the local constituencies, both Valley and Hill, there was provision for additional elected members representing commerce, education and the Manipuri Muslims.
28. The biggest casualty was Hijam Irabot, the leader of the socialist and peasant movements, who was forced to go underground: on Hijam Irabot see John Parratt and Saroj Arambam Parratt 'Hijam Irabot and the radical socialist-democratic movement in Manipur' in Internationales Asienforum (forthcoming).
29. Nari Rustomji, in his memoir, *Enchanted Frontier*, Calcutta, 1973, p. 89 described him as 'a senior Congressman of great ability and high ambitions.' E.T.D. Lambert's 'Special Report on Manipur' of 14.9.48, had a rather different view: of the man: he was, wrote Lambert, 'one of the nastiest pieces of work in Assam, a high grade opium smuggler and smooth individual with the tongue of a rattlesnake and the mind of a corkscrew' (O&IOL L/P&S/13/1803, Pol 4508/48).
30. According to Lambert for issuing over 500 illegal gun licences and racketeering in the issue of petrol coupons; but, as important, he clearly failed to exercise any diplomatic skills as Dominion Agent.
31. Despite the fact that relations between Bodh Chandra and his brother Priyabrata were cool, and that the Maharajah had tried to avoid appointing him as Chief Minister.
32. Hydari seems to have had a genuine concern for the state and related well to Bodh Chandra. He frequently visited Manipur for duck shooting at Lake Loktak, and it was there that he died. He was buried in Manipur. The course of the merger may well have been different had he lived.
33. MK. Priyabrata 'Reminisciences of the First and Last Chief Minister' in Naorem Sanajoaba ed. *Manipur Past and Present,* vol 1, Mittal, New Delhi, 1988, p. 139; Bhuban, *op. cit.* Pp. 115-6; also personal communication (1980) from the late Songaijam Nabakumar, a member of the Maharajah's staff.
34. MSA file DO 1986 P II/1 dated 23.3.49.
35. The Communist threat was greatly overplayed for their own political advantage by all parties at the time—the British, the Union Government, and the Manipur Congress, and also by the Interim Government: despite the connection of Hijam Irabot with Burmese Communist groups, the possibility of a Marxist takeover of Manipur was never remotely likely.
36. MSA file DO No 2088 P II/1 no date.
37. Bhuban, *op. cit.* 123 points out that his credentials were suspect in

that his rank was not earned in the Indian army, but in the service of the state of Jaipur, and that mainly for ceremonial duties.

38. Quoted in full by Karam Manimohan *op. cit.* pp. 334-5.
39. MSA correspondence of Prakasa to Bodh Chandra 14.4.49.
40. MSA Order 138 of 16.4.49 by Maharajah Bodh Chandra
41. MSA correspondence of Maharajah Bodh Chandra to Governor of Assam 25.6.49.
42. MSA correspondence of Prakasa to Bodh Chandra 4.7.49.
43. Karam Manimohan, *op. cit.* p. 347-8, also N. Joykumar Singh Merger of Manipur with India in Lal Dena, ed. *The History of Modern Manipur*, New Delhi, 1991, p. 184.
44. Lokendra, *op. cit.* p. 227.
45. MSA Resolution of the meeting of MLAs of the Praja Santi Party held on 25.8.49; also Karam Manimohan, *op. cit.* p. 352, Lokendra, *op. cit.* p. 226.
46. We cannot trace responses from any of the addresees to the Praja Santi's paper.
47. Priyobrata was an educated and calable man, and a former captain in the Indian army: his sympathies however leaned towards merger with India. He had got to know Rustomji while in Shillong immediately after the war.
48. Rustomji, *op. cit.* p. 109. Rustomji goes on to claim that he subsequently went to Imphal and told the Maharajah of the imminence of the enforced merger. We can find no confirmation of this in any of the Indian or Manipuri records, and such a claim can hardly be reconciled with what happened in Shillong.
49. Rustomji's claim (*op. cit.* p. 109) that he and Prakasa met the Maharajah on his arrival cannot be correct.
50. The details of events at Redlands are given in Bhuban's book, which is based on eyewitness accounts, including those of Gourahari and Anandamohan, both of whom were with the Maharajah during the negotiations. Bhuban himself is by no means antagonistic to the merger, which supports the essential trustworthiness of his account.
51. Bhuban (*op. cit.* p. 106) reports that Rustomji threatened that if Bodh Chandra did not sign he would never leave Shillong. At this the Maharajah turned to Prakasa and said he had not come there to talk to Rustomji but to the Governor. Prakasa then silenced his assistant.
52. Bhuban, *op. cit.* p. 108: according to Gourhari's account Bodh Chandra's insanity manifested itself again around midnight, when he proposed that he and his ADC should assassinate the Governor and then kill each other: this is supported by Songaijam Nabakumar (personal communication, 1980).
53. Bhuban quotes the text of the note in full, p. 109.

54. Source Bhuban: the urgency was stressed, 'immediately repeat immediately.'
55. Rustomji, *op. cit.* p. 109 euphemistically speaks of the Maharajah being 'honoured by a protective guard.'
56. Bizarre though the attitude of the Maharajah appears, there is clear evidence that the draft as signed by Bodh Chandra included several provisions which were omitted from the final version, including a clause which could be so interpreted. Article VI originally contained the provision 'it is also to be distinctly understood that should any circumstance hereafter arise by which the administration of the State now made over to the Dominion Government is to be reverted, then it should be restored to the Maharajah or his successors along with Manipur's original rights.' Additional clauses which do not appear in the final version included those safeguarding the priority of Manipuris for employment within the state, restricting immigration from outside Manipur, and continued Manipuri control of imports and exports (Article X): all these provisions were disregarded after October 1949. For the full texts of the sections omitted from the final version of the merger document see Karam Manomohan *op. cit.* pp. 428-29).
57. The last was violated almost immediately with the influx of appointees from India over the heads of existing Manipuri civil servants.
58. The best collection of papers making a strong defence of this case is the symposium Annexation of Manipur published by the People's Democratic Movement, Imphal 1995, being papers delivered mainly by academics and politicians two years earlier. The keynote address by Professor Noarem Sanajoaba, 'Manipurgi Lousinkhibagi Wathokta Achumba Thiba' (The Problem of the 1949 Annexation) (pp. 54-66) presents a trenchant analysis the issue from the standpoint of international law.
59. While it is true, as RK Jhlajit Singh points out in his strongly pro-Congress account in A Short History of Manipur (2nd edit. Imphal 1992) pp. 336-37 that there were some shortcomings in the constitution, especially in the prerogative it gave to the Maharajah to nominate the Chief Minister, his characterisation of it as 'a dangerous anachronism' is quite wrong: on the contrary it marked for the first time a break from a feudal monarchy.
60. Menon, *op. cit.* pp. 97, 112
61. *Op cit.* p. 128.
62. Which is what some did, though without a great deal of success: on the 'insurgency movements' see especially Phanjoubam Tarapot, *Insurgency Movement in North Eastern India*, New Delhi, 1993.

CHAPTER – 5

The Manipur Nation: A Position

CORE 1

Historical Evidence

> **"We had our independence for thousands of years, but our sovereignty was forcibly removed in 1949. So, our people are very eager to have their sovereignty again. It is our genuine demand and one day, I hope, we will be successful. Armed struggle is not the best way, but it is one of the ways."** [Leisemba, traditional king of Manipur, India. 9th March, 2007; in "a safe house for dangerous men" www.Theeconomist.com]

The State of Manipur, which lies in the latitude range of 23°83″ and 25°68″ (North) and in the longitude range of 93°03″ and 94°78″ (East), is one of the earliest States in the continent of Asia, including the Indian subcontinent. This ancient Asian State was known by different names to different countries that is—'Poirei Meitei Leipak' or 'Kangleipak' to the indigenous people of Manipur or Meiteis; 'Kathe' or 'Ponnas' to the Burmese; 'Hsiao Po-lo-mein' to the Chinese; 'Cassay' to the Shan; 'Moglai' to the Cacharis and Bengalis and 'Mekle' to the Assamese (as well as to the British in the 18th Century) in the pre-Christian period. Its location is identified with places within the jurisdiction of Tugma, Triglipton, Mareura and Kirrhadia according to the sources of Ptolemy. The Manipuri themselves knew the State by as many as 22 names in different ages and at different times. The early state of Pragjyotishpur or Kamrup, or present Indian state of Assam has been for millennia a buffer between State of Manipur and State of India known as Bharat for millennia. All the available maps available with India depict Manipur as an independent state till the annexation in 1949.

Table 5.1: Genealogy of Meidingu (Ningthou or Chiefs) of Meitei Nation (According to Chei'thaarol Kum'paba, the Annual Diaries of the Meitei)

No.	Name	Year wise period of their rule
1.	Nongda Lairen Pakhangba	33–154
2.	Khuiyoi Tompok	154–264
3.	Taothingmang	264–364
4.	Khui Ning-ngonba	364–379
5.	Pengsiba	379–394
6.	Kaokhangba	394–411
7.	Naokhamba	411–428
8.	Naophangba	428–518
9.	Sareimang	518–568
10.	Urakonthouba	568–658
11.	Naothingkhong	663–763
12.	Khongtekcha	763–773
13.	Keirencha	784–799
14.	Yaraba	799–821
15.	Ayangba	821–910
16.	Ningthouchen	910–949
17.	Chenglei Epan Lanthaba	949–969
18.	Yanglou Keiphaba	969–984
19.	Irengba	984–1074
20.	Loiyumba	1074–1122
21.	Loitongba	1122–1150
22.	Atom Yoiremba	1150–1163
23.	Iwanthaba	1163–1195
24.	Thawanthaba	1195–1231
25.	Chingthang Lanthaba	1231–1242
26.	Thingbai Selhongba	1242–1247
27.	Puranthaba	1247–1263
28.	Khumomba	1263–1278
29.	Moiramba	1278–1302
30.	Thangbi Lanthaba	1302–1324
31.	Kongyamba	1324–1335
32.	Telheiba	1335 –1355
33.	Tonaba	1355–1359
34.	Tabungba	1359–1394
35.	Lairenba	1394–1399

(Contd.)

Table 5.1 (*Contd.*)

36. Punsiba	1404 - 1432
37. Ningthoukhomba	1432–1469
38. Kyamba	1469–1508
39. Koiremba	1508–1512
40. Lamkyamba	1512–1523
41. Nong-en-faba	1523–1524
42. Kabomba	1524–1542
43. Tangjamba	1542–1545
44. Challamba	1545–1562
45. Mungyamba	1562–1597
46. Khagemba	1597–1652
47. Khunjaoba	1652–1666
48. Paikhomba	1666–1697
49. Charairongba	1697–1709
50. Garibaniwaz (Mayamba)	1709–1748
51. Chitsai	1748–1752
52. Bharatsai	1752 - 1753
53. Maramba	1753–1759
54. Chingthangkhomba	1759–1762
55. Maramba	1762–1763
56. Chingthangkhomba	1763–1798
57. Labyanachandra	1798–1801
58. Madhurjit	1801–1803
59. Chourjit	1803–1813
60. Marjit	1813–1819
61. Takuningthou (Heerachandra)	1819–
62. Yumjaotaba	1820–
63. Gambhir Singh	1821–
64. Jay Singh	1822–
65. Yadu Singh (Nongpok ChinglenKhomba)	1823–
66. Raghav Singh	1823–1824
67. Nongchup Lamgaingamba (BadhraSingh)	1824–
68. Gambhir Singh (ChinglenNongdrenkhomba)	1825–1834
69. Chandrakirti (Ningthempishak)	1834–1844
70. Nara Singh	1844–1850
71. Debendra Singh	1850–
72. Chandrakirti, KCSI	1850–1886
73. Surchandra (Chinglen Lanthaaba)	1886–1890
74. Kulachandra	1890–1891
75. Churachand Singh, KCSI	1891–1941
76. Bodhachandra	1941–1955

The State formation was completed in the early Christian era, when as many as seven indigenous nations amalgamated themselves to constitute the earliest Meitei State, which territorially fluctuated but extended beyond the present territory. The earliest settlers were the ancient Meiteis of the present valley area, and the peoples now recognised as belonging to the emergent generic post-British *Naga* and *Kuki-Chin* ethnic agglomerations. The early Meitei State which is presently known as Manipur is an Indian State of three major ethnic group of Mongolian race, namely, (i) the Meitei (valley Manipuri), and Hill Manipuris re-christened by the colonial British as (ii) the Nagas and (iii) the Kuki-Chins. There was a centralised Constitutional Government since 429 AD, according to a renowned Meitei historian and scholar, the late Oinam Bhogeswar. The history of Manipur had been documented in an ancient hand-written continuous chronicle known as *"Chei'thaarol Kum'paba"* (33 AD to 1950 AD). The English translation is available in the Indian Office Library, London, and other Archives of the United Kingdom, which still preserve a large number of historical documents, treaties and other official records pertaining to the relation of the State of Manipur with the British Government since 1762 AD till 1949 AD. These materials, including local and native, may be closely examined as historical records. Early and medieval Indian history has never included present Manipur as its component till India's annexation of Manipur in 1949. Even the Indian colonial historians admit this.

A centralised Constitutional Government had been functioning in the early State of Manipur invariably from 1100 AD, when the Meitei Meidingu Loiyumba had promulgated a political Constitution known as *"Loiyumba Shinyen"*.

The aforesaid constitutional Government continued from 1100 AD till the international conflict arose in between the Manipuris and the Burmese in the 18th and 19th centuries AD, when Meidingu Pamheiba alias *Garibaniwaj* invaded Burma in the 18th century several times with as many as 30,000 warriors. A large part of the Manipur territory was later ceded by the British government of India to Burma (now Myanmar)—the Kabo (or Kabaw) Valley, that had been a part of the Manipur Territory till the early part of the 19th century. The British gave annual revenue of Rs. 5000 to the Government of Manipur on behalf of the Burmese till the Indian annexation of Manipur in 1949. The Government of India ceded the Kabo Valley to Burma (present Myanmar) after signing an Indo-Burma agreement in 1953. The provisions of the unpublicized treaty are not yet made known to the people of Manipur as well as to the citizens of India.

After Burmese military occupation of Manipur for seven years in the period from 1819 to 1825, complete sovereignty was restored to Manipur following a bilateral treaty, The Treaty of Yandaboo, signed in 1826 between the British Crown representative and the representative of the Burmese Government. By this treaty, the Burmese power in Asia and the imperial colonial power of the British Crown had accorded multilateral international recognition to the independent and sovereignty of the early State of Manipur. In 1835, the British set-up in Manipur a Political Agency, which was supposedly a Consulate in that period and it continued for a long time. The British power and the Manipur power had continued the friendly relationship by mutually opening Political Agency. The Manipur Power opened the Political Agency of Manipur in the British Territory at Lakhimpur (Cachar) as well as at Calcutta. The Anglo-Manipuri friendship was established for the first time in 1762, when a treaty had been signed between the representative of Maharajah Jay Singh (*alias*) Bhagyachandra of Manipur and Mr. Harry Verelst, Chief of the Chittagong Factory on behalf of the British Crown on the 14th September, 1762. The treaty is a testimony to the independent, sovereign political Status of Manipur (known to British as Meckley). The basic parameters of an independent state, as stipulated by the Montevideo Convention, 1933, viz., (a) territory, (b) population, (c) government, and (d) capacity to maintain external relations, had been found in the State of Manipur. Manipur had, therefore, been recognized as sovereign state in as early as 1762 AD. The present Indian state did not exist in 1762.

There was mutually protective Anglo-Manipuri arrangement in between the Manipur Power when the British Viceroy had a summit meeting with Maharaja Chadrakirti of Manipur in August 1874. By this arrangement between the Manipur and the British powers, both the contracting parties had agreed to assist one another in the mutual and reciprocal interests of both the powers. The relationship broke down in March 1891, when the aggressive British army had initially been defeated by the Manipuri army on 24 March, 1891 and the Manipuri army had finally been defeated on 25 April, 1891. However, the British Queen did not annex Manipur to her empire. At her worst situation, Manipur remained an international protectorate.

Subsequently, the British had military occupation in the State of Manipur till 1907 by totally disarming the Manipuris to the last man. However, the Queen did not annex the State of Manipur as part of the British Colony to the British territory for the several reasons. The British Parliamentary Proceedings on the subject would be found in the Hansards of U.K. in June and July 1891. Even after the defeat of Manipur, it had not been annexed to or colonised by the British although the British Crown considerably interfered in the local administration of Manipur by assuming the latter as an International Protectorate. Manipur was not a part of India in this period.

From the Manipuri perception, it was a political intervention in Manipur's political sovereignty. Manipur had been labelled as a Native State in the subcontinent of India from the British perspective. Thereafter, in fact, from the Manipur perspective, Manipur had never been a constituent of India, as this Asian State of Mongolian race and Mongolian population is completely different from the other so-called Native States of the Indian subcontinent, which are truly the realm of the Aryan and Dravidian races. Further, the leaders of the Indian freedom fighters and the Congress Party, led by leaders like M.K. Gandhi, Jawaharlal Nehru and Sardar Patel had consistently defined the Native States of India as a blood-relation State, which means an Aryan or a Dravidian State. Since, Manipur is a Mongolian State; it had never been a part of Ancient State of the present British-created India. It is unclear how a Mongolian State could ever be considered as a constituent State of the Aryan and Dravidian peoples, who are racially integrated. The Manipuris continue to be an alien race. The colonial officials of India made attempts to dilute the independence of Manipur by citing her as one of the 560 native states.

the Manipur People—A Nation

The about 2.3 million indigenous Manipur people comprising of 31 indigenous peoples speaking Tibeto-Burman or Sino-Tibetan language having their common pedigree from a common Mongolian ancestor constitutes a *PEOPLE* or nation.

The indigenous Manipur people being the first settlers or, autochthones in the present territorial state had organized their own history and nation-state since 33 AD, independent of the historical experience of Indians.

No pre-, proto-history, ancient and medieval history of India including broad-based works of history written by India's first Prime Minister Jawaharlal Nehru, viz., *Glimpses of World History*, *Discovery of India*, *Autobiography*, have mentioned Manipur and her indigenous people even once. Even the history books, re-constructed with a view to incorporating India's recent territorial acquisitions and pre-1949 Maps included in the text books do not include Manipur. This gives testimony to the self-evident fact of Manipur people being alien, dependent and foreign to the Indian People.

The royal chronicle of Manipur—"*CHEI'THAAROL KUM'PABA*", which had recorded the genealogy of Manipur chiefs since 33 AD and proto-history of Manipur as recorded in "*KANGBALOL*"—which had noted the first proto-historical Meidingu Kangba of the then Manipur, had not mentioned any historical ties of Manipur with India. The historical records of neighbouring countries like Tibet or, Burma (Myanmar) have invariably corroborated the absence of Manipur-India historical ties, if any.

None of the Indian kings—Bharat, Ashoka, Chandragupta, Akbar to the last Indian emperor Bahadur Shah had any links with Manipur, let alone their temporary sway and administration. The British crown who ruled India since 1858, in similar tradition, did not rule Manipur till the lapse of British intervention or Paramountcy in 1947. Manipur had remained an international protectorate of the British till 1947.

The native states of India save Manipur had been the successors to the Sikh, Hindu or, Maratha empires, notwithstanding the British consideration and treatment of Manipur like any other Indian states.

The status of the Manipur people as a 'PEOPLE' is decided by the following criteria: *Firstly,* the indigenous Manipur people being Mongolians are racially different from the Indians who are Aryan-Dravidians. Dr. Sunitikumar Chatterjee, the most renowned Indologist in his major work—'Kirata Jana Krti' admits this distinction. *Secondly,* Dr. Grierson in his most authoritative volumes of the Linguistic Survey of India had recorded that the Manipur people are speakers of Tibeto-Burman language, unlike the Indians. *Thirdly,* as corroborated by all historical accounts of both Manipur and India, the people of these two countries had been distinctive, different and alien to each other in the last several centuries. *Fourthly,* Manipur state had remained independent of India till the latter had annexed the former. *Fifthly,* the Manipur indigenous people have been subjugated, dominated and oppressed by an alien, foreign government of modern nation-state of western origin which is represented by India.

Following the Indian annexation of Manipur, the demographic composition of Manipur has been dramatically altered during the more than half-a century old Indian annexation of Manipur. No better testimony could be addressed to this population grafting issue than by what the government of Manipur admitted in 1984 corroborated by the government of India's occasional statements on the subject. Subsequently, the pre-dominantly Mongolian population of the state has been considerably altered.

The Manipur people as a 'PEOPLE' had not been consulted at the time of Indian annexation of Manipur in 1949. This denial of popular consultation gives evidence of the Indian colonial character.

The Manipur people, who had not exercised their inalienable right to self-determination in 1949 has not abdicated this right in any sense of the term. This right of a people has to be exercised as yet.

The Government of India is run by the executive constituted by a President, a Union Cabinet of about 50 ministers, the Indian army led by hundreds of generals, an apex court—the Supreme Court of India and several organs and bodies created by the Constitution. No Manipur people had ever been inducted into these top echelons of power during the last half-a century. In a parliament of 793 Members of Parliament, only three members hail from Manipur. Besides, the local government and assembly have been held so as to masquerade a representative form of government at the local, state level. Similar elections have been held in East Timor also, before its independence, by Indonesian Government. Manipur is a *de facto* non-self-governing territory since the Indian annexation in 1949 and the Manipur indigenous people are non-self-governing people.

However, the state-of-the art colonial propaganda has successfully projected the non-self-governing people and territory of Manipur as one having a fully representative form of government and internal democracy, by stating that local elections are being held periodically, whereas, these farcical colonial elections, processed under the nose of the world's third largest army institutionalising large-scale corruption and bribery have not reflected the genuine wishes and aspirations of a people, let alone a plebiscite or referendum. 3,000 Indian dailies and powerful electronic multi-media cover-up the genuine aspirations of the non-self-governing indigenous people of Manipur. The Indian Colonial machinery has successfully divided Manipuri People into Meiteis, Nagas, Kukis so and so forth, thereby encouraging *balkanization* of the 2000-year-old territorial integrity of Manipur, whereas the boundary of Manipur can never be disturbed or altered to the prejudice of Manipur under *'Uti Possidetis Juris'* rule of International Law, that has been recurrently affirmed by the International Court of Justice.

The colonial, non-self-governing status of Manipur people would remain unaddressed as such, unless the UN includes Manipur in the mandate for de-colonisation by incorporating her in the list of non-self-governing people, through the good offices of the Special Committee on De-colonisation and the Fourth Committee of the UN General Assembly. The contemporary development of International Law has to take the publicists seriously. Jorri Duursman in his work —"Fragmentation and the international relations of Micro-States" observes—"Peoples who find themselves in similar circumstances as colonies will enjoy a complete right of self-determination even if they are not specifically mentioned in the list of Non-Self-Governing or Trust Territories." (Cambridge University Press, 1996 ISBN 0 521 56360 7, page 83)

The UN Declaration on Principles of International Law concerning Friendly Relations and Co-operation among states, 24 October, 1970 (UN GA Resolution 2625 Para. 6) provides that

> "6. The territory of a colony or other Non-Self-Governing Territory has, under the Charter, a status separate and distinct status under the Charter shall exist until the people of the colony or Non-Self-Governing Territory have exercised their right of self-determination in accordance with the Charter, and particularly its purposes and principles."

The above-mentioned principle is applicable to Manipur, which is a *de facto* colony or, Non-Self-Governing territory of colonial power—India. The UN and its members have the obligation to de-colonise Manipur either by enlarging or, modifying its mandate or, by way of appropriate intervention in order to eradicate colonialism in its wholeness.

The Government of India, on her own had accepted that the word "Peoples" applies to a large compact group, who made a conscious demand for the right of self-determination (see UN Doc. E/CN.4/SR. 2256 (1952) p. 5). The more than 2 million-strong indigenous Manipur people in their compactness within the territory of Manipur invariably constitute the 'People', as defined by India.

National Liberation Movement—Genesis of Modern Conflicts

In the late 1960s, National Liberation Movement of Manipur and militant resistance had been started by the Métier State Committee that militarily resisted the Indian forces. It was closely followed by the Revolutionary Government of Manipur (RGM). The nucleus of a sister liberation struggle had been seeded in 1964. After the dismantling and disbandment of the RGM, the Revolutionary People's Front (RPF, the political wing of the People's Liberation Army of Manipur) was formed on 25 February, 1979 and the PLA started operating for the liberation of Manipur from the Indian occupation army and Indian colonialism along with several sister organizations.

Professor Emeritus V.V. Rao of the University of Gauhati in his books on the North-Eastern India has recorded that the PLA has the broad vision encompassing the interest of all the colonised, subjugated people elsewhere, beyond the contours of Manipur.

The UN should have listed East Timor and Manipur in the same slot of colonised states or, people before two decades. Several national daily papers of Indian colonialism, however, flashed the international attention, as sought by PLA through all the embassies. The national liberation movement of Manipur has been consistently opposing the alleged colonial Government of India on political terms and had been struggling against the 'occupation army' of India on military terms since the time of the Indian annexation of Manipur in 1949 till today. The UN selectively took up similar cases by shelving de-colonisation of Manipur in the cold freeze. Ironically, the UN discriminates Indian colonialism against European colonialism.

Very few liberation movements in the world have been left outside the closest attention of the UN and her members except the half-century old National Liberation Movement of Manipur. The UN objective of eradicating colonialism by 2000 AD would remain a futility without de-colonising Manipur and her neighbourhood colonies of India like Assam, Nagaland and Tripura. The colonial Government of India had permanently perpetuated colonialism of Manipur by proclaiming the *national liberation movements* including the armed struggle triggered off by the PLA (RPF) since 1978 as unlawful organization under the Prevention of Unlawful Activities Act, 1967 and suppressing the human rights since 1958 by invoking the draconian law the Armed Forces (Special) Powers Act, 1958 (amended in 1972), the Punjab Security of State Act, 1953, the

Terrorists and Disruptive Activities Prevention Act, 1985 and the National Security Act, among other equally repressive laws. Absolutely in self-defence and self-preservation, the occupation army is resisted by the movement.

Socio-Economic and Political Colonisation

The people of Manipur have been deprived of their inalienable birth-right to determine their political and socio-economic status on their own due to Indian colonial process, subjugation, alien and racist national oppression. They have been deprived of their inalienable right to manage their natural resources as per their self-determination and this right has to be restored to them. Following the ICJ verdict, 1995 on Timor Gap Treaty, it is a criminal wrong for India to usurp the natural resources of Manipur. They have to exercise their inalienable right to self-determination for their permanent sovereignty over their natural resources, biomass, water-bodies, fauna and flora, among others.

The pre-dominantly Mongolian population of Manipur has been subjugated by the Indian racist and colonial regime which represents only the blue blood of the Aryan and Dravidian races. The administering power, i.e. the Indian regime has never established an institutional space for any indigenous people of Manipur who are of Mongolian origin in the highest decision making levels of government. The people of Mongolian origin are treated as subjects and subjugated race only to be ruled by the *occupation* army. Since 1949 onwards till today, not a single day has ever passed in Manipur without the repressive measures taken by the Indian army by torturing, insulting or extra-judicially murdering the indigenous people of Manipur. As cited above, a number of repressive laws or laws of legitimizing State Terrorism including the Armed Forces (Special) Powers Act, 1958, the Terrorist and Disruptive Activities (Prevention) Act, 1987 and several other draconian laws have been systematically introduced and enforced in the State of Manipur in order to subjugate the people of Manipur and incapacitate them from determining their own political destiny. The UN Human Rights Committee and global NGOs have denounced them as incompatible with the International Bill of Rights, 1966 to which the colonial government of India has been a party. The Government of India is accountable for enacting laws incompatible with the Covenants, ratified by her.

The colonial development process and economy had not been helpful to the people of Manipur. Not a single major industry, much less an important establishment has ever been established in Manipur. Whereas several billions of Rupees have been spent apparently on paper maintained for the record in order to refuel and recycle their colonial apparatus, quite a few families in Manipur are also used as colonial subsidiaries, the economic condition of the average people of Manipur specially those in the hill areas has not improved even up to the level of subsistence. People survive on grassroots in the Manipur hill areas because of colonial economic process. The Manipuri hills-people and valley-people are divided by the Presidential approval to a divisive law—the Manipur Land and Revenue Act, 1960 which does not accord uniform protection to the land rights of all the citizens and communities of Manipur. The system based on apartheid has been created.

The colonial economy of Manipur has pushed down 68 per cent of Manipur people below the Poverty line. Centre for Monitoring Indian Economy in 1992-93 indicated that whereas Indian state of Punjab has reached index of 205, Manipur's index is 71. As per the Asian Development Bank Report, 11 May, 1997, Manipur rice production in kg/hectare is 1400 (against Indian average of 1740), Road in 100 sq. km. in Manipur is 32.64 km (against Indian average of 62.82 km), Banking credit in Manipur is Rs. 44 (Indian is Rs. 1722.11), p.c.i. of Manipur is Rs. 5,326 (against Indian average of Rs. 6,929), Annual budget of Rs. 400+ crore is literally for the maintenance of 90,000 colonial Indian army, innumerable mercenaries, police, espionage, supporting pro-colonial families and half the budget allocation is not available due to colonial fiscal policy.

Proxy elections are conducted by spending crores of Indian Rupees in order to perpetuate colonialism through quislings, puppet regimes and fifth columnists under the proxy election process by way of misleading the illiterate electorate. The Indian colonial regime can in no way justify the electoral process whatsoever, since the people of Manipur cannot exercise their "independent political will" and resolve their destiny at the gunpoint of the massive, racist Indian colonial army and several thousands of mercenaries, subversives and spies. The colonial elections held in the mighty presence of occupation army, mercenaries and pouring crores of rupees for bribery have debarred the people to exercise their free will and no plebiscite on de-colonisation had ever been held. Alcoholics, drugs, heroin, brown sugar and narcotics are freely distributed to the voters in the colonial elections.

Right to Self-Determination

It is significant to reiterate the absolute commitment of the United Nations to eradicate colonialism in all its forms and manifestations by 2000 AD and to put in record the emergence of 135 independent states in conformity with the global de-colonisation process that sparked off since 1960s and 1970s. The official deadline for eradication of colonialism remaining unaltered, colonialism will be sustained in proximity-colonies of India like Manipur, Nagaland, Assam, Tripura and Jammu and Kashmir and nearly fifty other territories, many of which are incorporated in the list of 48 unrepresented peoples of the UNPO—the Hague based Unrepresented Nations and Peoples Organisation. These colonies will survive the 2000 AD UN deadline, unless the UN and its main organs initiate pro-active de-colonisation, as much as it did in 1960s and 1970s. The UN would not fulfil its objectives of total de-colonisation, in the event of sustaining the above colonies or, peoples who are yet to exercise their right to self-determination. India being a member of the UN De-colonisation Committee has to initiate de-colonisation of Manipur.

The Government of India has the treaty obligations to allow alien, dependent, subjugated and oppressed people like the Manipur people to exercise their inalienable right to self-determination, as the Government has rectified the ICCPR, 1966 and ICESCR, 1966, besides its being a regional power which facilitated national liberation and de-colonisation of several colonised peoples in the Third World. The UN Human Rights Committee in 1997, July has urged upon the Government of India to withdraw her reservation in respect of common article 1 of the ICCPR, 1966 and ICESCR, 1966. The government has to comply with this recommendation and report compliance by 2000 AD at the time of submitting the 4th periodic report to the UNHRC *vide* article 40 of the ICCPR, 1966.

Government of India's declaration in respect of her ratification of the ICCPR, 1966 on 10 April, 1979, is as follows:

> ICCPR, Article 1
> Para 10. It has been the position of India ever since its independence that adherence to self-determination is co-

> existent with the principle of sovereign equality. The principle of domestic jurisdiction of state as enshrined in the United Nations Charter is to be equally respected.
>
> Para 11. In conformity with this position of principle on self-determination, India made the following declaration in 1979 at the time of its accession to the International Covenant on Civil and Political Rights:
>
> "With reference to article 1 of the International Covenant on Civil and Political Rights, the Government of the Republic of India declares that the words 'the right to self-determination' appearing (in this article) apply to people under foreign domination."

The Manipuri people, who had never constituted a part of Hindustan or India or, British India had been placed under Indian foreign domination in the event of the annexation of Manipur in 1949. The caveat to the declaration makes room for according the right to self-determination to the people of Manipur. The Vienna World Conference on Human Rights, 1993 and the UN Human Rights Committee in July 1997 have mandated the Government of India to remove even this narrow caveat and accord the right to deserving people including the Manipuri people who had been sovereign for two millennia before Indian annexation. India's present stance prevents the worldwide de-colonisation process and hence, she owes an explanation for her defence of colonialism of Manipur.

India's Declaration stipulated that "Declaration contains enunciation of certain basic principles". Paragraph 1 declares, "The subjection of peoples to alien subjugation, domination and exploitation constitutes a denial of fundamental human rights." The people of Manipur obviously falls into the Indian enunciation of alien subjugation and domination. The colonial government of India has to prove that Manipuris are not alien to Indians.

The people of Manipur who are colonised by alien Indian administering power are people of non-self-governing territories as much as the East Timorese after Indonesian annexation in 1975 constitute people of non-self-governing territories. Indonesian elections had been held in East Timor since 1977, yet East Timor is recognised as non-self-governing territory by the United Nations. Similarly, colonial elections have been held in occupied Manipur by the Indian administering power without any prejudice to the sovereign political status of Manipur.

The ICJ in Portugal *vs*. Australia, 1995 has decided that East-Timorese have their *right to self-determination* erga omnes (against the whole community). Similarly, the people of Manipur have their *right to self-determination* erga omnes, notwithstanding India's preposterous prevarication against the colonised Manipuris.

Territorial Integrity

The colonial government of India defines in her 1950 Constitution, the territorial integrity of India in two places. Firstly, in the first schedule serial No. 19; Manipur is defined as "The territory which immediately before the commencement of this constitution was being administered as if it were a Chief Commissioner's province under the name of Manipur".

The first schedule itself clearly and categorically records that the territorial State of Manipur preceded the Constitution of India. No other constitutional provision has more clearly given testimony to the illegal annexation of Manipur than this provision. Before Indian Commissioner had occupied Manipur, she remained independent till 1949.

Article 1 of the Constitution of India defines the territory of India as follows: (1) India, that is Bharat, shall be a union of states. (2) [The states and the territories thereof shall be as specified in the first Schedule]. (3) The territory of India shall comprise—(a) the territories of states; (b) the union territories specified in the First Schedule; and (c) such other territories as may be acquired.

The state sovereignty doctrine has been enunciated in articles 2(4) and 2(7) of the UN Charter as well as by the UN GA Resolution 2625, Declaration on Friendly Relations, 1970. The Union Government of India pleads that her territorial integrity would be impaired if Manipur would be allowed to secede from the Indian Union. The argument may be further strengthened by citing the prevention of disruption of the "national unity and the territorial integrity" of India, as it is understood after the adoption of the 1950 Constitution (*see* Para. 6 of the UN GA Resolution 1514(XV) of 14 December, 1960). This argument is fallacious.

Aggression

All the available documents and records give eloquent testimony to the parameters of Indian aggression in Manipur. On 19 April, 1947,

Nehru sent threatening ultimatum to states. By an agreement reached on 2 July, 1947, Indian agency had been allowed to stay in Manipur. On 5 July, 1947, Hindu dictator M.K. Gandhi allegedly a pacifist communicated to Lord Mountbatten that state should not be given independence. Indian agent Akbar Hydari had abolished dominion agency in Manipur on 22 August, 1948. On 14 April, 1949, the colonial government of India asked the Manipur king to transfer all powers to an Indian Dewan under immense pressure and coercion; and the king was forced to appoint on 16 April, 1949 one Indian colonial Major General Amar Singh as Dewan of Manipur. Assam Governor Shri Prakasa sent a memo on 25 June, 1949 that India de-recognized the Manipur State Council and elected Manipur Assembly (read Parliament of Manipur). All the political institutions and municipal administration had been subverted by India's Assam Governor Shri Prakasa who also initiated the covert Indian aggression in Manipur.

The United Nations should invite all the Government of India's records concerning Indian aggression in Manipur for the period 1947-1949 and can easily determine the facts in no time. 9.05. Manipur in 1949 had no obligations under the UN Charter, but the Indian Dominion, being a member of the UN since 1945 has Charter obligations not to use force against Manipur and also to honour the territorial integrity of independent Manipur. Article 2(4) of the Charter determines this responsibility:

> "All Members shall refrain in their international relations from the threat or use of force against the territorial integrity or political independence of any state, or in any manner inconsistent with the purposes of the United Nations."

The colonial government of India has further violated article 1 of the UN Charter by committing aggression and breach of peace. The national liberation movement is exercising its right to self-defence and self-preservation, without any prejudice to the genuine integrity of India.

The UN General Assembly in its Resolution 3314(1974) defines aggression in article 1: "Aggression is the use of armed force by a state (read India here) against the sovereignty, territorial integrity or political independence of another state, or in any other manner inconsistent with the Charter of the United Nations." Further, Indian military occupation and annexation of Manipur by use of Indian forces constitutes aggression under article 3 of the Resolution 3314(1974), regardless of declaration of war.

The UN GA Resolutions 2625(XXV), 1970 and 2734(1970) provide that no territorial acquisition resulting from the threat or use of force shall be recognized as legal. Hence, India's military occupation of Manipur since 1949 till date is illegal and creates no legitimate claims of India over the sovereignty of Manipur.

Gross Human Rights Violations and Humanitarian Law

During India's repressive, colonial regime in Manipur, human rights violations have been massive, colossal, brutally de-humanizing and absolutely barbarian. Indian military occupation, compounded by the invocation of the world's most barbaric laws including the Armed Forces (Special) Powers Act, 1958 for half a century in both the hills and plains of Manipur and shielding the entire genocidal pogroms from the glaze of independent international media by prohibiting any foreigner to step into Manipur under the *Restrictive Areas Permit Act* without the closest scrutiny of the Home Ministry of India, resulted to unprecedented state terrorism, repression and barbaric human rights violations.

The Government of India and her defence forces which are under obligations after Government of India's accession to the Four Geneva Conventions, 1949 and subsequent enactment of the Geneva Conventions Act, 1961 by the Indian Parliament, to fully comply with the humanitarian laws, had consistently breached the humanitarian laws by way of committing relentless state repression on the unarmed civilians of Manipur and captured combatants or *hors de combat* of the Manipur National Liberation Movement. Even the ICRC has not been allowed to visit Manipur, since the Home Ministry refused to lid off the Auschwitz iron curtain of Manipur. No force-commander or even a single military General has ever been punished for the breach of the Geneva Conventions, 1949 or, the Geneva Conventions Act, 1961 passed by the Indian Parliament. No other testimony could be more appropriate than citing the Government of India's refusal to sign, accede and ratify the two "Protocols Additional to the Geneva Conventions of 12 August, 1947", 1977 and the Rome International Criminal Court (ICC) treaty, July 17, 1998. The leaders and cabinet of the Gandhian state of India, who led the Non-Aligned Movement and the global de-colonisation

Movement had been deliberately committing "war crimes", "crimes against Humanity", "Genocide", and "Aggression" in Manipur for half a century, while the international community chose to remain a silent spectator for half a century.

Article 1(4) of the First Additional Protocol, 1977 provides legal protection to peoples, who are "fighting against colonial Domination and alien occupation and against racist regimes in the exercise of their right to self-determination", but the occupation army of India has been ceaselessly torturing by using 3rd degree methods, arrested POW guerrillas. The RPF—Revolutionary People's Front of Manipur and its military wing PLA—People's Liberation Army has signed common article 3 of the Four Geneva Conventions in 1997 and has been strictly complying with the International Humanitarian Laws, but the Indian security forces have routinely committed grave breach of the Geneva Conventions. Thus, criminals are awarded and rewarded profusely and ostentatiously by the President of India (read Union Cabinet) in public annually for committing heinous crimes against mankind in Manipur, people who are citizens of India. The national media regularly project Manipuri freedom fighters as criminals and terrorists. This hatred campaign helps the genocide while promoting impunity.

Emerging Dimensions of Political Positions

So far, as described and compiled from various documents, records, statements and publications, the Manipur national position is clear *vis-à-vis* international and customary law. In this context, the UN's endeavour to eradicate colonialism can be materially achieved only after de-colonizing proximity or, neighbourhood, colonialism in the Asia-Pacific region, beyond the scope of the classical European Salt-water or Blue-water colonialism model. Indonesia and India, which are considered to be world-leaders in neutrality movement, had non-self-governing territories or, colonies like East Timor in Indonesia and Manipur in post-1949 India.

Whether the de-colonisation agenda of the international community is considered to be completely or not may, in the end, not be the deciding factors for lasting conflict resolution or lasting peace in Manipur. Claims based on certain aspirations of peoples should be broadly understood and acknowledged without a concerted and covert drive to "manage" the conflict for a lasting destabilization of the State and the region as a whole. It is, at the end of the day, merely "buying time", and cannot develop into the win-win situation of the peoples and the governments. The fact remains, as enshrined in every lofty document, Charter and Constitution of the world that the rights to self-determination and sovereignty are indeed inalienable. How States and peoples work through these core human rights in praxis is the challenge, and here, civil society has a recognizable and undoubted role to play.

However, in the current global context and developing changes in our environment – financial, economical, climate and ecological – such a position as described is only one position among several. Arguably, such a political and legalistic position may be overtaken by emergent understanding, realities and changes that have global dimensions that may bring before us an imperative to challenge this legalistic position and seek solutions or outcomes that can better address the emergent issues and needs. Manipur needs to reflect on some important emergent imperatives *vis-à-vis* its held position since the middle of the last century.

Firstly, the paradigm on which development itself is modelled is being strongly challenged today; this is something that the UN and other institutions of the UN family still do not and are facing difficulties to integrate with existing institutionalised arrangements, practice and standards. The legalistic position described pegs itself on an increasingly questionable development model, where economic and social development policies and practice are described within delineated territorial boundaries, known as States. A legal position should fundamentally reflect certain aspirations of the peoples, aspirations that are closely intertwined with daily livelihoods and choices, natural and cultural heritage, knowledge and intellectual pursuits. As the theoretical model underpinning development shifts away from utilitarian economics-based and basic needs-based models towards a freedoms and capabilities model for the present and future generations, a political position may have to be comprehensively and inclusively reviewed.

Secondly, the freedoms of individuals and collectives today are being increasingly curtailed by threats and changes of global dimensions but with very significant local impacts or consequences. Globalisation, driven by neo-liberalism and new market-driven *economism*, has made State boundaries and protectionism increasingly redundant and ineffectual. The "rules of the game" are changing even as the struggle of Manipur's self-determination is being played out.

The constituency is no longer a territorial limit but a conceptual limit. Concepts of ecological and natural limits to development, the now undisputed evidence of global warming and climate change due to anthropogenic causes, the rights of collectives and communities are the new "frontiers" of States. In this compelling perspective of the new order, a position based more on pre-dominant legal frameworks created and interpreted by the very States that had colonised most of the world should be viewed by a great degree of caution.

Thirdly, the indigenous peoples' problematic also imposes many new dimensions and challenges to existing political positions. New frontiers of rights are now being posited in the international community, and this problematic now is a major preoccupation of the United Nations and its member States. On the other hand, the human rights framework or discourse is itself being expanded to include a significant section of the world's population that had become more and more discriminated and marginalised. The threats to the indigenous peoples are not imaginary, and many face extinction of their populations, territories, cultures and knowledge. This new rights dimension also challenges the indigenous peoples themselves as it exerts tremendous tensions and pressures on pre-existing perceptions and traditionally held beliefs or practices that impact on held positions. The nation of Manipur, an indigenous state, existed before such dimensions emerged and began to influence people's perceptions about themselves and aspirations.

Finally, if Leisemba's words are to come true, the future of the Manipur Nation itself may need to be viewed through a more enlightened framework that would include the current perceptions of its peoples and the international community, and not just base itself on narrow orthodox legalist model that may be already soon in disuse.

NOTES

1. Compiled and presented by the Centre for Organisation Research and Education at "Training on Conflict Resolution and Peace Building Capacities", Guwahati, India, on 24-31 March, 2007. The chapter is a compilation based on various sources, government, non-government, media, official and people's archival materials, etc. The views and opinions expressed in this chapter are not necessarily those of the Centre for Organisation Research and Education or any of its members.

CHAPTER – 6

Narratives of Self-Determination Struggles in Manipur

Lokendra Arambam

Introduction

This chapter begins with an anecdote from the apocalyptic literature of the 18th century Manipur. Maharajah Garibniwaz (*alias* Pamheiba 1709-1748), one of the greatest kings of independent Manipur, who had engaged in relentless warfares with Burma and other states of the Northeast was also involved in unleashing a regime of personal power to induce drastic domestic changes in the realm, notably in culture and environment which brought disaster to the polity. Obsessed with the newly developing theory of the divinity of monarchs and exercise of absolute power, he took advice from an Indian Brahmin from Shyllet (now in Bangladesh) to introduce amongst his subjects the worship of Rama, the warrior prince of Ayodhya. To convert the population into the sect of Ramandi (Rama worship), he used force excessively to have them forego their already established indigenous religion (Pakhangba and Sanamahee worship). He destroyed the sacred precincts of the indigenous deities, broke into pieces the iron statue of the Lord Sanamahee (creator of the Manipur Universe and Household God), organized ceremonious state burning of the religious manuscripts known as Puyas, and tortured large masses who conscientiously objected to the forcible conversion into Hinduism. Tired and exhausted in the resistance to state authority, the Meetei clan elders agreed to acceptance of the change in religion, for at least seven generations from thence.

In local organicist thought and belief of equating the state with a house or human body metaphorically, the event came to be understood as opening of the Western Door (Nongchup Thong Hangba), a term coined by the wisdom teacher of the king and leader of the cultural resistance—Lourembam Khongnangthaba. He was fondly remembered as Chingoo Khongnangthaba (elder noble, Planter of the banyan Trees). The opening of the western door in the geo-body of the indigenous realm was deeply lamented by Chingoo Khongnangthaba and his followers as a deep tragedy. Since his ultimate advice to royalty on matters of state and culture before the entry of Brahmin advisers was now no longer appreciated by the monarch, the mystic sage withdrew with his six disciples in a conclave and spoke about the future and the change that was to ensue. His revelatory sayings were recorded in pen and paper by the disciple Konok Thengra, in the presence of five others, for future generations to know the reality of the transformations.

Using short, enigmatic and symbolic riddles the sage spoke about the opening of the western door. *"Two prototypes of the deity Shani (the evil eye, the Hindu God of catastrophe) had arrived, trudging along the Ngaprum Chingjin roadways (in the western hills). Now the capital Kangla is on fire. Different types of humans, some scantily clad shall rub shoulders with the autochthons. Later on, another horde of tall, broad eared, red faced ones shall enter and in the confrontation and struggle, the natives shall move with prostrate bodies (predicting the oncoming Anglo-Manipuri war of 1891). Stone from the northern hills shall spread in the roadways of the land. New capital shall be built east of the Sanjenthong bridge (In 1908 the princely abode was built by the conquering British). Fish shall attend to the duties of the realm (alluding to emergence of slippery officialdom). The garden fences shall eat up the vegetables. The Chinga Hillock in the south shall turn to markets (it happened in the late twentieth century!) Stone chips shall float. Cotton will sink. On the broad highways the big trees shall vanish. The flash floods shall have no ends. The standing trees shall fall on their trunks. On the pastures floating weeds shall rush into rapids. Huge migrations shall arrive even before the mid-day meal. The flies shall swarm the markets. At those times on the mounds of Moirang, a pregnant woman shall be attacked by beasts. At these times the Jackal shall leave faeces on the gold dish. The shine of gold shall wither. Imitation gold shall become valuable. Slangs and curses shall replace decent speech. There shall be no stable religious values. People shall die as they stand. Women shall shed their morals. Servants shall increase in numbers without masters. Sons shall be born without fathers. No distinction of the trees from the woods shall occur. There shall no more be the understanding of the ultimate and the divine."*[1]

Though it is difficult to explain the occult lives and mental states of these eighteenth century seers and mystics, these medieval elites in the moral and ethical universe of Manipur were deeply affected by the traumatic experiences of the onslaught of the Indic forces within the body polity of the ancient Asiatic kingdom. Many of the predictions of the wisdom teachers revealed profound truths in the changing dimensions of the historical experiences of the people resultant from the Indic connection.

However, interestingly, a contrasting world view just emerged through the efforts by more spiritually engaged successors and statesmen like Maharajah Bhagyachandra (*alias* Chingthangkhomba 1763-1798), grandson of the monarch Garibniwaj. Chingthangkhomba effected an alternative historical experiment by compromising the already established local religion with a much softer, benign form of the incoming world religion. i.e. Vaishnavism and Krishna worship. The conflict between the local and the world religion was resolved with a harmonizing synthesis. He also innovated a structural change in the social system by incorporating Indian Brahmins through marriages to native women, though these incoming demographic elements and their descendants rose in Kraton status in subsequent social developments. His identification of the ancestor-God Pakhangba (serpent dragon father) with the incoming God Krishna or Govinda ushered in profound spiritual developments (though non-adherent Meetei populations along with tribal communities in the hills were beyond the pale of this experience).

What the mystics in their dreamlike visions envisaged were not the simple forthright issues of the religious contradiction (which expanded later on), but deeper and more enthralling problems of civilizational difference, i.e. the way how as people they look up to their own worlds, and of their self-conscious evolution as societies of the future. There seemed to be in the inner world and psyche of the Manipuri an intense self-pride and resilient character enriched by severe historic experiences of war, both of victories as well as defeats, of their struggles of survival against subjugation and domination by greater powers like Burma and the British Empire. The legacies of independent decision-making and engaging with the realities of their destiny were handed down to their future generations as their polity was developed by themselves through a long process of war, confrontations or compromises, marriage alliances and adaptations to the vagaries of the environment. Though the national polity they developed in the 18th century was built on the dynastic principles of feudal power and benevolent despotism, the polity achieved a certain status of prestige and recognition in the comity of nations. The balance of power and international diplomatic relations were amicably organized through bilateral relations based on the values of blood and kin. Many Manipuri princesses of the royal family were married to regional monarchs of those days, and other princesses of distant kingdoms were married into Manipuri royalty. Manipur in fact had blood relations with the Burmese, the Shans, the Ahoms, the Tripuris, the Dimasas etc. through the circulation of royal princesses, and much racial inter-mixtures had entered into the fluid social structures without adherence to caste hierarchies.

Since Manipur also grew as a warrior state with inbuilt mechanisms for withstanding forces of violence since the 15th century, certain moral principles of human conduct, and customary laws of martial engagements were developed to avoid the scourge of violence. There were laws of duels and challenges (Chainarol), where personal engagements were more welcome to avoid group calamity. In the spear challenge, the opponent was given the right to have the first throw of the spear. Heads were given willingly by the loser of the personal combat, and victuals prepared by the spouses of the warriors were shared between the rivals. However, principles of dignity, valour, chivalry and sacrifice were imbibed in the personal character of the Meetei warriors, just like the Samurais of Japan. Fighting for the state, the community and the village were fond values in the personality of the Meetei warrior, but with self regulatory disciplines to curtail violence and respect for the customary values of their opponents as well. Trust and good faith were some of the choicest values in the conduct of conflict and its resolution. Systems of reciprocity as to what is being expected from the other for what is done to them was respected and acknowledged. Violence against each other's communities, and the pains thereof could be assuaged through smoking of the peace pipe through respect for each other's customary traditions of re-establishment of friendship.

Rituals were elaborately organized when one representative of the offending community could subscribe to the customary laws of friendship and trust of the other, whatever inconveniences the ritual may perpetuate. What is, therefore, built into the tradition of war is a strong sense of mutual respect, tolerance for the other community and expectation to be respected by the same. Strong notions of the laws of equality and parity of justicial treatment were inbuilt into the civilization of the people. Principles of honour and dignified treatment to the foes were preserved in traditional thoughts and behaviour, disrespect to which was resented.

Though the state is small by present day standards, its size in the 18th century was outstandingly large, probably through the warlike efforts and expansive energy of the martial people. British cartographers in the 18th and 19th centuries left imprints of the huge territorial dimensions of the Manipur Kingdom, though such enumerations are now best left alone, considering the contentious logic of land and territoriality disputes, which are enhancing ongoing processes of conflict.

What the opening of the western door ushered in was a violent overwhelming of life processes of the indigenous people and an exogenous restructuring of their world views, which resulted to antagonistic contradictions of vertical forms of conflict between non-state actors and the Indian state in later stages of history. Though the ancient mystics saw vague visions of the forthcoming modernization processes and its ruptures, without being rationally interpreted at that specific period of time, future inheritors of Manipur's history could now visualize the current environmental disaster, the loss of indigenous economy and its subsequent deprivations, the contentions demographic pluralism of the present, the loosening of women's morals, the bastardization of the population, the development of corruption and sleaze, the penetration of deceit and falsehoods, the manipulation of socio-economic and cultural processes when the subjects were not given the power of agency. These trends were to influence the history of the region in the next two hundred odd years of Manipur's life world, where the vision of the mystics were found to be true and revealing.

Brief Background of Insurgency Studies

International scholarship and national representatives of academics and journalists, as well as Indian officials who held gubernatorial posts, retired police intelligence officials and bureaucrats who had served the institutions of state in the more recent past in the decades of violence and turmoil had delved in the problems of these insurgencies especially in Northeast India, with varying approaches and angles of interpretation on their experiences of the phenomenon. Understanding the politics of the so called *'ethno-national movements'* were important for reasons of state, for supporting concerns of national security, for perfecting the rough and tumble contours of nation making processes of the post colonial Indian nation-state. Others from the international fraternity were also deeply concerned with the instabilities of the world order, the rise of ethnicities after the cold war, and their impact on global peace and security, hindrances to human development and democratization of various communities and peoples who had been left out of the global processes of change. There were fresh necessities to reduce violence and proliferation of conflict. Humanitarian institutions, the UN agencies, and departments and institutions of international universities had mushroomed worldwide *'to seek to prevent and transform conflict, to understand the interplay between conflict and development, to help societies create sustainable futures for themselves'*.[2] Many international centres for peace and conflict studies had burnt midnight oil *'to seek ways to understand and address conflicts over security, identity and distributive justice'*.[3] The writer would be happier to join the issues of understanding of conflict of embedded world views and their intractable dynamics through supporting the works of inter-cultural conflict specialists like Kevin Avruch (1998), Oscar Nudler (1993) and others to probe the phenomenon of political violence between antagonistic cultural worlds of the Indian state and indigenous non-state actors of today.

What is essentially a basic impediment to the understanding of Manipur insurgencies is a regular absence of authentic voices and narratives from the region especially from those in the processes of the movements themselves, their version of the struggles and articulations of their actions. These lacunae in proper sourcing of information on these movements may probably be due to the logic of the criticality of the struggle, that many of these outfits were banned through strong domestic laws of the Indian state, that they live a life of secrecy and silence, lest they be victims of exposure and punishment. Over the years, writings about these movements were from the efforts of researchers, casual interviewers from radical medias, who meticulously prune documents, handouts and press communiqués, and find opportunities to talk to surrenderees or protagonists in base areas in the interiors or foreign sanctuaries. Other researchers from international communities do research from in depth surveys into both government or non-government sources, and collect scientific data from incidences of violences, links these datas relevant to the study of the dynamics of societal conflicts. International researchers are supposed to be more qualititatively engaged in cross-disciplinary research on societal conflicts linked up with issues of state failure and minority rights etc. But even international researchers sometimes wrongly reported on Northeast insurgencies when it was submitted that independence aspirations of some major outfits in Manipur like UNLF and PLA were due to the refusal by the Government of India to recognize their demand to be given Scheduled Tribe status.[4] Sometimes innovative theories of greed and grievance are alluded to ongoing movements, where concerns of material benefits and lucrative manoeuvres from the development investments by lavish largesses from the state are being taken advantage of in the name of self-determination.

What is most understandable of the culture of the Manipur insurgents are probably that the silences of the more established outfits are, apart from these habitual culture of silence, due to the nature of contemporary Indian state's strong surveillance systems, and that their regime of repression is harsh. Due to the problems in their internal processes of struggle itself, since their supposed enemy is strong and heavy, dysarchic tendencies work in the mental attitudes, behaviours and actions of the non-state antagonists. This syndrome leads to intense segmentation and fragmentations within the movement themselves, which prevent them to speak or act as mandated representatives of the people. Ideological as well as personal equations are of significance since the mutual positions of friendship or trust are often undermined due to the severity of stress, intrigue and possibilities of betrayal. Activists of the struggle seem to keep a civilized silence not to hurt or undermine the other outfit, even though there seemed to be strong differences in their outlook to the struggles. Respect for the other is a silent code inherited from traditional values and behaviour, but which had now been usurped by contemporary tensions of mutual suspicion, mistrust and disbelief, since subtle ploys and dangerous penetrations of the long hands of the state and its myriad agencies to split, destroy and devastate the collective spirit of these people reached the inner depths of the social and political society. The late Madame Indira Gandhi's dictum to corrupt and weaken the Northeastern peoples seemed to have worked well. Recent attempts by these outfits to undertake a collective resurgence to form a United Front of NE insurgencies may yet open up new dynamics of the struggles for conflict watchers to analyze the patterns thereof, but contemporary manoeuvres by the Indian state to pre-empt these undertakings in the new geo-strategic shifts *vis-à-vis* China's looming threat, which make problems of NE insurgency a vital subject of intense ramifications. '*The Iron Fist in the Velvet Globe*', which was coined by General J.J. Singh (now Governor of Arunachal Pradesh) to define the changing doctrines of sub-conventional warfare of the Indian Army therefore poses delicate problems in a highly surcharged, corrupt socio-political order amidst rapidly transforming traditional ethnic societies in the borderlands of South Asia and South East Asia.

What possibly be the root cause of these Manipur insurgencies? Could we have a bird's eye view of its more recent past, or was it embedded in the contradictions of colonialism and imperialism that overwhelmed various parts of Asia, Africa and Latin America that changed the forces of historical development of these regions? The author of this chapter had an opportunity to provide an overview of the impact of these world forces as they affected the Northeast thus '*imperialism and colonialism rapidly intervened amidst pre-colonial societies whose equilibrium was based on values of a different kind. It created discontinuities, ruptures and fissures in tribal and ethnic polities, whose earlier relationships were based on natural organic laws of blood, kin and face to face interactions in society and polity. New structures through economic integration to the over wielding imperium where impersonal laws based on capitalist transactions created new forms, new relationships, exploitation of resources, commodification of land and people, and divisions in society through class, groups and sections with differing perceptions on the world. The succession to this colonial project was organized by the modern Indian state without much structural changes. New world outlooks, however, were shaped by elite stakeholders in the modernity project, who emerged in the cultural and social transformations in the light of rapid decolonization movements in the global world. The processes of modernization through education, economic transaction and mobilization of group resources, acquisition of wealth, power and territory became new engagement thereby rupturing old relationships. An undefined individualism nurtured by the capitalist transformation and democracy was also shaping up, and at the same time the new challenges thrown up by the economic and social processes paved the path for elite formation, who would soon utilize 'primordial and collective symbols' in the race for power, resources and status in the decolonizing world. These modern elites were different from the blood and kin traditional aristocracy (who were merged into the new social structures in the process of democratization), and they started re-negotiating their historical and political space in the modern context. The issues of identity, for re-invented groups and collectivities, and for the new individuals were to become features of the modernity project. The response of different ethnic societies and the texts of these responses differ due to the environment, culture and subjective experiences of the people themselves. All the ensuing disequilibria, social and political unrests, therefore, are complex interplays of the changing character of these ethnic societies in vital relationship with the pre-dominant presence of the new Indian state negotiating their own self-perpetuation as a South Asian global power, whereby the Northeast is subsumed to the status of a periphery in the new 'Pan-Indian imperialism'. These issues are, however, not to be reduced to simple oppositions between two entities, the core and periphery, but also between peripheries themselves, which are complex dynamics created by the system'.*[5]

Narratives of Recovery of Identity and Dignity

Defeat at the hands of British Empire and the loss of freedom of the ancient Asiatic state and its people in the Anglo-Manipur war of 1891 left deep scars in the hearts and minds of the Manipuris. A deeply trusted friend and ally in the past, who helped liberate the state from the bondage of the Burmese (1819-1826), had now turned into a hated foe, with superior military resources at their command. Her Majesty's Government declared war on Manipur on April 11, 1891. The charges were waging war against Queen Victoria and for murdering five British officials (including the Chief Commissioner of Assam, a British colonel), who went to Imphal in March 1891 to intervene on the issue of a palatial revolution in the state. Within two weeks of the invasion of the state from three sides, they were able to break the resistance of the natives. The last encounter was at a village called

Khongjom, 22 kms. south of Imphal, where the Manipur soldiers engaged in a brutal hand to hand combat with the imperial forces. The British were victorious, the river Khongjom running red with Manipuri blood. The direct clash of Manipuri swords with the Empire's bayonets lasted from 8 AM in the morning till 5 PM in the evening. The Gurkha regiments later in history celebrated this victorious anniversary, remembering the battle in Manipur as one of their hardest engagements in history. Victoria crosses decorated their officers, and acclaimed the victory as a glorious saga of imperial expansion with courage and bravery worthy of the Empire, while from the point of view of the natives it was a heroic sacrifice for the cause of the peoples' freedom (Mao-ze Dong is learnt to have included this event in the second phase of National Liberation Struggles of the Asian peoples against the white Europeans, similar to those of Cambodia and the Philippines).

What the Empire did after the conquest of the state was first the occupation of the sacred capital of Kangla by its military forces (till 2004, when it was handed over to the state by the Assam Rifles!), raising of the imperial flag on 27th April, 1891, and physical destruction of all symbols of native authority and pride of the vanquished nation. The leaders of the rebellion were arrested, a British court of trial was established, presided by a military officer. They tried the leaders of the war under British laws, found them guilty of waging war against Her Majesty's Government, and executed them (two in front of the public and three inside the jail). A few other princes were deported to the Andaman and Nicobar Islands for life imprisonment. The properties of the nobles were confiscated and auctioned. The common people were forced to carry supplies of salt and other materials to the imperial garrisons spreading all over the Northeast.

The economy was integrated into that of the empire. To run the imperial economy Marwari merchants were kept in the town with their families protected by the imperial soldiers. For restructuring of the land revenue system and introducing the concept of private property and for educating the natives in the ways of the Empire, Bengali officials and teachers with their families were brought in within the British Reserve (which is now the Kangla Fort), establishing a colony of the *'Babu'* which came to be known as Babupara (the residence of the Babus or gentlemen). Deliberate contentious pluralism was foisted on the traditional social fabric earlier based on the organic pluralism of the autochthons, who later on were to change into assertive ethnicities.

A new lineage not in conflict with the Empire was chosen to rule the state (now an Indian princely state) under separate terms of engagements known as sanads. *'The British government undertook to defend the ruler and his lawful successors from external or internal attack and not to interfere in the domestic concerns of his state except in the event of gross misgovernment. The ruler, for his part, accepted what came to be called the 'suzerainty' of the British crown and agreed to surrender all controls of his relations with other states to the 'Paramount Power', to provide military forces if required for the defence of India, and to co-operate in the extension of communications and other matters affecting India as a whole. Thus on the one hand the rulers or, to give them their present day collective title the Princes, retained their domestic autonomy quamdieu se bene gesserint, their territory did not become British soil, and their subjects did not become British subjects but remained their own subjects'.*[6] Thus a new social, economic and political order was restructured to implement the white man's global mission, tutoring the natives into the realm of colonial modernity.

The Second World War (1942-1945) intervened where the land, people and its resources were completely embroiled with the violences of the global conflict. The war dislocated the economy and stirred the placid social structures to new orientations of greater mobility and more thrusts towards self empowerment. At the near end of the British imperial power, the traditional monarchical principles declined, and in the valley, the rise of democratic aspirations as against the feudal dynastic system heightened as a result of the Hinduized association with mainstream India. The pattern was such that while in the valley there were rising anti-monarchical and democratic movements (encouraged by the Gandhian movements), a wider contextual experience, the surrounding hills were progressively getting into the form of ethnic selfhoods, with difference from the others, and the passion for recognition of their economic and political privileges on the basis of difference and ethnicity. Tighter ethnic consolidation was effected amidst various groups. These trends were re-negotiated by the Maharajah Bodhchandra Singh (1941-1955) through conciliation and compromise. An attempt to self-empower the natives were made to deal with the new freedom secured by the sudden departure of the British in 1947, and a first democratic constitution under the principles of the constitutional monarchy of Britain was adopted in 1947, and a first democratic assembly was elected in 1948 with election held under adult suffrage. However, under the new manoeuvres by the succeeding Dominion of India after the Empire's withdrawal from India, Manipur was merged into the new state under controversial circumstances in October 1949, and the Assembly was dissolved, with a Chief Commissioner's Province as a *'Part C State'* reducing the traditional status of the ancient kingdom into an obscure and backward part of the Indian Union.

Two trends are noticed in the struggles by the natives to resist the exogenous onslaughts into their universe. The first was the development of the spirit and actions of anti-colonial struggles, defying enforcement of outside will on the life world of the people. The first resistances were seen on the actions of the native women in the valley, who resisted the introduction of the rupee as medium of exchange, and later refused have their men obey the imperial orders for reconstruction of burnt houses of colonial officials in 1904. It was known as the first women's war of 1904. While the men in the valley were forced to contribute manual labour to collect timber and bamboos to reconstruct the burnt out bungalows of colonial officials, the women in the markets stopped the men, and threw their materials into the river. The initiative of women were understandable, since many of the princely families had been punished severely during the last war, there was an environment of fear and repression and conspiracies were in the offing, and incendiarism were symbolic protests against the Empire's authority over the natives. Force was exercised to suppress the agitation by the women, and in the struggle, a sixty-five year old woman lost her teeth! This was the first instance of the assault on the body and integrity of the women through colonial rule, and eleven princes were arrested and deported outside. In 1939 again during the women's great struggle for food security some twenty-one women suffered bodily wounds from bayonet attacks by the imperial forces, and some twelve women experienced life in colonial jails. Periodic resistances by the peasants on the introduction of forced labour was evident in the valley, while in the hills arms resistance again developed amidst the hill peoples notably by the Kukis in 1917-19, and the Nagas in 1929-1934. British intrusion into the hills to secure revenue through house-tax, and the Empire's demand to have the hillmen serve as corps in the First World War emboldened the native of the hills to resist the imperial orders, and war and confrontation were the result. The British took two years to quell the Kuki rebellion, and in the other punitive expeditions from 1932 to 1934 against the Zeliangroung Nagas, a seventeen year old maiden named Gaidinlieu emerged like Joan of Arc in Manipur to continue the resistance after her cousin brother Jadonang, the leader of the movement was arrested and hanged by the British in 1931. She was however arrested after a skirmish in Pulomi in 1934 and interned in Indian Jails till she was released after Independence of India. Jawaharlal Nehru, the Prime Minister of India gave her the title of *'Rani'* in 1937, in order to honour her spirit of struggle for Independence.

All these aforesaid struggles were local responses to the colonial penetration into the domestic spaces of the indigenous peoples, when the British Empire intruded into their traditional world, dividing them, re-structuring their lives to meet the economic and social needs of the empire to which the natives struggled to save their culture and traditions and their original way of life. The pacification of the hills, one by one, village by village and community by community through the exercise of military power and force amidst slowly emerging ethnicities informed the colonial intrusion and alteration of their lives in the image of an imperial *'other'*. This othering was gradually supplemented by the spiritual transformation effected by the teachings of Christianity which was to become a major ideological development which was to have widespread ramifications in the worlds of the hill people in the future.

These internal awakening in the lives of the autochthons and their immediate reactions to the physical presence of the power and institutional forces of the empire and its dynamic tension in stirring up responses and reactions amidst ethnic societies were indeed natural outpourings of autonomous energy experiencing this impinging impact on their traditional dignity and identity as people. These resurgent energy were however weak and fragile compared to the resources of force and ideological power accompanying the conquering entity. Memories of these struggles, the pain and sacrifices of the autochthones in their physically withstanding the forces of the repressive *'other'* were sustained in the ballads, oral traditions and folklore of these societies, which was to be re-consolidated in a more organized manner through the advent of more subjectivised experiencing of contradictions, and more globally aware resistances which was to become a second trend in the struggles of these natives, having a direct bearing on the modern insurgencies of the day.

The impact of the Second World War (1942-45) which embroiled the state in the violences of the global conflict, where the indigenous peoples had no virtual stakes, however helped them to become aware of movements of the worlds' peoples for self-determination, independence from the colonial enslavements for which the Asian peoples as a whole were struggling with national aspirations for freedom. The growing knowledge of global movements through the radio, newspapers, and other physical interactions with imperial or liberating agents emboldened the new political elites to develop new consciousness in their subsequent engagements for the future of their communities. Two leaders emerged in the Northeastern mountains and the valleys, in the current Nagaland and Manipur, whose experiences in the global movements separately left profound imprints in the emancipation struggles of their own peoples.

A.Z. Phizo of present Nagaland, while in Burma since the thirties experienced the liberating impulse of the Asian peoples, more especially under the leadership of the imperial Japanese Army in Burma. His arrest and incarceration by the British in Burma, due to suspected involvement in the war as a member of the Hikari Kikan, an intelligence unit of the Japanese army, and his subsequent release and return to his native home after the war resulted to tumultuous changes in the history of the Naga people. Zapu Phizo's experience of the Japanese concept of a new international order seeking *'co-prosperity for Asian countries'* which would share prosperity and peace under the Toa Shin Chitsujo or the New Order in East Asia Scheme would have inspired him on the issues of his peoples' freedom, that he released the suppressed energy of the people towards the cause of Naga Independence. His movements for the Naga cause was first the awakening of his own people's consciousness of the new future, attempted negotiations with the Indian leaders and the British authorities through discussions, delegations and meetings, but the intransigence of the Indian authorities prompted him to seek complete break of relationship with the Indian leadership in 1952, though the Naga National Council declared Naga Independence on 14th August 1947. The rest is now history. Police and army action by India began in 1952 and inevitable war ensued.

A.Z. Phizo's contemporary in Manipur Hijam Irabot, who experienced a different dynamic in his political life in the valley, provided the base modern concepts of Manipur's freedom. As a leader of the civil society movements in Manipur since the thirties, he had participated in the anti-colonial struggles and demonstrations in the princely state, established the first political demand for representative government as against the monarchical system in 1938, left his government job as Judge of the Sadr Panchayat Court as a result of the state's strict orders for government employees not to participate in political activities, and decisively intervened in the women's food agitation in 1939, known in Manipur history as Second Women's War or Nupilal. For his support to the women's movement he was arrested and sent to jail with a summary trial in January 1940 on charges of sedition, and transferred to the imperial Shyllet jail in East Bengal, where he was imprisoned for two years. His stint as a political prisoner in the colonial prison exposed him to the global emancipation movements of the oppressed peoples, under the ideology of Marxism-Leninism. He became a secret member of the Communist Party of India in 1943, spent two years in the Barak Valley in Assam being disallowed by the British authorities to enter his homeland. He continued to enhance the peasants and peoples struggles in the southern plains of Assam, and after his return to the homeland after the war in 1946, he re-organized the Krishak Sabha and the peasants movement in Manipur, established political party of the middle bourgeoisie variety (official communism was abhorred by the state's discourse), as opposed to the newly emerging Congress Party of Manipur. In the next few years of the globally enhancing national liberation struggles after the war, Irabot also organized the first modern armed opposition movement (1949-1951), under socialist ideological underpinnings, as part of the Indian Communist Party's armed struggle under the B.T. Ranadive line. He also became the first amongst the Northeasterners to link up the peoples struggle in Manipur with the Southeast Asian left wing movements in Burma, especially the Communist Party of Burma under Thakin Than Tun. Unfortunate death of Hijam Irabot in 1951 in Burma, and massive arrests at home and intervention by the Indian Army led to the decimation of the struggle for the establishment of an Independent Socialist Republic in Manipur. But adherents of the armed struggle refused to disavow the movement when the Communist Party of India denounced the B.T. Ranadive line and accepted the parliamentary processes, thereby creating a rift in the Communist Party in Manipur.

Post Merger Developments in the Armed Struggles

The death of Irabot in Burma in August 1951 was kept as a secret amongst his party cadres for quite long, and perhaps the Chief Commissioner's government as well as the Manipur public was not aware of the incident. Most of his comrades who had participated in the armed struggle against the Government of India had been arrested in the early fifties and contact with the leader was not possible in the circumstances. The Manipur-Burma borders were sealed by the Indian Army to prevent infiltrations of the Communist menace from Burma, and the valley was scoured by the Army and the Police to suppress the movement at home. It was much later that news of the sending of three batches of volunteers to Burma for training in guerilla warfare under the auspices of the Communist Party of Burma before Irabot's death was revealed.

The path of the armed struggle became a contentious issue amidst Irabot's followers due to the drastic change of the Communist Party of India's policies in the mainstream after the retirement of both B.T. Ranadive and Rajeswar Rao and handing over charge to P.C. Joshi who advocated the parliamentary line. A secret conference was held in a village called Porompat in 1953 where representatives of both sides thrashed out the issue in presence of a mainstream Communist Party leader. Mr. Lamabam Ibotombi, the General Secretary of the Party and his core colleagues refused to adopt the parliamentary line suggested by the mainstream party and they continued the struggle till 1955, and later in 1964 joined the CPI-M.

The facts of Irabot's armed struggle, and narratives of the work of the leader in his relationship with ethnic armed opposition groups in Burma, colloquially known as the White Flags (BCP) and the Red Flags (PVO) etc., the stories of his intervention amidst the mutual quarrels and disputes of the opposition groups during the Burmese civil war, the reported autonomy provided to the patriot from Manipur, with administrative jurisdiction over some areas of the Kabaw Valley which was handed over to him to facilitate the Manipur liberation struggle were not discovered till late in the official Communist Party's history, or it was deliberately suppressed.

The retrieval of his contribution towards the cause of the poor and oppressed classes and memories of his fight against the feudal monarchical regime and his social reforms was started by the Manipur CPI in 1981, with public celebrations and writings about his achievements. A small booklet published in 1981, however, included portions of the steps taken up by the party in Manipur towards the establishment of the Red Guards, their training programmes in Assam and its future activities, its commander being Thokchom Boro, a staunch and capable cadre of the party. Public awareness of Irabot's armed struggle line was however facilitated by a journal of the Pan-Manipuri Youth League (formed in 1968), *'Lamyanba'* which carried in 1972-73 the new truths of Irabot's revolutionary struggle against the Indian state, which the CPI did not want to preach. Also the Aryan theatre, an anti-establishment theatre group in 1976 produced a documentary drama of the late leader's armed struggles in the eastern and north eastern and south western portions of the valley, his liberation of certain zones, introduction of village co-operative movements, elimination of class enemies and the police and army atrocities on the people in the process of the suppression of the movement and his subsequent death in Burma. The group was welcomed in many of the village audiences when they saw the realities of their past struggles with the injustices perpetuated on them by the state.[7] Also the first small autobiographical account of Irabot in Manipur History appeared in 1977 written by his follower S. Chattradhari too and counter narratives of Irabot's disavowal of the armed struggle were sponsored by the official Communist Party of India in the next few decades.

The post-merger development of armed struggle in Manipur inferred through the states discovery of an underground organization termed the United National Liberation Front established in 1964 could be understood if we go back a bit in the historical experiences of the people in the pre-merger eras and study the episodes of social and political instabilities in Manipur on the sudden prospect of regime change. The likely departure of the British Empire, and aspirations of various political groups amongst the middle class, and the radically declining institutional structure of the traditional monarchy, along with the economic depression through the disturbances of the Second World War and extensive social and political agitations of the *'empowered'* democracy aspirants made the situation in Manipur fluid, tense and conflictual.

There were deep anxieties amongst the people as to how they would shape their own destinies after the departure of the British. The political officials around the king's circle were deeply concerned with feverish attempts to effect constitutional reforms which was inevitable in the changed circumstances. The reigning monarch Maharajah Bodhchandra (1941-1955) along with his elite officials, supported by the British experts attempted to rediscover the spirit of the 'people' as constituted by the Hills and the valley, after a long period of separation during the indirect rule of the British (1891-1947). A native constitution was drafted after a lot of tension amidst varying opinions and a first democratic election was held in June 1948, much before Indian elections were organized. A fifty three member state legislative assembly was constituted and inaugurated on the 18th October, 1948. A constitutional monarchy in the twice removed image of the British model was structured, but it was brutally dissolved by the Dominion of India's government after the merger of Manipur into India in October 1949.

The decline of the decision making power of the state and the associate rise of intense democratic aspirations were associated with intense rivalries amongst the political aspirants, not only ideologically, which were, however, vaguely conceived at that particular period of historical time, but also through intense personal hatreds, suspicious and mutual intrigues. Earlier during the British regime the people responded to the colonial experience either through resistance or through assimilation, but the empire did not directly impact Manipur with what was being done at the imperial centre in New Delhi or Calcutta. But the pre-merger period when the Empire was about to depart and the political vacuum in the bargain was filled with secret decisions and actions at the centre of India which undermined the aspirations of collective decision making on the proposed future of Manipur. Certain decisions purportedly taken outside of the state, notably in New Delhi, in the close environment of a distant unknown power, affected the local peoples actions and behaviour, that responding to the many proposals about the political futures of the princely states stressed the public sphere and the attempt to devise a united political party in the valley was destroyed through mutual intrigue amidst the aspirants. The historic meeting of 1946 when organizations like the Krishak Sabha, Nikhil Manipuri Mahasabha met, quarreled and went in separate ways was decisive in the advent of mainstream ideologies and ideas with the formation of the Manipur State Congress in 1946, the advent of the Socialist Party and the yet to emerge Communist Party under the leadership of Hijam Irabot, whose options and actions, instead of developing a strong political order with diverse democratic ideologies and debates turned into a vicious circle of intrigue, defamations and incriminations which vitiated the public sphere. Contesting opinions about Manipur's desire to integrate into India by the State Congress under the influence of

New Delhi, the Socialist Party's desire to integrate Manipur into Assam through the influence of Ram Manohar Lohia, Irabot's concept of Free Manipur in Free India (inspired by the Communist Party of India's constitution based on the Soviet model) and the Maharajah's patronage to develop a local regional party (Praja Shanti which shared power in the 1948 assembly) all created a disturbed and confused socio-political order in the few critical years of pre-independence and post-independence Manipur. Dissident ethnic formations in the hills were also visible, through the emergence of ethnic organizations in spite of the attempts by the political elite to devise a Manipur State Hill Regulations Act of 1947 for reintegration of the hills and the valley. The literacy rate in the immediate post-war period was only 5 per cent of the estimate five hundred thousand population figures. The local economy based on agriculture was insufficient and the state was brought into near bankruptcy through the peasants and peoples struggle for opposition to the feudal taxation systems.

Enter the Hegemon

Let us view the narratives of the new Indian state and its presence in the domestic spaces of the Manipur people. V.P. Menon, who as the new Secretary of the States Ministry, in a production of a white paper in July 1948, on integration of the Indian states while initiating the principles of integration and democratization brought forth the idea that *"The accession of Indian states to the Dominion of India was the first phase of the process of fitting them into the constitutional structure of India. The second phase which has rapidly developed during the recent months has involved a process of two-fold integration, i.e. consolidation of small states into sizeable administrative units, and internal integration i.e. the growth of democratic institutions and responsible governments in the states"*.[8]

Though these avowed principles fixed at the centre without as much consultation or informed consent of all the parties involved, the sheer penetration of these ideas into the distant peripheries created intense dislocation of the socio-political orders. No doubt the Dominion of India was able to secure the first step to integration through two agreements called the Instrument of Accession (1947) and Standstill Agreements (1947) with the Maharajahs' of princely states (which are simply preliminary arrangements which can be counter-manded by the local power authority at their discretion), and the second principle of external integration, namely the consolidation of small states into sizeable administrative units and its implications created intense crisis in Northeast India, especially Manipur, whose people were extremely sensitive about culture and traditions. This principle would have worked in the mainstream geography in the heartland where there were more unities of space, language and other factors without much of cultural dichotomies.

This second principle and proposals of amalgamation of smallest territorial regions for administrative unity were filtered to these northeastern regions through reports in the newspapers, which propelled a rumour effect in the minds of the natives. The Dominion agents conducted these integration activities in secret through bilateral relations, subtle persuasions, threats and intimidations, and in the case of Manipur through force and deceit. The idea and suggestion of amalgamation of these small regional units for a workable, viable administrative whole had earlier been mooted by the departing British officials who envisaged a crown colony consisting of the hill regions in the mountain chains of Assam including present day Arunachal Pradesh, Nagaland, Manipur and Mizoram along with borderlands of Northeastern Myanmar and the Chin Hills. As Irabot reported in his newspaper '*Anouba Jug*'[9] (1947) "*Beginning from the Sadiya Hills in northern Assam, the Naga Hills, Manipur, Lushai Hills, the Arakan Hills, the Chin Hills of Burma under the administration of a Commissioner*" had in fact in 1946 been rejected by the Nagas and the people of Manipur, as they objected to insinuation from the departing British authorities to self-perpetuate their hegemony.

The second principle through the initiatives of the Dominion agents came to be known through a report from the Shillong Times in 1948, which was a Congress Party proposal to amalgamate the princely states of Tripura and Manipur with the Lushai Hills (now Mizoram) and the Cachar plains because of their geographic contiguity in the south of Assam into a Congress province with Bengali and Manipuri as official languages. This idea was initiated by Sardar Vallabhbhai Patel, the Home Minister of the new government. This scheme was known as the Purbanchal Pradesh scheme. It had serious repercussions in Manipur, and objection to the scheme by Irabot and his party in September 1948 led to the final banning of Irabot's organizations the Krishak Sabha and the Praja Sangha, and Irabot was forced to go underground to avoid arrest. This event also paved the path for the destruction of democratic opposition to the schemes of the centre regarding Manipur.

One month before the Anti-Purbanchal demonstration by Irabot and the peasants of Manipur, in August 1948, Sir Akbar Haidari, the Governor of Assam made a sudden visit to the Maharajah of Manipur Bodhchandra Singh, without any public engagements. He in fact was insisting the local ruler to take urgent action on Irabot and his followers since he was suspected of subversive activities. The state council immediately passed a resolution after his departure to the effect that the Krishak Sabha was restricted to hold meetings or processions without the Councils permission. *"The Governor might have been greatly disturbed by Irabot's participation in the Second Congress of the Communist Party of India held at Calcutta from 28th February to 6th March 1948, which adopted the B.T. Ranadive's political thesis of violent insurrection in India on the line of the October Revolution of 1917 in Russia. Most probably the high officials of New Delhi had seriously considered the possibility of Manipur Irabot's leadership joining hands with the Communist insurgency in Burma".*[10] The centre's suspicious on Irabot and the possibility of a Southeast Asian Communist integrated movement was also one of the factors for the centre's underhand dealings to effect Manipur's rapid integration into India in 1949. This perhaps was contrary to the services of the neighbouring Government of Assam towards better understanding with Manipur for future relations with India in earlier times, and the Governor Sri Prakasa was to play a decisive role in forcing the Indian militaristic hand in getting Bodhchandra's signature to the Merger Agreement in September 1949.

The failure of the proposal in the second principle of external integration, as suggested by the States Ministry perhaps could have influenced the New Delhi authorities to improvise on the direct methods on the issue of internal integration, namely on the avowed principle of ushering growth of democratic institutions and responsible governments in the states. But this type of integration should be at the behest of the centre, without the necessity of understanding whether democratic institutions were already existing in the princely state or not. For the next decisive action taken by the Indian state was a complete denial of the existence of a democratic lawful legislative assembly in Manipur, and of the history and traditions of the land.

The centre's attitude forwards Manipur on the eve of the forcible integration was that Manipur's history was *'obscure'* and that it was a *'backward state'* with a small population size, and *'unviable'* in terms of modern development. *'It was also in view of its position as a border state and its underdeveloped character, it was decided to take over Manipur as a Chief Commissioner's province'*,[11] which has much more meaning than it is usually assumed.

Hard materialist and ruthless considerations of the states ministry was also that in 1943, the experience of voluntary integration of certain areas in a consolidated western India provided the principle that *'nothing which was not inherently capable of survival should be artificially perpetuated, and that the ultimate test of fitness for the survival of any state was its capacity to secure the welfare of its subjects'*.[12]

The attitudes, behaviour and actions of the high officials of the Indian state in dealing with the Maharajah of Manipur in his meeting with the Assam Governor Sri Prakasa at Shillong on September 18, 1949 are now revealed in the records now in the public sphere (*vide* M. Anandamohan – Shillong 1949, 2004). Immediately during the meeting the Maharajah was handed over a document of the merger of the state into India for his urgent signature. The Maharajah politely refused to sign the document without consultation with his people, and that he was now only a constitutional head. The persistent pressure also led to intense emotional breakdown of the Manipur king that the meeting was subsequently postponed on the next day. On the same day in the evening the Maharajah wrote an official letter to Sri Prakasa, the Assam Governor *"Now that the sovereignty of the state has been vested in the people it would be in the fitness of the things to hear the peoples voice and learn their sentiment so that the line of action may not be in any case unconstitutional"*.[13] However, on the same day, the Governor Sri Prakasa sensing a fear that the Maharajah may slip away sent an urgent telegram to Sardar Patel.

> "H.H. threatens returning to Manipur without holding any discussions or signing the agreement. H.H. must not under any circumstances be allowed to return to Manipur with his advisors and I have accordingly instructed police to detain here his party if they attempt to return before signing of agreement.
>
> Please telegraph immediately repeat immediately authority for detention of H.H. and advisers under Regulation II or whatever other means you consider might be appropriate.

> *Have already warned Sub-Area to be prepared for any eventuality in Manipur. Grateful for further instruction. Ends".*[14]

Details of the conversations, the planned preparation of House arrest of the Maharajah, the preparatory trip of Sri Prakasa to Mumbai to meet Sardar Patel, and the often quoted sound byte of Sardar Patel *"Isn't there a Brigadier in Shillong?"* and other details of the negotiations are revealed in the autobiographical account of M. Anandamohan, who as ADC to the Maharajah accompanied him to the fateful Shillong trip 17-21 September, 1949. Moreover substantial military preparations were made with additional postings of military detachments over and above the Assam Rifles for any eventuality during the take-over of the Manipur Administration on October 15, 1949.

The post-merger management of Manipur as a Chief Commissioner's province, as a simple district territory and simple police district as a Part *'C'* state under the constitution manifested the *'othering'* of a racially and culturally different community under the direct Indian regime, secured through the critical exigencies of the political crisis. The erstwhile efforts at self-governance and peoples democracy by the indigenous communities were hastily brushed aside, the administration of the princely state taken over, a military official appointed as the first Chief Commissioner, and the indigenous bureaucracy and police were transformed through the appointment of Indian officials at the top hierarchy. All the earlier traditionally enacted laws were promptly abolished, especially the restriction of entry of foreigners and Indians were removed through the abolition of the Foreigners Registration Act of 1947, and the door was open to free entry of economic migrants and partition refugees and other laboureres which was to transform the demographic structure of the land. Through the introduction of the Merged States (Laws) Act of 1949, laws that had been framed by the British Government for the administration of Indian provinces were imported wholesale, many of them unsuited to local conditions and their impersonalized legal systems were to become contradictory applications to the indigenous practices and customs. The intense social and cultural contradiction was evident in the behaviour and attitudes of high officials towards the native subordinates when the new administration, with the help of the military, paramilitary and police forces were engaged in the ruthless suppression of Irabot's Communist movement.

The integration of Manipur into India had in fact been facilitated by the urgent concerns of the Dominion of India with fears and apprehensions of the Nehru Government about Communism's infiltration into Manipur from the Burmese side (the border state syndrome), deep suspicion over the manners, behaviour and character of the native Mongoloid population[15], and the Indians' ruthless pragmatic economism which prompted them to stop *'artificial propping up of unviable state system'* (underdeveloped economic character of Manipur). This third principle would, however, be surprisingly contradicted during the high tide of Manipur insurgencies in the last forty years or so, when India had to continually sponsor the artificial propping up of the economy and polity as a counter insurgent measure. The transformation of the Northeastern states into special category status in the late nineties (the Dev Gowda principle), massive investments of party funds in periodic *'democratic'* elections, held under heavy security protection, and ruthless utilization of sleaze and force in the conduct of the system were instant reminders to the hegemonic penetration of the Indic way into deeply stressed indigenous responses to the change.

What the young protagonists of the new insurgencies experientially felt and understood was that Manipur and its self-development could not be externally propelled through mechanically induced materialism, which is known now as *'vulgar evolutionism'* in the Marxist Jargon, but the basic cause of development of a thing is not external but internal, through its own way of finding the dynamics of self-growth, or its own dialectic.[16] This movement of attempting to discover the self and its dignity was, however, met by the Indian state in a variety of ways ranging from sheer repression through force, or through reconciliation or co-option, or through inducements, or corrupting influences to splitting of the subjects, i.e. the four precious principles of statecraft of Kautilya.[17] The patterns of its self-generating movement for the recovery of the land was seen through the first emotional attempts to revive the memories of ancient historical sacrifices of the people in the wars against imperialism and colonial subjugation of the land. The fight of the Manipuris against the British Empire, the sacrifices of the native patriots at decisive battles, and the imperial acts of hanging of the patriots like Tikendrajit and Thangal were celebrated as public days of mourning. Native plays and ballads of these patriotic sacrifices were deliberately encouraged. The late sixties and seventies were filled with re-energization of the energy and activism of youths and students, who became active agents against economic exploitation, developing corruption of the political and business classes, and overall marginalization of the natives. An intense re-energization of the local vernacular journals, the exposure of the behaviour of the military on the rapes of indigenous women, the relentless crusade against Indian officials and bureaucracy's corruption, and the fight against economic strangulation by Indian merchants, the discovery of the losses of native cottage industries, the captive market in operation to consume surplus products of mainstream manufactures and commercial products, and all vestiges of the emergence of a second colonialism through the Indian dispensation were brought into the public sphere. There was a generational change in the attitude, behaviour and actions of the youths, and the patterns and motives of the debates were distinctively transformed from those of the pre-merger days. Increasing use of excessive force became a feature in the repressive activities of the state, evident from the dealings against student strikes in 1952. The first *'massacre'* of civilians by the instruments of state through indiscriminate firing where four people including a girl student were killed occurred in the valley during an artificial famine of 1965. New paradigms of protests were intensified through more participation of youth and students in the agitations. In 1969, during the visit of Madame Indira Gandhi at Imphal, firing against the crowd led to the death of six civilians. Massive burning of the Khwairamband Bazar in 1973 in the wake of an Indian merchant's alleged molestation of a native woman right in the heart of the town reflected an intense dislike for and protest against Indian rule through their native compradors. All these manifestations of protest and eruptions of public anger against the authorities and violent student agitations through destruction of government properties (cars, buildings etc.) in the seventies were indicative of the rapidly developing secret insurgent forces. Deep hatred of the *'Mayang'* (outsider) was built fast into the psyche of the new generations which was similar to the attitude and feelings of the native Burmans against Indian merchants and business classes during the halcyon days of Burmese nationalism.

Without as much activation of the *'democratic'* public sphere, the local government under the centre's directions were responding to the development through increasing use of the armed forces in aid of civil authority under the Armed Forces (Assam and Manipur)

Special Powers Act, 1958. Democratic apprenticeship of the state through gradual increase of the status of the state from a Chief Commissioner's province to that of a Union Territory and later to a full-fledged state in 1972, had in fact nothing to do with the secrets and violent confrontations engaged in by the army, first with the aroused ethnic insurgents in the hills through military operations in specific areas like Ukhrul, Tamenglong, border areas in the Southeast near Burma and India and later in Assam-Manipur borders of Jiribam etc. during the sixties till the seventies. From a supposedly brief and temporary measure for countering the Naga insurgency in the hills of Manipur the notifications of the use of the act, announcement of disturbed conditions when the rural areas in the Meetei inhabited villages were suddenly incorporated into the scheme of counter-insurgency with its concomitant effect on civilian populations in 1979. Some sixty Meetei inhabited villages in the valley were declared *'disturbed'* on account of *'an unprecedented upsurge in the commission of crimes, such as killing of innocent persons as also police officers, robbery, looting, dacoity, abduction, sedition, offences under the Arms Act and harbouring and rescuing of criminals and attempts and incitement to commit the above and other offences and terrorizing peaceful and law-abiding citizens and disturbing the normalcy of life and public tranquillity endangering the lives of civil authority, the use of Armed Forces in aid of Civil Power is necessary'*.[18]

This was in response to the first armed strike in 1978 by the Lhasa trained outfit of the Peoples Liberation Army (PLA Eastern Region) against the local police and paramilitary forces and a series of brilliant interventions to raise arms as well as morale of the people which ushered in the modern classical period of urban insurgency. Raids against armed installations of paramilitary forces, shooting of soldiers and police officials, and engagements with the state forces even in the nooks and corners of the town, rapid shooting down of Indian soldiers and dashing get-away after loot and arms, vehicles etc. relentless hit and run tactics, demonstrations of intense sacrifices *'lifted the low morale of the citizenry during the three decades of India's 'occupation' of Manipur'*. Red star shaped balloons floated in the sky on top of trees in the roadsides to signal the rise of the liberation forces, pamphlets were strewn to propagate the actions and victories in the liberation struggle, which with the violent increase of confrontations ushered in the period of armed conflict.

The methodologies of the combing operations under the massive intervention of the military ruthlessly, considering the intensity of the resistance, were accompanied with all the unaccounted freedom in shooting, killing and torture which are yet to be fully documented in the history of the conflict. Sudden arrival of the troops in the localities of suburban populations as well as in the villages, collective herding in of native men and women civilians, introduction of black masked captured insurgents (nicknamed Zorros) to identify active insurgents hiding in civilian families, and whisking away of supposedly innocent young men aroused the collective anger of the women, thereby introducing the Meira Paibee movement. In the eyes of the women of the state, armed confrontation between the sons of the soil and their opponents, i.e. the state forces are legitimate and understandable in the ethics of war under local traditions. But unjustifiable and morally deplorable acts of wanton arrests of the innocent, enforced disappearances of young and old, ruthless elimination of school going students and heaping of indignity on the bodies of women are unpardonable crime which should be resisted and perpetrators punished. Definite clash of values were involved in the dynamics of the conflict.

Vigilante actions against the night raids became a feature of the collective women's movement. Lighted bamboo torches filled the night sky, unending processions following processions illuminated the urban and rural landscapes since the eighties. Sudden attacks against soldiers by armed insurgents were rapidly followed by reprisal actions against village populations nearby, suspecting the support of the nearby villagers. This ensued the killing of innocent civilian men and women. Protests against rape during combing operations, molestation and hurt accompanied these methods of extra-judicial execution, torture and elimination of armed opponents. Physical resistances by women to prevent arrest of young males resulted often to indiscriminate firings and a series of *'massacres'*, which reflected the genocidal mentality of the soldiers, and mowing down of volleyball players, medical students and ordinary villagers etc. resulted from the violent conflict since the eighties.

Physical actions against these aroused women, whom the sepoys derisively termed the *'Petticoat Soldiers'* included releasing of dog hounds to bite the women, throwing of grenades to disrupt congregations, gushing of vehicle smoke to disperse the crowd and even physical bouts with the soldiers accompanying such resistances, and bodily wounds from bullets from the firing, dislocation of shoulders and joints and even death were the result. The movement consumed a lot of women's lives, some from intense physical and mental deterioration through the confrontations leading to unknown ailments like vomiting of blood and other such complications.

Most of the violent engagements between the Indian state's forces and the non-state actors in the early years of insurgency were staged in the flat plains of the geography of the valley, while the hill insurgents used the topography of the rugged terrain, though the intensity of the confrontation were qualitatively different, but with similar effects on the native populations. In the valley, this spatial dimension of the struggle was qualitatively advantageous to the Indian counter-insurgent forces, who managed to eliminate and neutralize the cream of the leadership of the insurgent groups. Yet the daring and courageous sacrifices, their deaths in the battles were eked out in the folk memory of the peoples for long. For those in the Peoples Liberation Army who sacrificed their lives, their families and friends erected red memorial tombs and mortuary relics in areas of engagements, and at the family gates of the patriots' homes. But these tombs and memorials were wantonly destroyed and vandalized by the state forces.

Untold stories of tales of capture, arrest and torture also emerged which were yet to be completely documented by human rights groups. Narratives of the experiences of torture, the incarceration of captives, and third degree methods for intelligence gathering and inhumanity to insurgent women captives were subsumed in the environment of fear and silence. The sacred and ancient capital of Kangla, the deeply revered centre of the Manipur universe which were occupied by the paramilitary forces since the 19th century – its activities later emerged during the peak of counter-insurgency as prototype of Guantanamo bay, where secret tortures were perpetuated to arrested insurgents. Tales of electric shocks, suffocation through dripping water, hanging upside down and brutal kicks and butting etc. and repeated dipping of nude females in the sacred ponds and such tales secretly emerged in the subaltern narratives which are as yet to emerge in the public sphere through proper investigation in the human rights annals of Manipur.

These incidents and details are highlighted to reflect on the human side of the conflict. After the first phase of the decade of the eighties when the confrontation with the forces of the centre was the main subject of the insurgency story, we witnessed the rapid emergence of equally committed groups in the valley who used the remote areas as well as nearby foothills to withstand *'the forces of occupation'* of the Indian state. Tales and narratives of meetings and serious discussions, of aims, objectives and methodologies of struggle had filled the rumour mills of the population, and at the same time the continuing superiority of the enemy forces, and the pressure of the counter-insurgent action, and the violence in the nature of confrontations led to serious splits in the ranks of the insurgent forces which gave the decade of the eighties an agonized experiences of the people in the human costs involved. But these agonies and pains in the social fabric did not influence the people to demand peace or stoppages of the violences in the nature of the vertical conflict.

The dynamics of the insurgency expanded in multiple dimensions in the nineties through structural changes in the processes of the struggles within, and large scale exogenous secret interventions by the state, not only to suppress the movement, but help change its directions to weaken indigenous resistance—notably the transformation of the conflict itself into horizontal ones. These structural transformations were also perhaps induced by the stress and strains of the neo-liberation schemes of the economic policies of de-regulation of protection tariffs and opening up of global capital with its logic of crippling of unprofitable economy and the corporate takeover of the development progammes under the Look East Policy of the Government of India. Though rigorous research is yet to be undertaken on the issues of the direct impact of the overall transformation of national economic policies on the insurgent movements of the Northeastern region, a strange development of the times was the rapid transformation in the politicization of the ethnicities and sharpening of ethnic divide in the region, along with mutual arming of small ethnic groups for protection of identities and for development of ethnic territoriality and exclusivist demands for control over resources.

Two factors are hypothesized for the development of in-group solidarity and out-group hostility amongst the indigenous populations of the Northeast. The first factor was a gradualist sharpening of the subjective development of ethnic selfhood which began as peaceful political awakenings through democratic representations to the government authorities and mutual consolidation activities into a critical period of the necessity to have militant actions through the use of violence and accentuation of the political and military strength of the ethnic self. This feeling and rapid transformation of the mindset of ethnic political organizations coincided with the rapid expansion of the political and military strength of the NSCN (IM), who, regarded as *'the mother of insurgencies in Northeast India'* by the Indian media started encouragement of ethnic armed allies in their strategic scheme of access to international arms, resources and geographic advantages of rapid movement between base areas transcending regional borders, and at the same time helping spread of the concept of Nagalim in the affinal communities of Manipur.[19] This internal movement of ethno-national identification coincided with a reverse attitude towards major armed outfits like the UNLF who, by 1991 started armed intervention against the state after prolonged, quite preparation politically and militarily through support of the NSCN (K), a rival to IM since 1988, and the Kachin Independence Army (KIA) in upper Burma. The ethnic cleansing organized by the NSCN (IM) in 1992-96 resulted to intense inter-community hatreds and rivalry in the Congress (I) led government too. The tension in the political classes and their inability to rise above ethnic prejudices and the increase of violences at the grassroots led to the fall of the R.K. Dorendra Ministry in 1994. The imposition of President's Rule in the state, however, could not also bring reconciliation amidst the communities.[20]

Coincidentally, the ethnic hostility wave and mutual violences by one community over the other followed in rapid succession when the entire state was drawn into the tragedies of inter-community clashes when insurgency and counter-insurgency activities were at its height in the nineties. The ethnic clashes of the Naga-Kuki communities were soon followed by the Meetei-Meetei Pangal (indigenous Muslim groups who were descents from intermarriage of Meetei women with incoming migrants) clashes in 1993. In June 1995, there was a sudden eruption of Kuki and Indian Tamil clashes at Moreh, an active international trade centre between India and Myanmar, which had been officially inaugurated in 1994-95. Again there was another chain of intra Kuki-Chin Mizo communities clash when Kuki-Paite violences erupted in 1997-98.[21] These types of inter-ethnic and intra-ethnic violences, were substantially intensified during the harsh transition into global economic processes where smaller as well as bigger ethnic communities were stressfully engaged in conflictual contestation for resources and profit. The post 1992 period of violence was accompanied by emergence of various armed groups within the affected denominations of ethnicity, sprung up in the highly surcharged atmosphere, with contesting claims to identity, aims, objectives and purpose of the organizations with relentless claims over land, territory and collective rights of the communities. The social history of the region was no longer the same in inter-ethnic and inter-community relations once violences were perpetuated on the bodies of men, women and children, whatever justification being given on the interpretation or cause of the conflict.

The second factor in the over-all transformation of the character of the local insurgencies and methodologies of counter-insurgency was the spatial involvement of the rugged western mountain terrains through the activities of the UNLF and their fraternal organizations when they took up arms in 1991 following the trail set by the PLA and the PREPAK in the eighties in the valley. This movement professed to bring the western hill ethnic groups together through mutual support and help in training and development of a defensive base in the *'impregnable natural defences'* in the hill cliffs, and their ability to strike at the security forces at will. Apart from the presence of groups who supported the leadership of NSCN (IM) in the western hill ranges, the impact of a new plains insurgent group in the hill terrains necessitated a sharpened orientation of counter-insurgency measures to take advantage of primordial prejudices and passions of ethnicity. *'Ethnicity became an ardent ploy as the best and effective means of using the hill populations against the Meetei non-state actors who had substantial control of major spaces in the hill terrain. The art of mountain warfare cultivated by the Meetei nationalists could be countered by strategic methodical approaches for military presence in the hills and unprecedented civic action programmes to 'convert' the local populations. The Assam rifles became a friend of the hill people in the post-nineties when the mother of all insurgencies, the NSCN (IM) agreed to sit on the negotiating table in 1997, and enter into political dialogue with the centre. The prolongation of armed resistance by the Meetei armed opposition groups could be countered by meticulous weaning away of tribal groups and communities from the logic of ethnic unity'.*[22]

As the author wrote in 2007, *'over the last three or four years, the military engagements of the Indian security forces with the Meetei-non-state armed opposition groups had revealed patterns of progressive linkages between armed conflict and politics of ethnicity. Since the end of 2003, the thrust to secure the Manipur hills to restore civil administration and exercise area domination over the western ranges of the Manipur state, there were slow, periodic, inch-by-inch, yard-by-yard occupation of strategic mountain villages, flushing out of Meetei insurgent outfits who had earlier entrenched themselves in the rugged mountain terrains, mingling with the 'neglected' and 'marginalized' hill people. Earlier stories of mutual support between the ethnic populations of the hills and the valley, stories of help in arms and equipment, and training of ethnic brothers by valley insurgents, stories of development interventions by militant cadres in areas where state presence was negligible – all these were suddenly transformed into chapters of spite and hate campaigns over the valley people by the hill civil society organizations. The turmoil in the lives of ethnic populations caused by these unfortunate incidents of armed conflict between the instruments of state and non-state actors were suddenly catapulted into chaotic disequilibrium and massive uprooting of life's rhythm. Stories of displacement, collective exodus into neighbouring hill townships and villages, incidents of physical harm and decapacitation in landmine explosion, charges of rape and criminal assaults over the bodies of tribal women – all these concomitant agonies were brought into the public sphere in a confusing amalgam of doubt, distrust and heightening ethnic differences over perceptions on truth and reality. The earlier balance between ethnic brotherhood were substantially damaged as a result of the military engagement of the Indian security forces with the Manipur nationalists in the rugged hill terrains of Manipur. For the Indian state, the operations against the Manipur militants in Operation All Clear (2004), Operation Tornado (2005), Operation Dragnet (2006), etc. were meant to clear the western ranges of the Manipur Hills for restoration of civil administration as well as the destruction of Meetei hegemony over the hill peoples. The highlander ethnic psyche was thus aroused to see the lowlander valley people as oppressive others'.*[23]

The Iron Fist in the Velvet Globe

Now in the 21st century, the Indian state had substantially transformed its military doctrine, and its philosophy of engaging with insurgency. Earlier in 2004, during the enquiry by the Jeevan Reddy Committee in the wake of the Manorama agitation, the Ministry of Home Affairs of the Government of India had submitted to the Jeevan Reddy

Committee that the Armed Forces and the other forces of the Centre would be progressively withdrawn from the Northeast, once the capabilities of the state armed police are up to the required standards. Until then the forces operating in the Northeast will require both the authority and legal safeguards provided in the *'AFSPA'*.[24]

New precepts of tackling of insurgency however was initiated under the guidance of General J.J. Singh (now Governor of Arunachal Pradesh), in 2009, which transformed the methods and principles of counter-insurgency, now known as Doctrine of Sub Conventional Operations (DSCO). It was reported to do away with the earlier hesitation of fighting shy of committing troops to prolonged internal society duties and now commit fully to the fact that sub-conventional wars are here to stay as a form of warfare and will seek, increased involvement of the armed forces in times to come. *'The doctrine emphasizes that South Asia is the epicenter of global terror and hence, the future can only be more grim-terrorists armed with improvised nuclear, biological and chemical weapons, asymmetric threats with transnational signatures, meaning the masterminds would be based in foreign lands. All of these will call for the army's support'*.[25] That means the Army shall stay permanently in the Northeast, but with a different *avatar*, that with ***'The Iron Fist in the Velvet Globe'***. The 76 page doctrine, compiled by the Shimla based Army Training Command was introduced by General J.J. Singh as *'a collective wisdom based on the experiences of five decades of fighting low-intensity conflict, including proxy war, counter-insurgency and limited conflict'*. It recommended old fashioned boots on the ground to relently hunt down terrorists, using high technology and intelligence, but without alienating the civilian populace. The Indian Army Chief's policy of the velvet globe with the iron fist clearly eschews massive force in favour of *'people centric operations'*. *'The SCO doctrine predicts the emergence of religious, cultural and socio-economic faultlines as the cause for future strife. The army will fight these wars with a nimble iron fist – the focus is on manoeuvre warfare as opposed to attrition warfare. Simply put, small teams of highly trained troops will constantly try to outwit the enemy'*.

'Among the doctrine's other directives is the need to reorient the soldiers mindset from 'fighting the enemy' to fighting his 'own people', namely terrorists hiding among civilians. The army hopes to fight this guns and roses war through manoeuvres and force multipliers, like surveillance devices, helicopters for troop insertion, drones and

dogs. Earlier we would directly confront terrorists. Today, we use an indirect approach' says General J.J. Singh.[26]

This new doctrine seems to be an adaptation from the American counter-insurgency operations (COIN), but with substantial difference in motivation and applications. In the words of Sameer Lalwani *"Despite Indian official doctrine formally espousing this concept and some contentions that India has seen COIN as a political rather than military problem, a closer look reveals that the Indian approach may be better characterized as a strategy of attrition with the deployment of 'raw state coercion' and enemy-centric campaigns to suffocate an insurgency through a saturation of forces. At times it may involve the co-operation of elites to 'buy-out' and contain an emergency".*[27]

To quote him further *'The co-operation and transformation of insurgents into local assets was a tactic employed both in Punjab (called 'CATS' for Covert Apprehension Technique) and Kashmir (Ikhwanis). Turning insurgents was sometimes achieved through money as well as abduction and torture, but these tactics eventually led to new problems, such as increased criminal activity and corrupted security forces, for the respective governments. Moreover, the highly kinetic approach of both campaigns entrails tremendous brutality, torture, disappearances 'encounter killings', and mass graves that created a litany of human rights investigations and public disaffection, and today continues to fuel simmering resentment and potentially violence.'*

"A slight variant of this approach – the buy-out and political incorporation of insurgents – has enabled India to keep a lid on a whole host of insurgent separatist movements in the seven states of India's eastern extremity, India's Northeast, since 1956. Yet while eliminating the prospect of separatism, it has perversely created spirals of insecurity, splinter groups (there are more than 100 district armed groups in the Northeast), and a dysfunctional insurgent political economy of violence, development aid, and interminable militia politics".[28]

The experiential world of the people of Manipur under the altered dynamics of insurgency and counter-insurgency in this first decade of the 21st century could be narrativised through new trends and patterns of social, political and militaristic behaviour of the stakeholders in the conflict and their impact on the polity. As we witnessed in the post Manorama tragedy agitation and peoples' protests with self-immolation of a student and nude protests of women against the soldiers in 2004, there was a sudden shift in the conduct and behaviour of the Indian security forces. There was a temporary retreat of these forces from public visibility and major responsibility of shouldering work for the security of the state and maintenance of law and order were empowered to the police personnel and the rapid action forces (Commando units) of the local government with extensive increase of equipment, arms and funds (with very little training on ethics and human rights). This newly empowered local forces interiorized the behaviour and conduct of the central forces, occupying the temporary space in the vacuum created by the retreat of their patrons, and in the severe intensity of the violence, became monsters and blood-thirsty maniacs of counter-insurgence, manifested in the alleged gang-rape of a school teacher girlfriend of a local insurgent who was killed in the gunfight along with his enemy police officer of the Commando unit (Naobi incident – 2006). The *'police modernization'* which was the official term of the new activity also incorporated recruitment of special police officers from affected villages, an imitation of the Salwa Judum experience of recruiting peasant populations in Chhattisgarh to serve as instruments of counter-insurgency which again intensified the ruptures in the social fabric. The activities of these empowered instruments of the local state were mired in controversies of encounter killings, alleged release of black-masksed rogues for loot, ransom, torture and unprecedented killings. Tense civil society agitations for the next five years were accompanied by extensive state repression and brutalization of the public sphere. The result of these confrontations were the alleged killings by the state forces of some three persons a day climaxing with the Rabina and Sanjit *'massacre'* of 2009 (exposed by *Tehelka Magazine*).

This newly emerging form of state violence was however enacted in a totally new environment of the estranged hill populations under the altered context of ethnicized political agitations in 2010, when the northern hills were protesting against the Manipur Government's action to prevent the leader of the NSCN (IM) Mr. Th. Muivah to enter his homeland Ukhrul, which resulted in state firing and killing of two Naga youths. The two victims were martyred in the cause of the demand for political separation of the hill populations from those of the valley, another heightened emotional twist to the tense ethnic relations of the state.

The deliberate withdrawal of the Indian security forces from public visibility in the wake of massive anti-AFSPA agitation in 2004 was substituted by a new form of intervention through development funding by the Centre. Apolitical economists in the local university were surprised by the pouring in of extensive construction projects by the Centre to the state, which were inproportionately balanced to the scarce measures for public welfare or other productive investments for developing the workforces of the region. This was in fact part of the massive accentuation of the WHAM project (Winning the Hearts and Minds of People), as constituent of the counter-insurgency programme. Huge incentives were given to university academics, media persons, artists, sportspersons, and public women Meira Paibees, being incorporated in the overall military's civic action programmes. Deliberate efforts were made to cultivate the so-called *'elites'* of the public society leaders to ingratiate the institution of the military into the ruptured emotional spaces in the hearts of the people. The resplendence of grants and largesses only re-invigorated the structure of corruption already embedded in the polity. Periodic *'democratic'* elections to the new institutions for governance and power exercise became personal fields for manipulation, bribes and sleaze, and all other forms of epistemic violence were noticed in the frantic pursuit of power and legitimacy. The fatalistic, poverty-stricken, common male and female populations were sucked into the vindictive subterranean hostilities in electoral battles where slush money, deceit and lies, along with reckless use of gun and muscle power being traded against one another amongst the rivals in the murky electoral battles. *'The wrenching process of democratization and modernization'*[29] had been re-structured in a way where the spoils system had wreaked havoc amidst the critically dependent and sponsored economy of the era. The political leaders of the Centre along with the business classes in the metropolitan centre are no silent spectators in the overall stench of corruption in the state. They too are actively involved with their own *'levy'* systems from their indigenous wards as well.[30]

Concluding Observations

The complexity and intensity of violent relations between the Indian state and non-state actors of Manipur which we have witnessed being acted out for the last four decades in an environment of rapidly transforming ethnic societies within the *'hegemonic'* political structures of an advancing South Asian power within a fast globalizing universe, and the new geopolitical dimensions of intense global rivalry between India and China, and the underlying vulnerability of the Indian state's hold over Northeast India's populations had signaled grave unease on issues of peace and human security of this strategic region. The necessity of the Indian states' continued hold over the Northeast as a defensive fortress, which require permanent militarization of the area, and the stubborn resistance of the indigenous non-state armed groups, especially from the valley of Manipur, to the relentless onslaughts over the socio-economic and civilizational fabric of this ancient Asiatic state have not yet been objectively studied by students of conflict studies and international enthusiasts for global security and international peace and harmony, though there had been outstanding contributions from excellent conflict analysts over the years.

Most of the literature that has been produced over the years has argued from the angle of having accepted the international state systems of national sovereignty emerging out the global catastrophies of the Second World War, thereby acknowledging the independence and integrity of the sovereign nations in the post colonial world. The problems that had emerged in the Northeast was of rather a different category that India had acquired and inherited these territories from the disassembling British Empire artificially and there had been colonial origins of the Indian state's so-called legitimacy over the Northeastern peoples. Certain historically independent states, and other quasi-independent and stateless communities alike were, in the words of Benjamin Reilly *'forcibly incorporated into one unwieldy unitary state'* (referring to the Indonesian condition which is similar to India's), and the claims of people like the Nagas who refuse to accept that they are Indians, and the Manipuris who challenge the foundations of the modern Indian state that they had been illegally and unconstitutionally brought into the Indian political fold under duress and through militaristic means had not yet been properly addressed in contemporary conflict analysis discourse. Most of the conflict studies that had emerged in the international discourse about the Northeast, therefore, accept the Indian state as *'given'* and that attempts to analyze the contemporary conflict should be with a view to understand the problems of conflict, of historical grievances and what not, yet provide ways of means of bringing *'the secessionist elements'* within the constituted order with certain dignified measures of reconciliation or compromise. This is the fundamental problem in understanding the nature of the Manipur insurgency. This also explains why the insurgency in Manipur had lasted so long, in spite of the lumpenization within their ranks, splits and fragmentations due to sheer weight and pressures in the unequal balance between the vertical antagonists.

Another difficulty in properly assessing the problem of Manipur is the avoidance of the word *'conflict'* in the political vocabulary of the Indian state while addressing the issues of insurgency in Manipur or the Northeast. For the Indian state the issues of *'serious internal disturbance'* necessitate the use of the armed forces in aid of civil power of the affected states, and that it is a *'law and order'* situation, a state subject, but needing the assistance of the central forces through an enabling law known as the Armed Forces Special Powers Act of 1958, amended in 1972. For members of the conflict studies communities, the word *'conflict'* is freely used in studying and analyzing the conflict situations when incompatibilities between the state and other forces or communities reached a certain threshold when armed violence became a necessary tool for resolution of their deep antagonisms, but the Indian state, through sheer statecraft ingenuity uses the words *'internal disturbance'*, an official term perhaps invented by the erstwhile member of the Constituent Assembly in the pre-republic debates Sir Alladi Krishnaswamy Aiyar, and later incorporated in Article 352 and Article 355 of the Constitution of India.

This semantic privilege utilized the Indian state by disacknowleging the armed conflict situation veritably serves two useful purposes, one in the eyes of the international community deeply conversant with International Humanitarian Laws and the Laws of Non-International Armed Conflict as laid down in Article 3 of the Geneva Conventions of 1949, and in Article 1 of the Additional Protocol II of the same. The non-signing of the Additional Protocol of the Geneva Conventions as well as the Additional Protocols of the ICCPR of 1967, therefore, can be explained by the active realities of the internal conditions of armed dissidence over the years, which enables the Indian state to avoid international complications, therefore, hiding the lethality and intensity of the *'hidden wars'* being waged by the state to suppress armed rebellion. Major independent governments and members of the UN fraternity are, therefore, unaware of the incomplete processes of the Indian nation state formation in contemporary times, though UN treaty bodies are aware of massive human rights violations by the state over its population.

The other purpose concerns the domestic lives of its adopted *'citizens'* of the Northeast, and more particularly the general population of Manipur, who are persuaded by the discourse of the state that life should go on as usual, that the political violence perpetrated by non-state actors are only a vocation of a few disgruntled, misguided elements who are out to disturb the peace and benign developmental activities of the empowered government. This silent but effective propaganda lulls the senses of the majority of the population, more particularly the emergent young generation who had been disassociated from connection with their elders, deeply engrossed with tradition and customary laws and values of the past, yet unable to intervene in the changing dimensions of the pulls and pressures of the market, which the young senses as their privileged domain, thereby enhancing the *'distantial divide'* amidst generations on values and principles, over and above the critical challenges of class, ethnicities and cultures spawned by the system. Understanding laws of conflict for mitigating injustice is absent in the current official Manipur discourse.

Domination of thoughts, cultures and beliefs, exuding from the centre of power and perpetrated by the *'elites'* in our societies is not the only phenomenon. What is more dangerous, in the words of Chandra Muzaffar, a Malaysian intellectual, is that *'we are being told that we live only at a particular moment in time. That is very dangerous in terms of our notion of what we are, what our roots are and what will be in the future. The idea that is being conveyed is that only this moment counts and nothing else. This is one of the dimensions of globalization that is not very well known. There is an attachment, almost obsession with the present. You do not relate to the past. If you do not relate to the past, you cannot build a future that is rooted in your own tradition'*.[31]

Apart from the heavy social impact of globalization which kills indigenous initiatives, induces a spirit of numbness and stupor, reduces the population to a position of passive, opiate onlookers without a stake in the exogenous transformations witnessed in the military-corporate takeover and re-colonization of the land, destroying landscapes, shattering the architectures of tradition, displacing large masses from their natural homesteads through forced reclamation of their lands, and specters of developmental violence through exploitation of the natural resources without prior inform consent of the people. All these remind again the words of the geographer Neil

Smith, which was quoted by Edward Said thus *"Capitalism historically has produced a particular kind of nature and space, an unequally developed landscape that integrates poverty with wealth, industrial urbanization with agricultural diminishment. The culmination of this process is imperialism, which dominates, classifies and universally commodifies all space under the aegis of the metropolitan centre"*.[32] For India, in relation to the Northeast including Manipur, a hideous form of domestic imperialism is revealed.

Two years ago (in September 2010), the Chairman of the proscribed outfit UNLF, R.K. Meghen (*alias* Sanayaima), was reported missing in Bangladesh. Complaints were lodged by the family to appropriate authorities as well as the UN Working Group on Enforced Disappearances. After a complete silence for some two months, the sleuths of the National Investigation Agency of the Government of India 'arrested' him at Motihari in Bihar. Now he is facing trial. This case of 'extraordinary rendition' (he was reported to have told the NIA Court at Guwahati that he had actually been arrested at Lalmati in Bangladesh and brought to Motihari in Bihar. There is no extradition treaty between India and Bangladesh, and the UN Working Group had issued notices to both governments), is not new in dealings by the Indian state with Northeastern political dissidents.

Surprisingly, recently the NIA in framing charges against the head of the UNLF in the NIA Court at Guwahati, submitted that *'the activities carried out by the United National Liberation/front (UNLF) are for bringing sovereignty in the State of Manipur'*.[33]

In his meeting with the national media in the sidelines of the court, R.K. Meghen stated *"the UNLF do not accept the charges terming him as separatist, insurgent, secessionists as Manipur was not part of India and Manipur has its independence for more than 2000 years"*.[34]

He further said that *"UNLF have nothing to demand from the Government of India but instead is fighting to regain the lost sovereignty"*.[35]

Barbara F. Walter in her references to the Minority at Risk (MAR) data codes cites things like remembered kingdoms from the pre-nationalist era, that groups with active separatist movements deliberately reconstruct and emphasize past *'independence'* as a means to mobilize support. *'If it is true, then it is the desire for self-determination that is causing groups to define territory as having been 'lost' rather than the other way round'.*[36] One can imagine the innate biases of conflict analysts who have deep pro-state leanings citing datas and raw materials of conflict in order to use the fact to suit the theories.

Indeed, the need of the day is for the international community as well as lovers of peace and humanity to consider the issues of *'armed conflict'* that is prevailing in Manipur and the Northeast and deeply ponder over the resistance by minority nationalities for over four decades, in spite of the unequal balance of forces and departures by the state from the international principles of proportion. They should also consider the relentless onslaughts over the right to life and dignity of the indigenous peoples. It is necessary for the Government of India to accept that there is *'armed conflict'* in the region under international paradigms of understanding the phenomenon. That the dissident forces are well organized groups with capabilities and commitments to international codes and conducts of war and are still holding on to precious unreported areas in the territory of conflict, withstanding the armed might of one of the strongest military powers of Asia. That since the conflict has been on for the last forty years, one should take first steps for minimization of violence, especially over the bodies of civilians and non-combatants through the humanitarian intervention of the International Committee of the Red Cross and Red Crescent in Northeast India. International intervention under the *'Responsibility to Protect'* on issues of human security should be given more teeth, rather than leaving it as wishful thinking since respect for state sovereignty seems to be the abiding principle of international relations. But when the principles of state sovereignty is challenged and questioned on its basic foundations, other paradigms of conflict study and analysis are called forth for understanding and resolving problems of dignity and distributive justice.

NOTES AND REFERENCES

1. N. Manijao, *Matamgi Khonglei Takpa Puyasing*, Sanakonung, 1998, p. 16.
2. J. Josep Hewitt, Jonathan Wilkenfield, *et al.*, *Peace and Conflict Executive Summery Centre for International Development and Conflict Management (CIDCM)*, University of Maryland, USA, 2008, p. 16.
3. *Ibid.*, 2008.

4. B. Lucina, Does Counterinsurgency Theory Apply in Northeast India, *India Review*, Routledge, London, 2007- 6:3.
5. Lokendra Arambam, 'Identity, Violence and Cultural Production in the Northeast', *Safdar Hashmi Memorial Lecture Janam*, New Delhi, 2004.
6. Reginald Coupland, *The Indian Problem 1833-1935*, Oxford Clarendon Press, 1942.
7. Lokendra Arambam, From the Frame to the Water: Recovering Indigenous Spaces for Performance, in, Anmol Vellani Ed. *Beyond the Proscenium: Reimagining the Space for Performance*, IFA, Bangalore 2010.
8. *White Paper on Indian States*, July 1948, p. 15.
9. *Anouba Jug* 1947, quoted by K. Manimohan Singh, *Hijam Irabot Singh and Political Movements in Manipur,* 1989, B.R. Publishing Corporation, New Delhi.
10. K. Manimohon Singh, *Hijam Irabot Singh and Political Movements in Manipur*, B.R. Publishing Corporation, New Delhi, 1989.
11. V.P. Menon, *The Story of the Integration of the Indian States*, Orient Longmans, New Delhi, 1955.
12. *White Paper on Indian States, July 1948.*
13. K. Manimohon Singh, *Hijam Irabot Singh and Political Movements in Manipur*, B.R. Publishing Corporation, New Delhi, 1989.
14. M. Anandamohon Singh, Shillong 1949, *Keishamthong Elangbam Leikai*, Imphal, 2004.
15. *Patil's letters to Jairamdas Doulatram*, successor to Sri Prakasa as Governor of Assam, 1950, in, M. Anandamohan Singh, Shillong, 1949, Appendix 10.
16. Mao-Ze Dong, On *Contradiction,* 1955.
17. Subir Bhaumik, *Insurgencies in India's Northeast 'Conflicts Co-option and Change,* 2007, East West Center, Washington.
18. *Manipur Gazette Extraordinary*, 27 September 1979. From Chirom Ranjit, *Unrest in Manipur,* 2004, Annexure vii (1).
19. Subir Bhaumik, *Insurgencies in India's Northeast Conflicts Co-option and Change,* 2007, East West Center, Washington.
20. A. Koireng Singh, *Ethnicity and Intercommunity Conflicts—A Case of Kuki-Naga in Manipur*, Akansha Publishing House, New Delhi, 2008.
21. *Ibid.*
22. L. Arambam, 2007.
23. *Ibid.*
24. Jeevan Reddy Committee Report of the Committee to Review the Armed Forces (Special Powers) Act, 1958, Government of India,

Ministry of Home Affairs, New Delhi, 2005, Human Rights Alert, Imphal, 2006.

25. *India Today Group,* September 15, 2012.
26. *Ibid.*
27. Sameer Lalwani, *India's Approach to Counter-insurgency*, Massachusetts Institute of Technology, New York, 2011.
28. *Ibid.*
29. Benjamin Reilly, Internal Conflict and Regional Security in Asia and Pacific, *Pacifica Review*, Vol. 14, Carlas Publishing, 2002.
30. Ved Marwah, *India in Turmoil,* Rupa & Co., New Delhi, 2009.
31. Chandra Muzaffar, *The Asian Future – Dialogues for Change 2,* Santi Prabha Dhamma Institute, Bangkok, 200.
32. Edward Said, *Culture and Imperialism*, Vintage, London, 1993.
33. *Imphal Free Press*, Popular English Daily, Imphal, 29 September 2012
34. *Ibid.*
35. *Ibid.*
36. Barbara F. Walter, *Information, Uncertainty and the Decision to Secede*, Graduate School of International Relations and Pacific Studies, University of California, USA, 2006.

ANNEXURE 1

Why Manipuris Fight for Right to National Self-determination

FOREWORD

The Manipuri people have a recorded history of about 2000 years. Many strands, cultural and ethnic, have combined over the centuries and through many struggles, to form the distinctive political and cultural identity of the Manipuri people. They value their freedom and the independence of their country more than anything else. The Manipuri people fought against invasion by the Burmese and drove them out of Manipur in the beginning of the 19th century; they fought against the British imperialists in 1891 even though they knew well that they stood no chance militarily. The period of the British colonial rule (1891-1947) also witnessed many mass uprisings.

The government of newly independent Dominion of India annexed Manipur in 1949 through intrigue and treachery. They snuffed out the elected legislature and government then functioning in Manipur and have imposed ever since their own colonial rule.

Manipur and the contiguous Indo-Burma Region are closed to the outside world; foreigners cannot enter this area without special permission from the Indian government. As such, the economic plight of the indigenous peoples in the Region, the unending overflow of immigrants from the Indian subcontinent and consequent demographic imbalance and threat to the distinctive identities of the indigenous peoples, the rapid environmental degradation from reckless exploitation of its natural resources, the black laws which make a mockery of international norms on human rights but have been imposed on the people to buttress the colonial regime, and even the brutal acts of repression perpetrated openly by the Indian Occupation Forces (IOF)—these get hardly known to the world outside. However, to the peoples living in India's colonial backwoods, there is no alternative to taking up arms in defence of human dignity and in the interest of generations yet to come.

The Manipuris are a peace-loving people and they want a peaceful resolution of the problem. They have till now exercised utmost restraint despite provocation and countless human rights violations by the Indian Occupation Forces. It may not, and cannot, continue as such for all time to come. The Manipuris therefore appeal to the world community to do all they can to enable the Manipuri people exercise their right to national self-determination so that they can freely determine their own political status and pursue in peace their economic, social and cultural development according to their own genius.

This booklet is intended primarily for those who are not already familiar with the history of the Manipuri people and the background to their ongoing struggle for freedom and independence. We hope this will lead to a better understanding of the problem in our Region and, perhaps, to a redefining of the concept of colonialism *vis-à-vis* the indigenous peoples. The booklet has been updated in this edition incorporating the popular uprising against Indian military repression and the '4-Point Proposal' of the UNLF for resolving the Manipur-India Conflict.

Place : Kangla
19 March, 2005

Sana Yaima
Chairman
United National Liberation Front, Manipur

I. A BRIEF HISTORY OF THE MANIPURI PEOPLE

Introduction

'Manipur' is the ancestral territory of the 'Manipuri' people. Manipur is presently under Indian colonial rule. It is situated in the northeast corner of India and bounded in the east by Myanmar (Burma). The present territorial area is 22,327 sq. km. It lies within 23.83°N to 25.68°E latitude and 93.03°E to 94.78°E longitude. A fertile alluvial valley extends north-south in the middle and it is surrounded on all sides by hill ranges forming a part of the eastern Himalayas. Though constituting only about 12 p.c. of the total geographical area, the valley is settled by more than 75 p.c. of the total population of 2.3 million (2001 Census).

The Royal Chronicle *Cheitharol Kumbaaba* maintains an uninterrupted historical record of the land and its people since 33 A.D. Throughout the history, the valley was, and continues to be, the core region where the distinctive Manipuri culture and way of life took shape and where political developments having repercussions throughout the Indo-Burma Region often originated.

Among the Manipuris, the *Meiteis* form the predominant ethnic group and they traditionally inhabit the valley. The surrounding hill ranges are settled by many tribes. They are broadly grouped together and known as the Naga and the Kuki tribes. While the Meiteis thrive on wet cultivation, the tribal population subsists largely on the slash-and-burn technique of cultivation and depends heavily on the valley for their needs. In recent decades, however, the steady influx of immigrants from the Indian subcontinent into the hill areas and into parts of the valley and also the internal migration of tribes from the hills to the valley, have disturbed the traditional settlement patterns and demographic balance both in the hills and the valley of Manipur.

The tribal ethnic groups have their mutually distinct cultural heritage. The members of a tribe communicate among themselves in their own dialect, but the Manipuri language is the *lingua franca* used for inter-tribal communication and by all Manipuris settled inside and outside Manipur. The tribal dialects are in varying stages of development; they are all written in the Roman script. The Manipuri language had evolved from Meiteilon, the native language of the Meiteis, which is written in its own script. All the tribal dialects as well as the Manipuri language belong to the Tibeto-Burman family of languages, just as all the indigenous ethnic groups in Manipur are of the southern Mongoloid stock racially.

Of the 18 'national languages' constitutionally recognised in India, the only language from the Tibeto-Burman family so recognised, though done so under political compulsions of the ongoing liberation struggle, is the Manipuri language. Anybody whose mother tongue is Manipuri language or who identifies himself/herself as a Manipuri, whether living inside or outside Manipur, belongs to the Manipuri people. There are about three million Manipuris in the world today. The Manipuris as a people are thus bound by a common racial origin, a common language and culture and by inheritance of a common ancestral territory now called Manipur. The following paras give a brief account of how their distinctive identity was forged and how they rose time and again against all odds throughout their long history.

Early Historical Setting

The origins of the Manipuri people are filled with myths and legends. One of them relates to three brothers who went in different directions from a place called Makhel in the northern hills of Manipur. The youngest of the brothers is said to have gone to the valley to become the ancestor of the Meiteis while the remaining brothers became those of the Naga tribes. Another common myth among the people is that of human beings originally coming out of a big cave.

Manipur lies on an ancient trade route linking South-east Asia with South Asia and beyond. Scholars agree that waves of migration from the north and the east brought the Tibeto-Burman speaking peoples to the region in the prehistoric times. Archaeological evidence also point to the fact that the present valley was under water during the quaternary period and that the earliest human settlements in the hills gradually extended downwards and to the valley over the centuries. A successful response to the historic challenge of draining the valley and consequent transformation from food-gatherers and hunters to sedentary cultivators gave birth to a rich culture and a distinctive way of life.

During the early centuries of the Christian era, seven major exogamous clans struggled fiercely for power and supremacy in the valley. The *Ningthouja* clan emerged victorious. Under its leadership, a larger and composite Meitei identity was forged out of the clans through a long historical process. Many tribal elements from the hills and many streams of migrating people naturally became a part of the cultural melting pot. The hill tribes in the interior regions maintained a subordinate relationship to the more powerful Meitei king. The consolidation of the Meitei State was more or less completed by the 12th century. It then embarked on a process of territorial expansion from the next century onwards.

The Meiteis emerged as an important player in the regional political arena by the 15th century, particularly during the reign of King Kyamba (1476-1508). The boundaries of the Meitei kingdom expanded in the east up to the west bank of the Chindwin River (in Myanmar today) and were recognised as such by other powers in the region. The Meiteis were also known variously to the neighbouring peoples during the early period. They were the *Kathe* to the Burmese, the *Cassay* to the Shans, and the *Meklee* to the Ahoms.

Manipur as a Sovereign State

A steady migration of non-Mongoloid peoples from the Indian subcontinent, Brahmins and Muslims in particular, began in the 16th century. They were subsequently assimilated into a larger Manipuri society. Under the impact of these migrations, however, the cultural complexion of the indigenous society underwent far-reaching changes. A pluralistic society and polity emerged. The Meitei kings began to assume Hindu names and titles. The kingdom itself came to be known as '*Manipur*' during the 18th century, even though it was still referred to as 'Meckley' in the treaty of alliance signed between King Jai Singh and the British East India Company in 1762.

The 18th century also witnessed the zenith of Manipur's power and influence as a sovereign state in the Indo-Burma Region. During the reign of King Pamheiba @ Garib Niwaz (1709 to 1748) the Manipur cavalry frequently raided deep inside the Burmese territory and gave a deathblow to the ruling Toungoo dynasty of Burma. The sacking of Sagaing in 1738 was the most remarkable event of the Manipuri attacks into Burma. The territorial extent of Manipur also spread far beyond the present boundaries. The Burmese retaliated in good measure when their opportunity came.

A schism occurred in the Manipuri society with the advent of Hinduism under royal patronage since the time of Garib Niwaz's reign. The Meitei followers of the indigenous faith, with its accent on ancestor worship, strongly resisted the imposition of the new religion on the people. It was taken as erosion of their distinctive culture and national identity. The religious dissension not only sapped the vitality of the people but also blurred their political vision. In fact, the national disunity and a corresponding discord among the Manipuri princes were principal factors that invited the Burmese invasion to Manipur with its disastrous consequences. When the Burmese forces also began to pose a threat to the eastern frontier of the British Indian Empire, it led to the First Anglo-Burmese War.

The Burmese forces invaded and occupied Manipur for seven years (1819 to 1826). The **Seven Years' Devastation**, as the period is known in history, marked a turning point in the fortunes of the Manipuri people. The Burmese pursued a policy of genocide on the Manipuri people and adopted scorched earth policy that thoroughly devastated the land. Thousands of Manipuris were taken prisoner and carried away to Burma as slaves; many more fled the country. A sort of Manipuri 'Diaspora' took place. Their descendants are still settled in large numbers in other States of 'northeast India', in Bangladesh and Burma. Those who stayed behind used guerrilla tactics to harass the Burmese occupation forces. However, it was not until Gambhir Singh, a Manipuri prince who fled from Manipur, raised a force called the Manipur Levy with British help in Assam and fought the Burmese who were ultimately driven out of Manipur in 1826.

Gambhir Singh was recognised as the king of independent Manipur by both the British and the Burmese under the *Treaty of Yandabo* (1826), which ended the First Anglo-Burmese War. However, the Manipuris as a people were at the nadir of their power and influence. They could not resist effectively when the Kabaw Valley, a strip of Manipur territory on the border, was 'made over' to Burma in 1834 by the British Indian government. The British adopted the policy of appeasement at the expense of Manipur to safeguard the northeast frontier of British India, to which the latest addition was Assam in 1826. The British did not feel secure enough by an independent Manipur as a buffer state because, despite its long record of antipathy to Burma, Manipur was then very weak. Manipur was compensated for the loss of her territory by a monthly allowance of '500 sicca rupees' to be given to the Manipur king until such time the Kabaw Valley was reverted to Manipur. Gambhir Singh died of heart attack on the same day the Kabaw Valley was transferred to Burma.

Extremely depopulated and economically ruined, a majority of the Meiteis began to take refuge and find solace in the escapist *Vaishanava* cult of *Hinduism* from Bengal. The Manipuri ruling class began to find living under the British imperial umbrella convenient for them, even though Manipur was referred to by British authorities as 'an Asiatic power in alliance with the [British] Queen'. A British Political Agent was posted at Imphal, the capital of Manipur, from 1835 onwards to facilitate a friendly intercourse. A Manipur representative was similarly posted at Calcutta. The Manipur king collaborated with the British imperialists on subjugating the neighbouring peoples, such as the Lushai and the Naga tribes outside Manipur, in the second half of the 19th century. When the British encouraged the emigration of certain non-Naga tribes from Burma in order to exploit their traditional hostility to the Nagas, the Manipuri ruling class did not protest against the imperialist policy. Such co-operation with the imperialists earned for the Manipur king a British knighthood, but it alienated the Meiteis from the neighbouring peoples.

Manipur's usefulness to the British as a buffer state between Burma and the British Indian Empire and as the cat's paw in their colonial expansion vanished when the British annexation of Burma was completed in 1885 and Manipur remained as the only independent kingdom in the midst of a vast British Empire. Many unreasonable and unfriendly demands were soon made on Manipur by the British Indian Government to give an excuse for the annexation of Manipur. In their moment of truth, the Manipuri ruling class called on the national feelings of the Manipuri people to meet the imperialist designs. The Manipuris, of course, knew that they were no match against the British might. But it was a measure of their pride as a nation that they deliberately chose open confrontation with the British rather than succumb tamely to their ploy.

So, five high-ranking British officers specially sent by the Governor General to the Manipur king for political arm-twisting were beheaded inside the palace compound. And when, as expected, the British retaliated by dispatching three army columns to Manipur, all sections of Manipuris fought pitched battles in the hills as well as in the valley against the invading British forces. The outcome of the war was, of course, a foregone conclusion. The Manipuri forces were defeated in what came to be known in history as the *Anglo-Manipur War of 1891*. Yet, it was the finest hour for the Manipuri people.

Manipur Under British Colonial Rule

The British hanged the Defence Minister and younger brother of the King, along with the General of Manipur army, in a public square to intimidate the Manipuri people. Many others, including the King, were exiled or imprisoned for long years. Manipur's ancient and holy seat of power, the Kangla, became the new barracks for the British occupation forces. An annual tribute, a heavy fine and other punitive measures were imposed to subdue the rebellious masses. Significantly, however, Manipur was never annexed to the British Indian Empire.

The British imperialists put on the Manipur throne a distant relative of the deposed king as ruler of the state. The ruler was assisted by a Durbar. However, real powers were exercised by the Political Agent and by the President of the Durbar, who were invariably British officers. The latter was personally made responsible for administration of the hill areas. In other words, nearly 90 p.c. of Manipur's territory was deliberately kept outside the jurisdiction of the native ruler.

Drastic changes were made in the administration to facilitate better collection of the revenue and to consolidate their colonial rule. Importance was subtly given to inter-tribal differences and rivalries in the hills. The British rulers also gave indirect encouragement to Christian missionaries who came to fulfil the White Man's Burden among the tribes in the hills. The subsequent religious differences between the tribal converts to Christianity and the Meitei converts to Hinduism were then exploited to cause social and political friction among the Manipuri people. The policy of divide-and-rule was given a further refinement when the 'prestige' of the native ruler was propped up by turning a blind eye to his imposition of feudal and Hindu orthodox values and practices on the people. This served the useful purpose of diverting the attention of the people from the colonial masters to the oppression by their puppet.

Manipur was important to the British as their strategic outpost in the Indo-Burma Region. Little attention was therefore paid to direct economic exploitation of the state as was usually done elsewhere. However, the indirect British colonial administration, through a native ruler and the tribal chiefs, extracted a heavy price from the people in the form of compulsory free labour in the construction of roads for use by the occupation army and in supplying rations to far-flung army outposts. Heavy taxes were also levied for payment of the annual tribute and the punitive fine and for contributions towards maintenance of roads, etc. Such measures angered the Manipuri public.

Struggle Against Colonial Rule—Early Phase

Public resentment against the colonial rule was evident as early as 1904 when the capital's main market and the residences of some British officers were destroyed by fire during the night under suspicious circumstances within the span of a few days. The Political Agent ordered the male inhabitants of Imphal to rebuild the residences at their own cost. Six Manipuris who were alleged to be ring leaders in the acts of arson were also ordered to be expelled from Manipur. An agitated public could no longer take such high handedness lying down and decided to defy the orders. And in a manner, which is still peculiar to Manipur, the women took the lead in the mass struggle. Thousands of them converged on the Market Square in Imphal and demanded to meet the Political Agent for withdrawal of the orders. The police were ineffective against the massive outburst of pent-up fury. The colonial administration and the normal public life were completely paralysed. The British had to beat a hasty retreat and cancel the orders.

The colonial masters had learnt a lesson. But the exigencies of the First World War prompted the British to raise a labour corps from among the Naga and the Kuki tribes of Manipur. Though much against their will, the first batch of some 2000 recruits were sent to France in 1917. However, when the British proceeded to recruit and send another batch, the Kuki chiefs did not obey the orders. The Political Agent took this an issue of prestige and sent troops to punish some of the more rebellious tribal chiefs. In the hilly tracts where the Kukis routinely shift their settlements from place to place, the British found them more elusive in the prevailing atmosphere of mutual suspicion and antagonism. So, what began as a limited measure to teach a lesson to some Kuki chiefs, snowballed to a big punitive expedition against the Kukis in general with the participation of many British forces from India and Burma. The expedition continued, despite considerable casualties on both sides, till the last of the leading Kuki chiefs was captured in 1919.

From this bitter experience with the Kukis, the British appointed more British officers in the hill areas to ensure strict control over the people. The co-operation and assistance they received from the then native ruler was a crucial factor in their success and therefore, a Knighthood was conferred on him in appreciation of the services rendered. And mindful of the geopolitical importance of the valley and of the need to keep the majority Meiteis settled there in good humor, the British rulers began to make other 'friendly' gestures also, like reduction in the amount of annual tribute, relief from contribution to maintenance of roads, easier terms in loan repayment, etc. More funds were made available for more extensive administrative machinery.

Struggle Against Colonial Rule—Later Phase

The spontaneity of the earlier struggles against the colonial rule gave way to more organized movements in the 1930s. One such movement was that of the Zeliangrong Naga tribes in the western hills of Manipur. As Christianity under colonial patronage began to challenge the traditional values and ideals of the tribal people, this mass movement under a charismatic leader was in the beginning a movement for reform in the traditional religion and society. The British rulers were uneasy at its mass support and became really worried when it gradually transformed into a movement against the British colonial rule. The leader told his followers to stop paying taxes, to disobey unjust laws, to fight against all foreigners and to struggle for a 'kingdom promised long ago by God.' The British suppressed the movement ruthlessly by hanging their leader in 1931 and his more prominent followers were imprisoned for long years.

More sustained struggles against the colonial rule became possible with the emergence of educated native elite who had been exposed to the Indian freedom struggle during their study in Indian colleges and universities. It began as a non-political pan-Manipuri movement to bring all Manipuris, inside and outside Manipur, under one banner. They combined this with reformist zeal against the oppressive feudal and Hindu orthodoxy of the puppet ruler. In the 'petition phase' of the struggle, they submitted all kinds of petitions to the British rulers but mainly for various constitutional reforms in Manipur. This kind of passive and elitist protest was rudely shaken by an upsurge of mass indignation against colonial exploitation.

The immediate provocation was an artificial scarcity of rice, the staple food of the Manipuris, during harvesting season and the consequent jump in prices in 1939. This was caused by the unrestricted export of rice from Manipur by Indian traders who, along with the Bengali clerks, were appendages to the British colonial rule. They were settled in large numbers inside the British Reserve, an extraterritorial enclave in Imphal, which came under the direct rule of the Political Agent. While the Bengali clerks were petty tyrants in government offices, the rich Indian traders were sharks in the colonial economy.

In 1939 also, as it was in 1904, the first explosive reaction against the colonial regime came from the women of Manipur. As if out of nowhere, thousands of them gathered in Imphal and demanded immediate stoppage to the export of rice from the state by the Indian traders. In the course of their demand, they braved rifle butt and bayonet charges by the occupation forces, they lay down on the road in front of trucks loaded with rice for export, and they even compelled the high and mighty Political Agent to go with them to the rice mills and cut off their power supply so that the wily Indian traders would not be able to process rice for export even secretly. The fierce intensity of their anger, though brief, unnerved the colonial masters and their Indian lackeys so much so that the events came to be known in history as the **Nupi Laan** (Women's War).

Unlike in the previous occasions, the mass struggle continued with widespread disobedience movement with active participation by men. The social, economic and political superstructure carefully built up in Manipur on feudal and colonial foundations, simply collapsed in the frenzy of a mass defiance of colonial authority in the next few months, And the awe in which the British rulers were held by ordinary Manipuris was gone for ever in the aftermath of the Nupi Laan. The nature of the struggle in Manipur was obviously influenced by the civil disobedience movements in India under Mahatma Gandhi's leadership. But, being motivated by local issues and in the absence of any links organisationally between them, the movement in Manipur was not a part of the Indian freedom struggle.

It was during such a politically fluid condition that the Second World War broke out and the Japanese dropped their first bomb on Imphal in 1942. Manipur was then quickly drawn into the vortex of war. From a transit route for hundreds of thousands of refugees fleeing from the advancing Japanese forces in South-east Asia and from a camp for the retreating Allied Forces, Manipur itself was turned into a prime target for the two contesting armies. After fierce battles on Manipur soil in 1944, the Japanese advance was checked for the first time by Allied forces on the outskirts of Imphal and, in a decisive turn in the fortunes of the War in Asia, it was rolled back until the Japanese were finally defeated.

Never before were the Manipuris so intensely exposed to the ravages of a modern war. The business of day-to-day survival took precedence over anything else for the majority of the people. But, to the more politically conscious Manipuris, men and women who actively took part in the Nupi Laan and in the subsequent disobedience movement, the Japanese forces were seen as liberators. They went underground and mobilised the public to provide food, shelter, information, etc. to the Japanese forces. Despite the strict wartime surveillance by the British, they established pockets of influence in the valley. The local support enabled the Indian National Army led by Subhas Chandra Bose, an ally of the Japanese, to raise for the first time the flag of their 'Provisional Government of Free India' on Manipur soil. They announced it as the beginning of the end of British colonial rule in the Indian subcontinent.

Of course, the hope of liberation from colonial rule was dashed with the Japanese defeat. But it soon became apparent that the British had neither the energy left nor the inclination to continue ruling over an increasingly hostile Indian people. When the modalities for the transfer of power were finally worked out, the Native States like Manipur, administered by the native rulers under British paramountcy, were given the option to remain free or to join one of the two Dominions, namely, Indian and Pakistan.

Back to Square One

When political developments of such historic significance were taking place around them rapidly, the Manipuris were still recovering from the traumatic experiences of the War and were trying to bring back some normalcy to their lives. So, war compensation, to them, was perhaps an issue more important than political happenings elsewhere. Besides, while the old social values and mores had been swept away by the War, new ones were yet to take roots. During such a period, Maharaja Bodh Chandra, the then young and inexperienced native ruler of Manipur who was put on the throne by the British on the death of his father during the War, signed the Instrument of Accession (see Appendix I) on 11 August, 1947 acceding Manipur to the Dominion of India, just three days before the long-awaited dawn of freedom. Nobody knew how and under what circumstances he signed, or was made to sign, the document which put the clock back in Manipur and placed the Manipuri people once again at the mercy of the new rulers in New Delhi. However, under the terms of the Instrument of Accession, the Maharaja of Manipur retained the sovereign power to reject 'any future constitution of India'.

Manipur's political relations with an independent India were still the same as they existed under British paramountcy. Under the terms of the Instrument of Accession, the Indian government was responsible for Defence, External affairs, and Communications and the Maharaja enjoyed considerable autonomy in internal administration. A leader of the Indian National Congress from Assam was appointed the Dominion Agent in Manipur to look after India's colonial interests, just as the Political Agent did regarding British colonial interests. The Political Agent had functioned during the British Rule under the direction of the Governor of Assam in Shillong who was in overall charge of the Indo-Burma Region in his capacity as Agent to the Crown Representative in India. The Governor of Assam now had similar responsibilities as Agent to the Government of India. The Governor now reported to the Minister of States, Government of India. Almost everything remained unchanged, including the occupation of the Kangla, the sacred and ancient seat of power of Manipur kings, by an Assam Rifles battalion.

There were, however, significant changes in Manipur's internal administration and politics. The long-standing public demand for a 'full responsible government' in Manipur, which was disrupted during the War, had gained political momentum once again when the winding-up of the British Indian Empire became imminent. A Constitution Making Committee headed by the President of the Durbar, a British officer, was, therefore, constituted by the Maharaja by the end of 1946. The 15-member Committee included five elected members from the valley, five nominated non-officials from the hills and officials deputed or nominated by the government departments concerned. After years of procrastination on the issue, there was a sense of urgency all around. A draft Constitution incorporating the basic structure of a responsible government was ready a few days before the transfer of power by the British.

But the Maharaja was reluctant to outright introduction of a responsible government. In the meanwhile, the Durbar was abolished and replaced by an interim Manipur State Council as the hub of administration in the wake of the transfer of power. With a Chief Minister at the head, the Ministers in the Council were appointed by the Maharaja and they were responsible to the Maharaja. The Maharaja-in-Council had both legislative and executive powers over the whole of Manipur.

Political Polarization

The most vocal element in the protest over delay in adoption of the Constitution was the Manipur State Congress, a political party which came into existence overnight in the second half of 1946. Its leaders had a political godfather in the Dominion Agent, a veteran Indian Congress leader. They resorted to demonstrations, picketing government offices, and other forms of agitation to dislocate normal life in Imphal. The Manipur State Congress was later affiliated, in 1948, to the All India States' Peoples' Conference, a front organization of the Indian National Congress for the people in Native States.

The role of the Manipur State Congress was that of a usurper, for the demand for a responsible government had been spearheaded since 1938 by a broad-based political movement under the charismatic leadership of Hijam Irabot. The Manipur State Congress was nowhere on the political scene when Hijam Irabot was sentenced to three years' imprisonment in 1940 for leading the Nupi Laan and the mass disobedience movement that followed. The British rulers incarcerated him at the far away Sylhet Jail (now in Bangladesh). On being released from the jail, he was not allowed to enter Manipur. He was re-arrested and detained in the Silchar Jail (now in Assam state) till the end of the War. No other political leader was so popular and respected among the Manipuri people, and for that reason so 'dangerous' to the British, as Hijam Irabot.

During the years he spent in jail, Hijam Irabot had the opportunity to interact with Indian communist cadres and to study Marxism-Leninism. As a result, he became a committed Marxist with a radically changed political outlook. But Hijam Irabot's political line was conditioned by his long experience in political organization and his intimate knowledge of the Manipuri people and society. He did not, therefore, subscribe to the then prevailing communist dogma originating from Moscow and being obeyed *in toto* by the Indian communists, even though he was organizationally associated with the Assam unit of the Communist Party of India. For this, in October

1949, he was subjected to self-criticism by the party and he confessed that he had been following the political line of Marshal Tito of Yugoslavia. Translated into ordinary language, it meant that Hijam Irabot was a Manipuri nationalist who also believed in the revolutionary tenets of Marxism-Leninism.

When Hijam Irabot was allowed to return to Manipur in 1946, he did not reveal initially his new political ideology but quietly went about organizing the peasants at the grassroots in a class struggle against the feudal land owners whose class interests were best represented by the opportunist and urban based leaders of the Manipur State Congress. Most of his political colleagues and followers of the pre-War period belonged to the petty bourgeoisie and they were now regrouped under one banner. Hijam Irabot also tried to forge a political alliance of the peasants, the petty bourgeoisie and the tribal leadership for a national democratic revolution in Manipur.

So, when the British rulers left Manipur, there was a clear political polarization. The Manipur State Congress, which got all their political sustenance from India and represented the land-owning urban middle class, was on one side. In the Manipur State Council, where the feudal elite were entrenched, they also had an ally. There was, on the other side, Hijam Irabot's broad nationalist alliance of the petty bourgeoisie, the tribal people and the increasingly class conscious peasants. The contradiction turned into a class antagonism when the Manipur State Council, vested with enormous legislative and executive powers, felt threatened by the political awakening among the peasants and took up repressive measures in 1948 against the movement led by Hijam Irabot. He went underground in September 1948 to avoid being arrested on fictitious criminal charges.

Democratic Government and Constitutional Monarchy

The Maharaja-in-Council finally adopted the Manipur State Constitution Act, 1947 (See Appendix 2) and also the Franchise rules, which laid down, the details regarding conduct of elections. The salient features of the Manipur Constitution and the Rules were:

(a) a 53-member legislature, of which 51 members were elected from territorial constituencies on the basis of adult suffrage by secret ballot and the remaining two being representatives of Educational and Commercial interests;

(b) a seven-member Council of Ministers, consisting of six Ministers, including two Ministers reserved for the Hill people, elected by the legislature and a Chief Minister appointed by the Maharaja in consultation with the elected Ministers;
(c) a Maharaja who was 'Constitutional Head of the State', enjoying certain personal prerogatives and a fixed percentage of the state revenue as civil list and to whom the Council of Ministers was jointly responsible for administration of the state;
(d) a provision of the Fundamental Rights and Duties of the citizens which, among others, guaranteed the rule of law, equality before the law, 'freedom of thought, expression, belief, faith, worship, vocation, association, and action subject to law and public morality'; and
(e) a Judiciary, which was completely separate from the Executive.

There were about half a million eligible voters, adults above 21 years of age, in the electoral rolls of the 51 territorial constituencies. In view of the inadequate manpower and poor communication facilities, the elections were conducted in a staggered manner from June 11 to July 27, 1948 and the final results were published on 20 August 1948. The new legislature was ceremonially inaugurated by the Maharaja on 18 October, 1948.

The Manipur State Congress secured just four seats in the legislature, reflecting the big gap between their pretensions and the reality. A local party, with support from Independent legislators, came to power. The Maharaja appointed his younger brother as the Chief Minister and the new Council of Ministers were sworn in by the Chief Judge on 26 November, 1948. Thus Manipur became perhaps the first among the Native States to have a secular and democratic government within the framework of a constitutional monarchy (*see* Appendix 3). In a society which was steeped in feudal values and with an electorate which were largely illiterate, it was a bold and remarkable achievement.

Indian Intrigues and Annexation of Manipur

When the new Ministers were feeling their way in the government and when the legislators were busy debating on all kinds of issues in their new-found freedom and enacting basic laws urgently required for governance, the leaders of independent and resurgent India were consolidating the empire they inherited from the British. The so-called merger of hundreds of Native States, big or small, to the Dominion of India was on the top of their agenda. The process was nearly complete by the beginning of 1949. But the people and the government in Manipur were too absorbed in their respective local problems to fully appreciate the real strategic importance of Manipur to India's security and, therefore the necessity, from India's point of view, of annexing it as soon as possible. On the other hand, they contented themselves with an assurance given by the Indian Prime Minister Jawaharlal Nehru, in a letter to the Maharaja, that the integrity and distinct identity of Manipur would be preserved.

The first Indian move was planting a Trojan Horse in Manipur. The Governor of Assam, on behalf of the Government of India, insisted on appointing an officer called the Dewan to look after the 'treaty obligations' between Manipur and the Indian Dominion, on the ground that such an officer was essential at Imphal with the abolition of the Dominion Agency. The Maharaja reluctantly agreed to the proposal as the Chief Minister was to be appointed concurrently as the Dewan. But the Governor changed his mind soon after the appointment and told the Maharaja to appoint a person nominated by the Indian Government as the Dewan 'with full powers over the whole range of administration'.

The Government of India had no right to interfere in the internal affairs of Manipur like this under the terms of the Instrument of Accession. Clearly, the Indian political leaders who claimed to be the champions of democracy had no respect for the democratic government and institutions in Manipur. Through the Governor of Assam, they adopted the tactics of recognising the Maharaja only and nobody else. They now pressurised an inexperienced Maharaja into accepting a situation where the Ministers of a responsible and popular government were to take orders in day-to-day administration from an extra-constitutional functionary like the Dewan.

With the installation of a Major General as the new Dewan in April 1949, the denouement came quickly. The Manipur State Congress, which had been smarting from their election fiasco, soon began to whip up public emotions on the alleged oppression of the people in 'social and religious matters' by the Maharaja and demanded the Maharaja's head as well as the integration of Manipur with India as the price. To get over the last hurdle in India's colonial expansion, the Governor was now orchestrating the pressure on the Maharaja in Manipur through the Dewan on the one hand and, on the other, he applied guile and flattery so skillfully that he could pose as the Maharaja's saviour!

It was primarily to seek the advice of the Governor on a contentious legal matter involving the disqualification of a Minister by the Election Tribunal and also to entreat his 'saviour' to restrain the unruly Manipur State Congress that the Maharaja went to Shillong, the then capital of Assam State, in September 1949. The conspiracy hatched up in New Delhi and Shillong was thus working according to plan. The Maharaja's own plans, of course, fell apart. Instead of the benign Indian Congress freedom fighter whose sole concern in the past always seemed to be the Maharaja's welfare, there was now a Governor in his true colours telling a shocked Maharaja to forget about the popular government in Manipur and to put his signature on a prepared document ceding full and exclusive authority regarding the governance of Manipur to India.

There were indeed for some time all sorts of press reports and rumours about possible merger of Manipur into India. But in his naivety, the Maharaja could not have thought that it would come about in such an abrupt and treacherous manner. So, according to well-documented accounts of that sordid episode, the Maharaja was adamant in his refusal, insisting on first taking into confidence the popular government and legislature in Manipur. The Governor and his masters in Delhi then resorted to applying intense psychological pressures on the Maharaja. The Indian Army soon cordoned off the 'Redlands', the private residence of the Maharaja in Shillong, where he and his small entourage were staying. All means of communication with the outside world were totally cut off. Not so subtle hints of dire consequences in case of continued defiance and prospects of a much enhanced Privy Purse in case of compliance were conveyed to the Maharaja. On the third day of torture, the Maharaja broke down. And on the next day, 21 September, 1949, India got a new colony on its northeast frontier as the Maharaja signed the so-called 'Manipur Merger Agreement' (See Appendix 4). It looked as though the British were fools in 1891.

To the Maharaja's credit, he had signed the so-called agreement 'on behalf of himself, his heirs and successors' only. In other words, the Maharaja left the door open for the Manipuri people either to reject or approve of his action. Needless to say, the 'Agreement' was never ratified by the Manipuri people's elected representatives in the State Assembly nor approved by the then popular government in Manipur. Besides, being a document signed by the Maharaja under duress and in violation of the provisions of the Manipur Constitution, the 'Manipur Merger Agreement' was, and continues to be, legally invalid.

According to the terms of the 'Agreement', the formal annexation of Manipur took place on 15 October, 1949 amid tight security.

II. INDIAN COLONIAL RULE IN MANIPUR

The Background

India's struggle for freedom from the British colonial rule was a movement of historic proportions. With sacrifice and participation by millions of Indians under Gandhi's unorthodox leadership, it was an inspiration to all freedom-loving peoples worldwide. Not surprisingly, its impact on those Manipuris who were educated in India before the Second World War was considerable. Moreover, there had been cultural interaction between the two peoples for about two centuries. So the bulk of the Manipuris were not ill-disposed towards India or the Indians in 1949. Only the Indian rulers thought and behaved otherwise. They adopted underhand treachery to annex Manipur and India's very first official acts in Manipur were the dismissal of the popular government and the dissolution of the elected legislature. All powers were concentrated in a Chief Commissioner who, at the first opportunity, muzzled the press and banned all public meetings.

However, as perceived by the new colonial regime, the greatest threat to them was the peasant movement led by Hijam Irabot. This movement had acquired international ramifications after Hijam Irabot attended the Second Congress of the Communist Party of India (CPI) at Culcutta in March 1948 where he met with Thakin Than Tun, leader of the 'White Flag' Burma Communist Party (BCP). This development, with its potential for linking up Hijam Irabot's movement with other anti-colonial, nationalist and usually communist movements in South-east Asia which extended in a continuous arc from Burma to Indo-China, was a key factor in the hastening of Manipur's annexation by India overriding the popular sentiment against 'merger' and the Maharaja's sovereign power, under the terms of the Instrument of Accession, to reject 'any future constitution of

India'. In the Indian context too, the Second Congress was a landmark in communist movement in that the CPI decided to launch armed struggle against what they called the sham Indian independence and the bourgeois ruling class.

Hijam Irabot, then working underground, felt strongly against Manipur's annexation. The manner in which it was effected was, from his Marxist viewpoint, a further confirmation of the reactionary character of the Indian ruling class. So Hijam Irabot seized the opportunity provided by this tactical change in the communist movement and took advantage of the comparatively easy availability of arms and ammunition in Manipur in the after math of the Second World War. He then began to transform the anti-feudal peasant movement in Manipur into a guerrilla movement against the Indian rulers.

By the middle of 1950, his armed 'Red Guards' were in control of scores of villages in the Manipur valley. The colonial administration promptly declared them as 'disturbed and dangerous area'. The police and the paramilitary forces were then unleashed on the people to crush the movement. Hijam Irabot directed the struggle from his hideout in a Burmese village, which was facilitated by his cordial relations with the BCP. Unfortunately, he died in September 1951 due to illness, and the guerrilla movement also petered out in the next few months from lack of proper leadership. Though the armed struggle led by Hijam Irabot, the first of its kind in the Indo-Burma region, was not a success, its revolutionary legacy is still cherished by the Manipuri people.

Unlike the struggle in Manipur valley, which adopted a basically Marxist political line, there was also opposition to the Indian colonial rule on ethnic lines by many freedom-loving tribes. For example, the Naga tribes in what is now called Nagaland (then a part of Assam) began their own armed struggle for national liberation by 1956. There also, it was a story of brutal suppression by India's Occupation Forces.

The Watershed

When the mass of indigenous peoples in the Indo-Burma region were thus feeling alienated from India and the Indians, the Sino-Indian War broke out in 1962. A unilateral cease-fire by China saved this strategic region for India by a hair's breadth. This brought about a change in the attitude of Indian rulers to the region. There was now more of a carrot in addition to the big stick. A new State of Nagaland in the Indian Union was formed in 1963, followed by the States of Tripura, Manipur and Meghalaya in 1972. But it was too little and too late in the day for the Manipuri people.

A new generation of Manipuris, born during and after the Second World War, brought up without their parents' wishful thinking about India's freedom struggle but wiser from their own bitter experiences of the Indian rule, had come of age by the middle of the Sixties. They initially got their inspiration from the glorious past of the Manipuri people. More important, they began to realize the irreconcilable nature of the national contradiction between the Manipuris who have very close historical, cultural and racial affinity with the peoples of South-east Asia and the Indians who have their own rich and distinctive cultural heritage. They also realized that similar national contradictions prevailed in the Indo-Burma region with respect to other indigenous peoples.

The thought, feelings, aspirations and grievances of this generation of Manipuris found a concrete expression in, and were propagated by, the establishment of the United National Liberation Front (UNLF), Manipur in November 1964. Some veterans of the struggles led by Hijam Irabot also joined to lend their experiences to the organization and to complete what they felt was their unfinished task.

To the new generation, the fundamental national contradiction between the Manipuris and the Indians explained why India's 'democratic' rulers had no qualms about trampling on Manipur's nascent democratic government and institutions in 1949; why they were interested only in the physical security provided by the Himalayan range which extends up to the Indo-Burma region, ignored Manipur's rightful historical claim over the Kabaw Valley while settling the India-Burma boundary and erected an artificial wall between countless families who have been living on the border for centuries; why India's professed ideals like anti-colonialism, secularism and socialism do not extend to the Mongoloid indigenous peoples of the region; why India's armed forces behave and operate like an army of occupation; why this region is the least developed economically despite its rich natural resources and has instead become the dumping ground for Indian industries as well as the cheap source of their raw materials; why even the judiciary adopts a different norm on human rights for the peoples of this region; or why an ill-concealed attempt is being made to change the demographic composition of the region. The list seems endless. In short, the irreconcilable national contradiction explained why Manipur and the rest of the Indo-Burma region remain an Indian colony.

The Captive Market

The so-called development activities undertaken by India from the late Sixties onwards were naturally conditioned by considerations of India's security and territorial integrity. Priority was given to construction of roads in the border areas for better deployment of an ever-increasing number of Indian Occupation Forces (IOF) in the region. That the people could also use the same roads was an incidental benefit. With its vast untapped natural and mineral resources, with its perennial rivers, the Indo-Burma region has the potential to generate huge surplus power and become a well-developed region. But India's colonial rule has ensured that it remained the least developed and the most backward region thereby making it totally dependent on India. Not much attention was given to planned development of the human resources nor to modernization of the means of production. India was interested only in extracting the raw materials that its developing industries desperately needed, such as tea, oil and timber and in keeping the region as a captive market for their shoddy products. Consequently, it has caused an ecological disaster in the region.

In Manipur, for example, its handloom and handicraft industries, the traditional mainstay of livelihood in a majority of Manipuri families and famous for their exquisite workmanship, were allowed to be strangled economically by cheap, machine made goods from India. In the absence of irrigation facilities, multiple cropping was unheard of in Manipur's fertile agricultural lands even though their acreage was shrinking due to increased population pressure. Not long ago, Manipur used to export rice and many more items, but it is now compelled to depend on India for each and every item of human needs.

Under the circumstances, the more India invested money in Manipur's 'development' under its Five Years Plans, the more profit thus accrued to Indian business and industry. All the reins of the colonial economy are consequently held by their agents and collaborators in Manipur. What is more, not even 5 p.c. of the huge amount mobilized annually from Manipur by the Indian financial institutions and banks are reinvested in Manipur. By any yard stick for measuring human development, Manipur today is far below India's national average except for the literacy rate. At 60.96 p.c. (1991 Census), it is higher than the all-India average of 52.11 p.c. This happened despite, not because of, India's policies. Many private schools and colleges were established, particularly in the late Fifties and the Sixties, not only to provide more educational facilities for the rising generation but also to create the only avenue to employment for those who were already educated.

But there is a limit to how much employment can be provided in this manner. In the absence of meaningful development in agriculture and industry to absorb them, a massive unemployment among the educated youth is thus a natural corollary of 'development' under colonial rule. A tragic social consequence of this has been Manipur's educated but frustrated young men and women drifting to drugs in large numbers. So the world knows Manipur better today as the land with possibly the highest per capita concentration of drug addicts and the related HIV-positive cases in the world, not as the land from where the modern game of *polo* originated during the British Rule and where a glorious heritage in martial arts is still alive. Of course, from the ranks of the educated youth have also come the bulk of the patriotic freedom fighters who have vowed to destroy the evil colonial regime.

The real beneficiaries of the present regime are only a handful of persons who have managed to pocket a portion of the so-called development funds as they trickled down from New Delhi. Though their share of the loot is a small fraction of the amount that has gone back to Indian hands, it is enough to create this local elite who are servile and given to vulgar ostentation. They are the fountain of corruption, which has become endemic and pervasive, and of moral degeneration in the society. They belong to any ethnic, linguistic or tribal community in Manipur. The members of this class will be found in positions of power and influence, as 'representatives' of the people, as ministers, bureaucrats, police top brass, contractors and so on. Underpinned by the Indian Occupation Force, they are putting up the show of a democratic government in Manipur.

After half a century of colonial rule, there are only Indian collaborators in Manipur, not even a native capitalist class that can take advantage of new economic opportunities. Now, in the free-for-all environment of a liberalized Indian economy, the Manipuris and other peoples in the region are not going to have a level playing field for competition. The delicate balance in their natural environment will be under greater threat than ever before as the multinationals and the Indian capitalists spread their tentacles with renewed vigour into the region. The Indian colonial regime did not in the past protect the vital interests of the peoples in the Indo-Burma region. Neither can it be expected now nor in the future too. To see light at the end of the tunnel and for the sake of generations yet to be born, those living today have no alternative but to organize themselves and fight to end the Indian colonial rule.

The Challenge and the Response

The reply to India's colonial policies, practices and attitudes has been, therefore, the birth of many national liberation movements in the Indo-Burma region. And like any colonial power, India had resorted to brute force to pacify them, to wear them down by attrition and finally to bring them to total submission. India had also adopted the policy of divide-and-rule, had tried to placate a section of the population, had physically shut off the region from the world by restricting the entry of foreigners, had made a mockery of the internationally accepted human rights norms by such laws as the *Armed Forces Special Powers Act, 1958* which empowers any armed personnel to kill anyone with impunity, and had even tried to change the demographic composition of the region by turning a blind eye to illegal infiltration and settlement by co religionists from Nepal and Bangladesh.

Of late, special attention has been given to administer a heavy dose of propaganda through the government-owned electronic mass media. However, the outcome of all their efforts has been generally negative. Because, the economic exploitation, the indiscriminate arrests and physical torture in detentions without trial, of which anybody can be a victim, the enforced disappearances, the killing of innocent people in cross-fire or in fake encounters, the cynical destruction and looting of private property by Indian security forces during their operations, the cases of rape and molestation, and other innumerable harassment that ordinary citizens have to endure, are simply too harsh realities of daily life under Indian colonial rule to be glossed over by India's propaganda.

As India had unleashed state terrorism against the political movements of the indigenous peoples, this region had witnessed enough bloodshed and human misery during the last five decades.

But India had singularly failed in its efforts to get a military solution. Now, there is a growing political polarization. On the one hand, there are the lackeys of the colonial regime and, on the other, an increasing number of people who are alienated from the repressive Indian rule. To counter the growing unity and understanding among peoples and organizations in the region, India has perfected the technique of divide-and-rule, that old favourite of all colonial powers. Old wounds, ancient misunderstandings or any cracks in the society have been exploited to the hilt for the purpose. The hostilities in the late 1990s between the Naga and the Kuki tribes in Manipur which claimed hundreds of innocent lives on both sides including those of women and children, and now trying to pitch the Nagas against the Meiteis through the process of India-NSCN (IM) ceasefire, is a glaring example of how successful, and also how cynical, can India be in the pursuit of its colonial interests. Thus India has managed 'free of cost' to divert the attention of these tribes from their rulers in New Delhi to their own neighbours, at least for the time being.

The Struggle

Peace can once again return to the picturesque hills and valleys of the region, bring back the smiles to the people, only when India opts for a political solution to this political problem of the indigenous peoples in the region. So far, instead of accepting this reality, India has been pushing for a military solution thereby prolonging the armed conflict between the Region and India. Therefore, the organizations in the vanguard of the struggles for national liberation are compelled to fight for the right to national self-determination of their respective peoples so as to regain their freedom and independence. Against this background, the UNLF also has been spearheading the fight for the right of the Manipuri people to determine freely their own political status according to their own genius as guaranteed by the International Covenant for Civil and Political Rights.

III. HUMAN RIGHTS SITUATION IN MANIPUR

Introduction

A striking feature of the Indian political system is the wide gap between theory and practice. The Manipuri people had been painfully aware of this fact even when, in the first flush of India's freedom, its leaders were giving lectures to the world about the historical necessity of decolonization and of granting freedom to dependent peoples. Because, in sharp contrast to their outward postures, India had treacherously annexed Manipur on 15 October, 1949 and its very first official act were the dissolution of the elected State Assembly and the dismissal of the Council of Ministers. All legislative and executive powers were then concentrated in a Chief Commissioner appointed by New Delhi and he was responsible only to his masters. A semblance of these powers was restored to the Manipuri people when, in January 1972, Manipur was reluctantly granted the status of a 'State' under the Indian Constitution.

The Framework

The discrepancy between what is presented to the world and what actually happens on the ground, is glaring in the matter of human rights as well. The Indian Constitution has undoubtedly many features in common with the human rights standard accepted by the international community. In March 1979, India also acceded to the International Covenant on Economic, Social, and Cultural Rights and the International Covenant on Civil and Political Rights, with reservations, *inter alia*, on the Right of Self-determination but accepting nevertheless obligations under the above Covenants. India, however, has not ratified the Optional Protocol to the International Covenant on Civil and Political Rights. Then, under its municipal law called the Protection of Human Rights Act, 1993, a National Human Rights Commission and many State Human Rights Commissions, were set up recently including one in Manipur. Within such a constitutional and legal framework, there ought to be a reasonable observance of human rights in any part of India. But, as in other spheres of public life, there is a different standard even in human rights for the indigenous peoples in the Indo-Burma region.

A Different Standard

From the very beginning, the 'democratic' Indian leaders sought a military solution to a political problem concerning the indigenous peoples. The Armed Forces Special Powers Act, 1958 was enacted specifically for Manipur and the other six States in the region. It negates every constitutional and legal provision concerning human rights when a State or a part of it has been declared a 'disturbed area' under the Act, and this declaration is made by the rulers not for a few months to cope with an emergency but for years or even decades together. For example, the whole of Manipur has been a 'disturbed area' since 1980, with no sign of respite from it in the near future.

Under this Act, the subjective opinion of or a mere suspicion by a Non-Commissioned Officer of the Indian armed forces is enough for the arrest without warrant, torture and killing of any person even before he has committed any offence, and for the destruction of any property. There is actually no need for the Indian Occupation Forces to invent fake encounters to cover up their crimes, for the Act provides them legal immunity from any prosecution. The Act enjoins on the Indian Occupation Forces to hand over a person in their custody to the nearest police station 'with least possible delay'. But they ignore even this minor concession by the Act and routinely interrogate and detain persons arrested by them, interpreting the time-limit according to their convenience. Cruel and degrading treatment, torture, extra-judicial executions and 'disappearance' of innocent persons take place during such unauthorized detentions. But, under section 19 of the Protection of Human Rights Act, 1993, even the National Human Rights Commission is debarred from direct investigation into such flagrant violation of human rights by the India's armed forces.

In a 'disturbed area', the Indian armed forces are supposed to operate in aid of the civil authority. But, in actual practice, the deployment of armed forces personnel in large numbers with unlimited powers over a long period, against the background of an irreconcilable national contradiction between them and the indigenous Mongoloid peoples, has induced them to operate and behave as a racist army of occupation. The continued and deliberate defilement of the Kangla by stationing an Assam Rifles battalion, despite its incalculable hurt to the Manipuri psyche, is just a case in point. This itself has undoubtedly provoked many young men and women into joining the struggle for national liberation. Their arrogance and ill-concealed contempt for civilians have alienated the Indian Occupation Forces even from the local civil authorities to whose aid they are supposed to be operating.

In 1991, the Human Rights Committee of the United Nations not surprisingly remarked that several provisions of the Armed Forces Special Powers Act, 1958 seemed to be incompatible with those of the International Covenant for Civil and Political Rights (ICCPR). Again, in 1997, the Human Rights Committee endorsed the view that the problems in the region were 'essentially political in character and that the approach to resolving such problems must also, essentially, be political'. In this respect, the Committee had in mind, among others, the right to self-determination of peoples in article 1 of the Covenant.

The Committee regretted that the Armed Forces Special Powers had been applied throughout Manipur since 1980 and that India was 'in effect using emergency powers without resorting to article 4, paragraph 3, of the Covenant'. The Committee recommended that 'the application of these emergency powers be closely monitored so as to ensure strict compliance with the provisions of the Covenant'. Further, the Committee hoped that the provisions of the Act would be closely examined by the Supreme Court of India for their compatibility with the Covenant.

The Indian Supreme Court did not find the time to examine the constitutionality of the Armed Forces Special Powers Act and kept it pending for about two decades until international public pressure could not delay it any longer. When it gave its judgment finally on 27 November, 1997, the Supreme Court upheld its constitutionality *in toto* within India's democratic framework. It amounted to prescribing a different human rights standard for the Manipuris and other indigenous peoples in the Indo-Burma region; it could also be interpreted as judicial sanction to racial discrimination as the indigenous peoples of the region are mostly of Mongoloid origin.

The indigenous peoples of the Region are simply outraged by the Indian Supreme Court judgement. In a recent workshop for human rights defenders in India by the Amnesty International, it was decided to protest against the judgment and to observe every year 27 November as 'Anti-Armed Forces Special Powers Act Day' throughout the region.

The Terrorist and Disruptive Activities (Prevention) Act, 1987 (TADA) gave a similar licence to the civil police in regard to arrest and detention. However, being a law extended to the whole of India and the public outcry against its continuance being that much more effective, the TADA was allowed to lapse while another repressive Act, Prevention of Terrorism Act (POTA) has been repealed as a result of public outcry against the Act throughout mainland India. However, the Armed Forces Special Powers Act remained intact. Then there is also the Punjab Security of State Act, 1953 which has been extended to Manipur and it enables the rulers to impose *inter alia* collective fines on villages and towns.

The Torch Bearers

The Manipuri people naturally do not repose much faith in the Indian political and judicial system for the protection of their human rights. An association of like-minded lawyers in Manipur called the Civil Liberties and Human Rights Organization (CLAHRO), established in 1983, used to plead in the courts for victims of human rights violations by the Indian Occupation Forces or by the police. They are now resigned to their ineffectiveness and quite disillusioned with India's judicial system. Then, in 1993, the Committee on Human Rights (COHR) was formed in Manipur as an apex body of many NGOs active in human rights. The COHR, unlike CLAHRO, relies more on creating awareness among the people to build up a mass movement against human rights violations. The trickle of information that the outside world now gets regarding the human rights situation in Manipur owes every much to these NGOs and human rights activists.

However, the vanguard in the struggle against colonialism from the time of British Rule down to the present is the ordinary women of Manipur. Today, in their respective localities, they keep all-night vigil with bamboo torches at the first sign of trouble from the police or the Indian Occupation Forces. They are called the ***Meira Paibis*** or, literally, the torchbearers. A mass of angry women participating in a rally or marching to any government functionary when they think a grave injustice or human rights violation has been committed, is a common sight. A glaring example—on 15 July, 2004 twelve *Meira Paibi Imas* (mothers) staged a historic protest against the rape and killing of a young woman, Thangjam Manorama, by the 17 Assam Rifles of the Indian Occupation Forces stationed at the Kangla in the heart of Imphal. The women protestors were so enraged and shocked by the barbaric act of the Indian soldiers that they unrobed their cloths at the gate of the Kangla and challenged the Indian soldiers there to rape and kill them also. Sensitised by this unique protest, the long pent up anger of the entire people of Manipur exploded in revolt against the Armed Forces Special Powers Act (AFSPA) in particular and the Indian colonial occupation in general. This is the beginning of a democratic struggle against Indian colonial occupation of Manipur.

IV. THE UNITED NATIONAL LIBERATION FRONT (UNLF), MANIPUR

The Premise

The armed struggle led by Hijam Irabot in Manipur was an exciting new experience to those who participated in it. But it had a comparatively short existence; by 1952 it was suppressed by police and paramilitary forces of the new colonial administration. Therefore, questions have been raised ever since about the cause of its failure. The obvious and most important one was the vacuum in leadership after the death of Hijam Irabot. But it was also distinctly possible that the Manipuris of that period were not fully prepared, socially and politically, for that kind of ant-colonial and communist armed struggle.

The armed struggles by many tribes in the Indo-Burma region on ethnic lines have been more resilient, though, in the end, the outcome has not been much different. While the ethnic bonds brought cohesion within the tribes and provided a critical psychological input during armed confrontations with the Indian Occupation Forces, that very ethnic character also tended to put others off. It became all the more difficult for a broader political concept or a new national identity to develop with the changing times. For the colonial power, it becomes that much easier to apply the policy of divide-and-rule, now divide-and-destroy, among them and then bring them to heel one by one.

When the United National Liberation Front (UNLF), Manipur was formally established on 24 November, 1964, it was with an acute awareness of these twin dangers: that of a liberation struggle going far too ahead of the people's level of political consciousness and that of being stuck in an ethnic groove.

Subsequent events and the experiences of the Naga and the Mizo struggles have borne out what the UNLF feared. Once in the forefront of armed liberation struggles in the region against the Indian colonial rule, the Mizos have been bought over by India with 'statehood' in 1987. In the case of the Nagas too, the then tired leaders of their armed struggle had capitulated to India with the signing of the so-called Shillong Accord in 1975. The Naga people owe it to the leadership in the undivided National Socialist Council of Nagaland (NSCN) for bringing them back to the path of a liberation struggle. However, the present leadership of the Naga struggle also may ultimately capitulate in the process of talks with India under the current ceasefire agreement.

The First Phase

The UNLF, it may be recalled, came into existence as the 'representative' organisation of a new generation of Manipuris who were born during and after the Second World War. It represented the hopes and aspirations of this generation for freedom and human dignity and it propagated their feelings against the Indian colonial regime. It also reflected their frustrations and grievances against their parents' generation and their disillusionment with what their parents stood for.

Because it was a time when Manipur and the Manipuri people have been systematically obliterated from the school textbooks; a time when children were ignorant of their distinctive and rich cultural heritage and of even elementary geographical and historical facts about Manipur. But they knew all about, say, the Indian film actors and actresses. It was a time when families of those martyrs in the Anglo-Manipur War of 1891 used to go on pilgrimage every year to Khongjom, the place where the last and decisive battle with the British forces was fought, and prayed in private for the souls of the departed and nobody took notice of. It was a time when sycophancy was a prerequisite qualification for climbing up the colonial hierarchy and when servility was the social norm.

It became apparent to the UNLF leaders that there was no alternative to a painstaking political socialisation of a whole generation with a new Manipuri political ethos and that there would be no quick-fix solutions. The means they adopted for the purpose was the establishment of front organisations in the late Sixties to reach out to all sections of the Manipuri society. These organisations had their own separate memberships, organisational structures and objectives. Most of them were pioneers in their respective fields. By dint of their sincere and dedicated service to the Manipuri society for about three decades, they are highly regarded by the people in their own right.

The effectiveness of the front organisations has been such that, following the ground swell of public pressure, even the colonial administration in Manipur had to adopt as their own some of the programme initiated by them. For example, the puppet government today officially observes the following Manipuri national functions: the *Khongjom Day* on April 23 to commemorate the Anglo-Manipur War of 1891; the *Patriots Day* on August 13 to pay homage to all martyrs of that War, as it was on this day in 1891 that the then Defence Minister and younger brother of the Manipur king and the then General of the Manipuri forces were hanged by the British in a public square; the *Women's Day* on December 12 to honour the brave Manipuri women who, in the Nupi Laan of 1939, led the mass defiance of British authority in protest against their colonial policies.

The Adventure

The multifarious activities of the front organisations also gave birth to a patriotic revolutionary generation of Manipuris by the late Seventies. Many from this generation began to look askance at the strategy and the pace of the UNLF. Thus came into existence a number of underground organisations in Manipur during this period, proclaiming their armed struggle for the liberation of Manipur from the yoke of Indian colonialism. Indeed, many of the members belonging to these patriotic organisations laid down their lives either in their sporadic attacks on or in counter-attacks from Indian Occupation Forces. The Manipuri public applauded the bravery and sacrifice of these patriots, as though a whiff of fresh air had come into the prevailing climate of corruption and sycophancy.

However, subsequent course of events proved that sacrifice alone was not sufficient and that a realistic strategy and tactics for liberation in the context of the Indo-Burma region as a whole was needed. This valuable lesson has guided the UNLF in its approach to the liberation struggle as a whole.

The Second Phase

The UNLF believes in the inter-relatedness and in the inter-dependence of all peoples in the Indo-Burma region. It believes that there is no scope for isolated ethnic struggles, however charismatic their leaders are or however powerful the organisations may appear at present. All must join hands together in a liberation struggle against our common enemy. But that depends on achieving a minimum level of political consciousness among all the peoples, such as the ability not to be a pawn in India's divide-and-rule policy. The UNLF also believes that the strategy and tactics of the struggle should be uniquely from our own practice and experiences, not something borrowed or transplanted from somewhere. The nature of the struggle will also be determined by the nature of the enemy. Taking all relevant factors into consideration, the UNLF decided in 1990 to begin the next phase of the struggle. While the valuable work of the front organisations will continue as before, the focus has shifted to armed propaganda. In fact, preparations for this phase had begun in the Eighties when the UNLF and the NSCN started co-coordinating in their activities. The basic objective of this armed propaganda is to consolidate the unity of the Manipuri people by raising the level of their political consciousness.

Therefore, in the early stages, armed actions by the UNLF were directed mainly against antisocial elements, particularly against those who committed crimes on women or exploited them for immoral purposes. They were given appropriate punishments after careful investigation. The UNLF also provides the 'cutting edge' to campaigns by the Manipuri public against rampant alcoholism, gambling, drug peddling and drug abuse. Having lost their faith in the kind of justice meted out by the corrupt colonial administration in Manipur, the people have begun to bring even their private and petty disputes to the UNLF for adjudication. It is a measure of their trust and confidence in the UNLF that its armed cadres operate freely among the Manipuri people today. Thus, having established a considerably vast area of mass base, both in the hills and the plains, the UNLF has now entered the next phase of the struggle to engage the Indian Occupation Forces in a full-scale armed struggle for national liberation.

Towards Unity

That the strategy and tactics of Manipur's liberation struggle should be charted in the context of the interdependence and inter-relatedness of all the peoples of the Indo-Burma region and of the common external enemy they confront today, is the basic political and military line of the UNLF. This demands unity first among the revolutionary organizations of Manipur. The UNLF, therefore, has all along taken the stand that all the genuine revolutionary organizations of Manipur should unite and fight together against Indian colonial occupation. Urged by this reality, the UNLF has been seeking possibilities of bringing about unity among the revolutionary organizations of Manipur. Other fraternal organizations have also been working for unity in their own ways. Their efforts, the hurdles they faced and the consequences thereof, are now a part of the history of the national liberation struggle of Manipur. This experience in the search for unity has provided invaluable lessons for the future.

Thus the common efforts of the People's Revolutionary Party of Kangleipak (PREPAK), the Revolutionary People's Front (RPF) and the UNLF brought them together in March 1999 to discuss the paramount necessity for unity among them. Ultimately, as the result of a long deliberation for 20 days, they committed themselves to fight together for the liberation of Manipur from Indian colonial occupation. Thus the *Manipur People's Liberation Front* (MPLF) was formed on 01 March 1999 to institutionalize their unity. The three parties also took the historic decision to unify, step by step, into a single party. The UNLF believes that the achievement towards unity in Manipur will give a new direction and impetus to the liberation struggle for the region as a whole.

The emergence of the MPLF has brought about a new revolutionary situation in Manipur. Now, the Manipuri people's national liberation struggle can be expected to make significant progress under a unified leadership.

The decision of the three parties to form the MPLF gave a new hope and a long awaited smile to the entire people of Manipur. There was euphoria all around. However, concerned peoples could not but ask some worried questions: Is the unity real? How long will it go? Will they not break up again...? For the MPLF, these are relevant questions to be answered in time, by deeds.

The Proposal

The peoples of Manipur have suffered for more than forty long years under Indian colonial occupation and military repression. Their fundamental human rights, both collective and individual, have been usurped by the rulers in New Delhi. In order to hold on to their colonial rule, India now deploys more than 50,000 military and para-military forces in Manipur alone. In their attempt to suppress our national liberation struggle the Indian Occupation Forces have committed summary executions of several hundred freedom fighters, committed massacres on many occasions while reacting to attacks by freedom fighters and many of our women have been raped in front of their family members. India also has lost many of their soldiers in the process of the so-called 'Counter Insurgency Operations'. India's military effort has only escalated the conflict rather than finding a solution thereby aggravating further the sufferings of our people.

In order to resolve the Manipur-India Conflict satisfactorily once and for all, the UNLF Central Committee announced a 4-Point Proposal on 31 January, 2005 as below:

1. To hold a PLEBSCITE under UN aegis so that the people of Manipur can exercise their democratic right to decide on the core issue of the conflict – the restoration of Manipur's sovereignty and independence.
2. To deploy a UN Peace Keeping Force in Manipur to ensure free and fair conduct of the Plebiscite.
3. UNLF to deposit all its arms to the UN Peace Keeping Force and India to withdraw all its regular and para military forces from Manipur before a deadline prior to the Plebiscite date to be decided by the UN.
4. The UN to hand over political power in accordance with the result of the Plebiscite.

The UNLF has made the above proposal so that our people, the ultimate authority of their own fate, could give their judgement on the core issue of the Manipur-India Conflict. We believe that the above proposal is the most democratic means to resolve the conflict, which 'the largest democracy in the world' should accept.

We, therefore, appeal to the international community in general and the United Nations in particular, to fulfil their moral obligation of protecting and upholding the rights of nations and peoples to determine their own future by themselves *vis-à-vis* the Manipur-India Conflict.

APPENDIX 1
Instrument of Accession

WHEREAS, the Indian Independence Act, 1947 provides that as from the fifteenth day of August, 1947 there shall be set up an independent Dominion known as INDIA, and that the Government of India Act, 1935 shall with such omissions, additions, adaptations and modification as the Governor-General may by order specify be applicable to the Dominion of India;

AND WHEREAS the Government of India Act, 1935 as so adapted by the Governor-General provides that an Indian State may accede to the Dominion of India by an Instrument of Accession executed by the Ruler thereof;

NOW THEREFORE I, *Bodha Chandra*, Ruler of MANIPUR in the exercise of my sovereignty in and over my said State do hereby execute this my Instrument of Accession and

1. I hereby declare that I accede to the Dominion of India with the intent that the Governor-General of India, the Dominion Legislature, the Federal Court and any other Dominion authority established for the purposes of the Dominion shall, by virtue of this my Instrument of Accession but subject always to the terms thereof, and for the purposes only of the Dominion exercise in relation to the State of MANIPUR (hereinafter referred to as 'the State') such functions as may be vested in them by or under the Government of India Act, 1935, as in force in the Dominion of India on the 15th day of August, 1947 (which Act as so in force is hereinafter referred to as 'the Act'); **and I further declare that the Dominion of India may, through such agency or agencies, and in such manner, as it thinks fit, exercise in relation to the administration of civil and criminal justice in this State all such powers, authority and jurisdiction as were at any time exercisable by His Majesty's representative for the exercise of the functions of the Crown in its relations with Indian States.*
2. I hereby assume the obligation of ensuring that due effect is given to the provisions of the Act within this State so far as they are applicable therein by virtue of this my Instrument of Accession.

3. **Without prejudice to the provisions of paragraph 1*, I accept the matters specified in the Schedule hereto as the matters with respect to which the Dominion Legislature may make laws for this State.
4. I hereby declare that I accede to the Dominion of India on the assurance that if an agreement is made between the Governor-General and the Ruler of this State whereby any function in relation to the administration in this State of any law of Dominion legislature shall be exercised by the Ruler of this State, then any such agreement shall be deemed to form part of this Instrument and shall be construed and have effect accordingly.
5. The terms of this my Instrument of Accession shall not be varied by any amendment of the Act or of the Indian Independence Act, 1947, unless such amendment is accepted by me by an Instrument supplementary to this Instrument.
6. Nothing is this Instrument shall empower the Dominion Legislature to make any law for this State authorising the compulsory acquisition of land for any purpose, but I hereby undertake that should the Dominion for the purpose of a Dominion law which applies in this State deem it necessary to acquire any land, I will at their request acquire the land at their expense or if the land belongs to me transfer it to them or such terms as may be agreed, or in default of agreement, determined by an arbitrator to be appointed by the Chief Justice of Delhi.
7. Nothing in this Instrument shall be deemed to commit me in any way to acceptance of any future Constitution of India or to fetter my discretion to enter into arrangement with the Government of India under any such future Constitution.
8. Nothing in this Instrument effects the continuance of my sovereignty in and over this State, save as provided by or under this Instrument, the exercise of any powers, authority and rights now enjoyed by me as Ruler of this State or the validity of any law at present in force in this State.
9. I hereby declare that I execute this Instrument on behalf of this State and that any reference in this Instrument to me or to the Ruler of the State is to be construed as including a reference to my heirs and successors.

Given under my hand this 11th day of August, Nineteen hundred and forty-seven.

Sd/- Bodha Chandra
Maharaja of Manipur

I do hereby accept this Instrument of Accession.

Dated this 11th day of August, Nineteen hundred and forty-seven.

Sd/- Louis Mountbatten
(Governor-General of India)

SCHEDULE

The matters with respect to which the Dominion Legislature may make laws for this State.

Defence

1. The naval, military and air forces of the Dominion and any other armed forces raised or maintained by the Dominion; any armed forces, including forces raised or maintained by an Acceding State, which are attached to, or operating with, any of the armed forces of the Dominion.
2. Naval, military and air force works, administration of cantonment areas.
3. Arms, firearms, ammunition.
4. Explosives.

External Affairs

1. External affairs; the implementing of treaties and agreements with other countries; extradition, including the surrender of criminals and accused persons to parts of His Majesty's dominions outside India.
2. Admission into, and emigration and expulsion from, India, including in relation thereto the regulation of the movements in India or persons who are not British subjects domiciled in India or subjects of any acceding State, pilgrimages to places beyond India.
3. Naturalisation.

Communication

1. Posts and Telegraphs, including telephones, wireless, broadcasting, and other like forms of communication.
2. Federal railways; the regulation of all railways other than minor railways in respect of safety, maximum and minimum rates and fares, station and service terminal changes, interchange of traffic and the responsibility of railways administrations as carrier of goods and passengers; the regulation of minor railways in respect of safety and responsibility of the administration of such railways as carriers of goods and passengers.
3. Maritime shipping and navigation, including shipping and navigation on tidal waters; Admiralty jurisdiction.
4. Port quarantine.
5. Major ports, that is to say, the declaration and determination of the ports, and the Constitution and powers of Port Authorities therein.
6. Aircraft and Air navigation; the provision of aerodromes regulation and organization of air traffic and of aerodromes;
7. Lighthouse, including lightships, beacons and other provisions for the safety of shipping and aircraft.
8. Carriage of passengers and goods by sea or by air.
9. Extension of the powers and jurisdiction of members of the police force belonging to any unit to railway area outside that unit.

Ancillary

1. Elections to the Dominion Legislature, subject to the provisions of the Act and of any Order made thereunder.
2. Offences against laws with respect to any of the aforesaid matters.
3. Inquiries and statistics for the purposes of any of the aforesaid matters.
4. Jurisdiction and powers of all courts with respect to any of the aforesaid matters, but, except with the consent of the Ruler of the acceding State, not so as to confer any jurisdiction or powers upon any courts other then courts ordinarily exercising jurisdiction in or in relation to that State.

APPENDIX 2
The Manipur State Constitution Act, 1947

Background

When the British paramountcy lapsed, the basic legal framework for the governance of Manipur was the revised rules for the Administration of the Manipur State which became operative from July 1, 1947. It provided for an interim Manipur state council consisting of a Chief Minister and six other Ministers who were appointed by, and responsible to the Maharaja. The Maharaja-in-Council exercised both legislative and executive authority over the whole of Manipur.

The detailed structure, powers and functions of the Chief Court and the subordinate Civil and Criminal courts in Manipur were already provided for under the Manipur State Courts Act, 1947. Similarly, the Manipur State Hill Peoples (Administration) Regulation, 1947 gave details about administration in the Hill areas of Manipur. So for the sake of continuity and possibly also with a view to complete their work within the short time at their disposal the 15-member Constitution Making Committee incorporated the existing laws and rules wherever applicable in the drafting of a new constitution for Manipur.

The Manipur Constitution, when it was finally adopted and enacted, formalized the transfer of powers from the Maharaja to the elected representatives of the people and confirmed the Maharaja's position as the constitutional head of the state. The constitution and the form of responsible government introduced by it for the first time in Manipur may appear rudimentary by today's standards but it was, in its historical context of a colonial and feudal society, a proud achievement of the Manipuri people.

Given below is the full text of the Manipur Constitution which was written in English and enacted as the Manipur State Constitution Act, 1947:

THE MANIPUR STATE CONSTITUTION ACT, 1947

Whereas it is expedient to enact a law for the governance of the Manipur state, His highness the Maharaja of Manipur is pleased to enact as follows:

CHAPTER I

1. Title: This act shall be called the Manipur State Constitution Act, 1947.

2. Extent and Application: This Act shall extend to the whole of the Manipur State inclusive of the Hill Areas saving that it shall not apply in any matter where a specific reservation of powers is made to any Authority in the hill under the provisions of the Manipur State Hill (Administration) Regulation, 1947.

3. Government of the State by His Highness the Maharaja: The territories for the time being and hereafter vested in the Maharaja be governed by and in the name of the Maharaja. All rights, authority and jurisdiction which appertain or are incidental to the government of such territories are exercisable by the Maharaja subject to the provisions of this Act.

4. Succession: Succession to the throne shall be governed by the Law of Primogeniture provided that the heir must be the legitimate son of a marriage recognized by the Council of Ministers. In the event of failure of heirs in the direct male line, His Highness the Maharaja shall, after consultation with the Council of Ministers and the Assembly, designate his heir.

5. Attainment of Majority: The Maharaja or his heir shall be taken to attain majority at the age of 21 years.

6. Council of Regency:

(a) Whereby reason of the Maharaja being a minor or whereby reason of any mental defect or grave bodily sickness as a result of which the Maharaja becomes permanently incapable of exercising his powers, the Council of Ministers shall take steps to set up a Council of Regency which shall exercise their powers in the State and shall continue in office for such time as the Council may determine.

(b) Notwithstanding the provisions of Sub-section (a) above, the Maharaja in consultation with the Council of Ministers may, at any time or for any reason which may appear suitable, set up a Council of Regency to exercise his functions.

(c) A Council of Regency set up under Sub-sections (a) and (b) may comprise one or more persons as may seem desirable. The Regent or Council of Regency shall before taking office be required to take an oath before the State Assembly to be loyal to the State and to observe faithfully its Constitution and laws.

(d) Where in any event it shall be necessary to set up a Council of Regency either for the reasons laid down in Sub-sections (a) and (b) above or for any other reason or where exercising his powers before such Regency can be set up, the Council of Ministers shall take whatever steps may be necessary for the governance of the State till such time as the Regency is created.

7. Failure of Heirs and Disputed Succession:

(a) In the event of failure of heirs in the direct male line and failure of the Maharaja to designate his heir under Section 4 above, a joint extraordinary session of the State Assembly and the Council of Ministers shall immediately be convened and shall remain in closed and continuous session till it shall have determined, by a 75 per cent majority of the members present and voting, the person to whom the throne shall pass.

(b) Where for any reason the succession to the throne is disputed, the Council of Ministers shall, on the death of the Ruler, take such steps as may immediately be necessary for the good governance of the State and shall refer the matter under dispute to the Chief Court for decision. Where any party is aggrieved by the decision of the Chief Court, an appeal shall lie to such authority as may be determined hereafter.

8. The Maharaja's Prerogatives:

(a) All family matters which are the Maharaja's sole concern as head of the Ruling Family, all matters which are his sole concern as the Defender of Faith and all matters connected with Titles, Honours and Palace Ceremonials shall be deemed to fall within the Maharaja's Personal Prerogative and in such matters the Maharaja shall exercise full discretion subject to the provisions of the Constitution and the laws of the State.

The Maharaja's Prerogative shall not however be taken to comprise any matter wherein the legitimate interests of the

State Administration or a civil right sustainable in a court of law is involved. It will be with the prerogative of the Maharaja to remit punishment and pardon offenders subject to the provisions of the Manipur State Courts Act provided that this prerogative shall not prejudice the right of any individual to compensation.

(b) It shall be the prerogative of the Maharaja and the Maharani that neither may be made answerable at Law or subject to any legal proceedings in the State Courts. Their persons and property shall be inviolable.

(c) Notwithstanding Section 8(b) above, it shall be lawful for the State Council in consultation with the Chief Court to draw up a statement of charges against the Maharaja or the Maharani where it is proved beyond all possible doubt that the Maharaja or the Maharani have been guilty of murder or of any other heinous offence or of any extreme political crime against the provisions of the Constitution.

(d) On a statement of charges being drawn up under clause (c) above, the Council shall present it before the Maharaja or the Maharani and require satisfaction. Should satisfaction be not forthcoming, the Council may refer the matter to such authority as may be determined hereafter.

CHAPTER II
Definitions

9. In this Act and the Rules issued thereunder, unless there is something repugnant to the subject or the context:

(a) State shall mean the Manipur State comprising the whole territory of Manipur as delineated in the maps of the Survey of India current at the date of this enactment.

(b) The Maharaja means His highness The Maharaja of Manipur, the Constitutional Head of the State.

(c) Chief Minister means the officer entrusted with the Chief Executive functions of the State.

(d) Minister means a member of the Council of Ministers appointed under this Act by name or by virtue of his office to administer certain branches of the State Administration and to perform the duties and exercise the power imposed and conferred upon a Minister by this Act and the Rules framed thereunder.

(e) Council means the State Council of Ministers constituted under this Act.

(f) Assembly means the State Assembly as constituted under this Act.

(g) Gazette means the official journal of the State by means of which important orders, notices, communiqués, etc., are published.

(h) Speaker means the President of the Assembly and includes the Deputy Speaker in the absence of the Speaker or, in the absence of both, a member voted to the Chair.

(i) Civil List means the appropriation of funds for the expenses of the Ruling Family and the Privy Purse of the Ruler.

(j) Privy Purse means such portion of the Civil List as is appropriated exclusively for the personal expenses of the Maharaja.

(k) Revenue includes all receipts of the State from the State Assets, from all Lands, Forest, Taxes, Penalties, Forfeitures, Escheats, Laps and other sources.

(l) Rules means any Rule issued under this Act.

(m) Fundamental Rights shall mean those rights which the State's people shall enjoy as of right under this Act.

(n) The pronoun 'he' and its derivatives are used of any person whether male or female.

CHAPTER III
The Executive

10. Council of Ministers:

(a) Subject to the provisions of this Act and subject also to the provisions of the Rules for the Administration of the Manipur State, the Executive Authority of the State is delegated to and shall vest in the Council of Ministers.

(b) Where under this Act or the Rules for the Administration of the State it is requisite that the approval of the Maharaja shall be taken to any measure, the Chief Minister shall seek the approval of the Maharaja in person or in writing and shall obtain the Maharaja's orders thereon. Should in any case the Maharaja's approval be withheld, the Maharaja shall be pleased to inform the Chief Minister in person or in writing and to communicate his reasons for withholding such approval in writing to the Council.

(c) The Council of Ministers shall consist of the Chief Minister and six other Ministers.

(d) The six Ministers on the Council shall be elected by the State Assembly subject to the provisions that two of these Ministers shall be representatives of the Hill people of the State elected in such manner as shall be laid down in the Rules of Business of the State Assembly.

(f) The Chief Minister and the Ministers shall receive letters of appointment over the seal of the Maharaja.

(g) The Chief Minister in consultation with the Ministers shall allot portfolios.

11. The Chief Minister shall be the President of the Council and the Vice-President shall be appointed by the Council.

12. The Council of Ministers shall have a common seal and shall be jointly responsible to the Maharaja for the Administration of the State.

13. The Council of Ministers and the Ministers individually shall exercise such powers and functions as may be assigned to them by or under this Act or by or under the Rules for the Administration of the State.

14. The quorum necessary for the transaction of business at a meeting of the Council shall not be less than three excluding the President.

15. The Chief Minister and Ministers shall, on taking office, swear an oath of loyalty and allegiance to the Maharaja in the following form:

> 'I (name of the Minister) having been appointed as a Member of the Manipur State Council, do solemnly swear that I will be loyal and faithful and bear true allegiance to the Maharaja, his heirs and successors and that I will faithfully discharge the duties laid on me under this Act'.

16. A Minister of the Council shall not be removable from office except in accordance with the provisions of the Chapter below.

CHAPTER IV
The State Assembly

17. There shall be constituted a State Assembly. The Assembly shall be elected for a period of three years and shall comprise Representatives freely elected by the people on an adult franchise and on the principle of Joint Electorates. Elections shall be in such manner and by such franchise as may be laid down under the Rules for the Representatives returnable from General, Hill and Mohammedan Constituencies shall be in the ratios of 30:18:3 respectively with an additional two seats for the Representatives of Educational and Commercial interests.

18. The State Assembly may debate all matters concerning the Government and well-being of the State which, in the opinion of five Members of the Assembly, it is in the public interest to debate. The Assembly shall tender such advice to the Council of Ministers in any matter in which a majority of the Members present are agreed on the advice which shall be tendered provided that no matter touching the Maharaja's Prerogative shall be debated and provided that the Maharaja may on the advice of the Council, veto debate on any matter where such course shall in the public interest be necessary.

19. The State Assembly shall not tender advice to the Council on any matter which is of primary concern to the Hill people unless such advice has the support of a majority of the Hill Representatives in the Assembly.

20. Subject to the provisions of this Act, the Assembly may make rules for regulating its proceedings and the conduct of business.

21. Where in any case it is required to pass a vote of no confidence against a Minister of the Council for his individual acts, a motion of no-confidence signed by not less than ten Members of the Assembly and laying out in detail the facts giving rise to the motion, may with the permission of the Speaker of the Assembly be moved. If such motion shall receive the support of at least 75 per cent of the Members present and voting, it shall be forwarded through the Chief Minister to the Maharaja who, unless there appear strong and valid reasons to the contrary which shall be recorded in writing, shall after consultation with the Chief Minister require the Minister against whom the motion has been passed to resign.

22. Where in any case the State Council or the Maharaja is in the special circumstances of any case unable to accept the advice of the

Assembly, the Maharaja or the Council as the case may be, shall communicate in writing the reasons which have led to such course and shall give facilities for personal discussion of the matter with a representative or representatives deputed by the Assembly.

23. Subject to the provisions of the Act and to Rules framed under it for the disposal of the Assembly business, there shall be Freedom of Speech in the Assembly and no Member shall be liable to any proceedings in any court in respect of any speech or vote given by him in the Assembly or a committee thereof and no person shall be liable in respect of any publication by or under the authority of the Assembly of any report, paper, vote or proceedings.

24. No Member of the Assembly shall be liable to arrest or detention in prison under a Civil process—

(a) if he is a Member of the Assembly, during the continuance of the Assembly;
(b) if he is a Member of any Committee of the Assembly, during the continuance of the meeting of the Committee.

25. The elected Ministers, the Speaker, Deputy Speaker and Members of the Assembly shall receive such emoluments as may be determined from time to time by the Assembly.

CHAPTER V
The Law Making Authority

26. The Law Making Authority in the State shall consist of the Maharaja in Council in collaboration with the State Assembly acting under Section 18 above.

27. When the Council or the Assembly consider that a law should be enacted the Council shall cause a Bill to be drafted, which shall be laid before the Assembly and a reasonable time shall be given for consideration thereof. The Council shall then cause to be made such alterations or amendments as may be deemed necessary in the light of the advice tendered by the Assembly, and the Chief Minister shall submit the Bill in its final form for the Assent of the Maharaja.

28. On the receipt of the Maharaja's Assent, the Bill shall be published in the State Gazette and shall become an Act having the force of law.

29. Should the Maharaja in any case withhold his Assent to a

Bill, that Bill shall lapse as if it had not been passed. If the Assent of the Maharaja is not forthcoming within one calendar month of the Bill being submitted to him, he shall be deemed to have withheld his Assent.

30. Where the Assent of the Maharaja to any Bill is withheld, the Council may cause the selfsame Bill to be introduced in the next session of the Assembly and if passed without amendment by 75 per cent majority of the Assembly, the Bill shall be certified over the Seal of the Council and shall become law.

31. Nothing in this Chapter shall be deemed to derogate from the absolute right of the Maharaja in Council to promulgate, in emergency case, orders having the force of law without previous reference to the Assembly where the public interest in their opinion, demands that such order shall be promulgated provided that the first opportunity shall be taken of laying the order before the Assembly for consideration. Any such order shall bot have the force of law for a period of more than six months.

CHAPTER VI
Finance

32. The Revenue of the State and such other receipts as may accrue from whatever source, less such reasonable percentage of the total real Revenue as may be reserved for the Civil list, are placed at the disposal of the Council for expenditure on the Government of the State in the manner prescribed by the State Account Rules saving that in every year a sum representing not less than 17.5 per cent of the average real Revenue of the State for the proceeding three years shall be allocated for expenditure on the welfare and administration of the Hill people.

33. The Minister in charge of Finance shall prepare an Annual Budget showing the estimated receipts and expenditure for the ensuing year classified under the prescribed heads of account and shall submit it to the Assembly within fifteen days of its meeting for the Budget Session along with a statement of account for the previous year.

34. The Assembly shall after considering the Budget submit it with their recommendation to the Council who, having made such modifications as may be deemed necessary, shall submit it to the Maharaja for approval. Where any delay occurs in the granting of Assent to the Budget by the Maharaja and where such Assent has not been obtained by the first day of the financial year, provisional effect shall be given to the Budget as passed by the Assembly and funds shall be drawn against its provisions as if it had received Assent.

35. The Maharaja's Civil List shall be fixed at a figure equal to 10 per cent of the real Revenues of the State over the preceding three years, provided that no extraordinary revenues shall be taken into account when determining this amount and provided that no State revenue in excess of Rupees twenty lakhs shall be taken into account in any one year. The appropriation to the Maharaja's Civil List shall be non-votable and shall not be the subject of debate in the Assembly.

36. No tax whatsoever shall be shown in the Budget and no tax shall be collected by any officer of the State or by any person unless such tax has been imposed by due process of law.

37. (a) There shall be a State Auditor who shall be appointed by the Maharaja in Council on a nomination to be made by the Comptroller of Audit, Assam or such other officer as may be deemed suitable. Such nominee shall be employed on contract for a period of not less than five years and shall be removable only by the Maharaja in Council in consultation with the authority making the nomination.

(b) The conditions of service of the State Auditor shall be such as may be prescribed by the Maharaja in Council provided always that he shall not be eligible for any office of profit in the State after his retirement.

(c) The Auditor shall exercise such powers and perform such duties as may be laid down in the State Account Rules.

CHAPTER VII
Hill People

38. The Council shall be responsible for the welfare and the good administration of the Hill people of the State and shall provide such funds for this purpose as may, subject to the provision of Section 32 above, be deemed necessary provided that the Local Authorities in the Hills shall exercise such powers of Local Self Government as may be laid down in the Manipur State Hill (Administration) Regulation, 1947.

CHAPTER VIII
The Services

39. The Council shall issue Rules regulating the conditions of service in the Departments of the State.

40. A Manipur State Appointments Board shall be constituted and the Council shall issue Rules regulating the constitution, functions and procedure of the Board. The Board shall consist of not less than three members, one of whom must be a Hillman, and a Chairman and shall be the final authority in all matters connected with appointments and promotions to the State Service except in so far as specific powers may be reserved under this Act or the Rules for the Administration of the State.

CHAPTER IX
The Judicature

41. (a) There shall be a complete separation of the Judiciary from the Executive.

(b) The Judicature of the State shall be as laid down in the Manipur State Courts Act, 1947.

42. The Chief Justice of the State and two Puisne Judges shall be appointed by the Maharaja in Council under the Royal Seal and shall hold office until the age of 65 years provided that—

(a) A Judge may resign his office.

(b) A Judge may be removed from his office by the Maharaja in Council only on the grounds of misbehaviour or of infirmity of body or mind.

43. A person shall not be appointed as a Judge of the Chief Court unless he—

(a) be a graduate in law and has held Judicial Office at least for five years, or

(b) is a Barrister qualified in England of five years' standing, or

(c) has for at least five years held Judicial Office in British India in a post not inferior to that of a Subordinate Judge, or

(d) has for at least a period of ten years been a Pleader of any High Court or of the Manipur Chief Court, or

(e) be a person recognized as having a special capacity for the exercise of Judicial Functions.

CHAPTER X
Fundamental Rights and Duties of Citizenship

44. All citizens shall be equal before the law. Titles and other privileges of birth shall not be recognized in the eyes of law.

45. The liberty of the individual shall be guaranteed. No person may be subjected to any judicial interrogation or placed under arrest or be in any other way deprived of his liberty, save as provided by law.

46. No person shall be tried save by a competent Court.

47. No person may be tried except by a competent Court who shall give full opportunity to such person to defend himself by a means.

48. All penalties shall be as determined by law.

49. Capital punishment may not be inflicted for purely political crimes.

50. No citizen may be banished from the State, expelled from one part of the country to another, and obliged to reside in a specified place save in such cases as may be expressly determined by law.

51. Every dwelling shall be inviolable save under express provision of law.

52. There shall be guaranteed to all people Justice—Social, Economic and Political; equality of status, of opportunity and before the law; freedom of thought, expression, of belief, faith, worship, vocation, association, and action subject to law and public morality.

53. The practice of Arts and Sciences shall be unrestricted and shall enjoy the protection and support of the State.

54. Without any prejudice to the communities concerned, public institutions shall be opened to all the citizens of the State.

55. (a) All officials of the State or of a Local Government shall be answerable before the law for their individual and unlawful actions.

(b) Where damage is caused to an individual by the act of an official of the State or an official of a Local Government, such individual may sue the State before the Chief Court and may seek redress save where such damage has been caused by a *bona fide* act of a State servant in pursuance of a policy duly laid down by a Competent Authority.

CHAPTER XI
General Clauses

56. Any provision of this Act may be subject to amendment by the Maharaja in Council provided that such amendment is laid before the Assembly and receives the support of at least 80 per cent of the Members of the State Assembly present and voting when such amendment is debated.

57. Where in any case circumstances arise which prevent the proper operation in law or in spirit of this Constitution Act, the Council may at their discretion refer the matter for decision to such authority outside the State as may be decided hereafter and the decision of that authority shall be binding.

58. The Court language of the State shall be Manipuri or English.

APPENDIX 3
The Representatives

The State Assembly

A peculiar feature of the elections to the State Assembly, conducted in a staggered manner from June 11 to July 27, 1948, was the principle of Joint Electorates. Under this system, separate General and Mohammedan or Hillman electorates in a territorial constituency elected their own representatives to the assembly. This legacy of the divide-and-rule policy of the British rulers was applicable to four constituencies in the Manipur Valley.

Particulars of the representatives elected by the people to the State Assembly are given below:

Sl. No.	*Name of Constituency*	*Name of the Elected Candidate*	*Remarks*
1.	Koirengei	Khwairakpam Chaoba Singh	General
2.	Khwai Lalambung	Khongbantabam Ibetombi Singh	General
3.	Lamsang	Wangkheimayum Tarpon Singh	General
4.	Patsoi	Khumanthem Golap Singh	General
5.	Sagolband	Arambam Ibungotomcha Singh	General
6.	Keisamthong	Elangbam Tompok Singh	General
7.	Yaiskul	Sougaijam Samarendra Singh	General
8.	Malom	Yumnam Megho Singh	General
9.	Utlow	Hijam Irabot Singh	General
10.	Nambol	Ayekpam Anganghal Singh	General
11.	Bishenpur	Khwairakpam Kamalakanta Singh	General
12.	Moirang	(i) Mairenbam Koireng Singh	General
		(ii) Teba Kilong	Hillman
13.	Thanga Kumbi	Wahengbam Gourakishore Singh	General
14.	Waikhong	Nongmaithem Toyaima Singh	General
15.	Kakching Khunou	Thokchom Shyama Singh	General
16.	Mayang Imphal	(i) Irom Merajatra Singh	General
		(ii) Md. Suleiman Mia	Mohamadan

(Contd.)

Sl. No.	*Name of Constituency*	*Name of the elected Candidate*	*Remarks*
17.	Wangoi	Nongmeikapam Iboton Singh	General
18.	Thoubal	Waikhom Mani Singh	General
19.	Wangjing	Laisram Chandramani Singh	General
20.	Khongjom	Mutum Khono Singh	General
21.	Sekmai	Khunbi Sorokhaibam Chourjit Singh	General
22.	Yairipok	(i) Waikhom Nimaichand Singh (ii) Md. Amjad Ali Mohamadan	General
23.	Irilbung	Moirangthem Gourachand Singh	General
24.	Lilong	(i) Md. Abdul Kadir Khan (ii) Md. Alimuddin	General
25.	Ningomthong	Khwairakpam Giri Singh	General
26.	Wangkhei	Laisram Achow Singh	General
27.	Khurai Lamlong	Ningthoujam Leiren Singh	General
28.	Sawombung	Maimom Modhumangol Singh	General
29.	Pangei	Takhellambam Bokul Singh	General
30.	Jiri	Sinam Sree Bijoy Singh	General
31.	Tengnoupal (1)	Mono	Hillman
32.	Tengnoupal (2)	Holpao	Hillman
33.	Hill Sadar	Ralengnao Khathing	Hillman
34.	Phaisat	Luying Hungyo	Hillman
35.	Ukhrul	Thisan Luikham	Hillman
36.	Chingjaroi	Miksha K. Shimray	Hillman
37.	Tolloi	Rungsung Suisa	Hillman
38.	Mao (1)	Mangpithang Kipgen	Hillman
39.	Mao (2)	(vacant)	Election could not be held.
40.	Tama	S.L. Lunneh	Hillman
41.	Tamenglong	Thanggoumang Sithou	Hillman
42.	Langkhong (1)	Buishing Kabui	Hillman
43.	Langkhong (2)	Kakhangai	Hillman
44.	Maite	Dr. L. Kampu	Hillman

(*Contd.*)

Sl. No.	*Name of Constituency*	*Name of the elected Candidate*	*Remarks*
45.	Thlanship	T.C. Tiankham	Hillman
46.	Senvawn	Tualchin	Hillman
47.	Churachandpur	Damjakhai Waiphei	Hillman
48.	Education	Chingakham pishak Singh	Non-territorial Constituency
49.	Commerce and Constituency	Ayekpam Gourbidhu Singh	Non-territorial Constituency

The Ministers

Members of the first Council of Ministers under the Manipur State Constitution Act, 1947 were:

1. Maharaj Kumar Priya Brata Singh - Chief Minister
2. Ralengnao Khathing - Minister
3. Arambam Ibungotomcha Singh - Minister
4. Ningthoujam Leiren Singh - Minister
5. Ayekpam Gourabidhu Singh - Minister
6. Teba Kilong - Minister
7. Md. Alimuddin - Minister

APPENDIX 4
The Manipur Merger Agreement

AGREEMENT made this twenty-first day of September, 1949 between the Governor General of India and His Highness the Maharaja of Manipur.

WHEREAS in the best interest of the State of Manipur as well as of the Dominion of India it is desirable to provide for the administration of the said State by or under the authority of the Dominion Government,

IT IS HEREBY AGREED as Follows:

Article I

His Highness the Maharaja of Manipur hereby cedes to the Dominion Government full and exclusive authority, jurisdiction and powers for and in relation to the governance of the State and agrees to transfer the administration of the State to the Dominion Government on the fifteenth day of October 1949 (hereinafter referred to as "the said day").

As from the said day the Dominion Government will be competent to exercise the said powers, authority and jurisdiction in such manner and through such agency as it may think fit.

Article II

His Highness the Maharaja shall continue to enjoy the same personal rights, privileges, dignities, titles, authority over religious observances, customs, usages, rites and ceremonies and institutions in charge of the same in the State, which he would have enjoyed had this agreement not been made.

Article III

His Highness the Maharaja shall with effect from the said day be entitled to receive for his lifetime from the revenues of the State annually for his Privy-Purse the sum of Rupees three lakhs free of all taxes.

This amount is intended to cover all the expenses of the Ruler and his family, including expenses on account of his personal staff and armed guards, maintenance of his residences, marriages and other ceremonies, etc., and the allowances to the Ruler's relations who on the date of execution of this agreement were in receipt of such allowances from the revenues of the State, and will neither be increased nor reduced for any reason whatsoever.

The Government of India undertake that the said sum of Rupees three lakhs shall be paid to His Highness the Maharaja in four equal installments in advance at the beginning of each quarter from the State treasury or at such other treasury as may be specified by the Government of India.

Article IV

His Highness the Maharaja shall be entitled to the full ownership, use and enjoyment of all private properties (as district from State properties) belonging to him on the date of this agreement.

His Highness the Maharaja will furnish to the Dominion Government before the first January, 1950 an inventory of all the immovable property, securities and cash balance held by him as such private property.

If any dispute arises as to whether any item of property is the private property of His Highness the Maharaja or State property, it shall be referred to a Judicial Officer qualified to be appointed as a High Court Judge, and the decision of that officer shall be final and binding on both parties:

Provided that His highness the Maharaja's right to the use of the residences known as "Redlands" and "Les Chatalettes" in Shillong, and the property in the town of Gauhati known as "Manipuri Basti" shall not be questioned.

Article V

All the members of His Highness's family shall be entitled to all the personal rights, privileges, dignities and titles enjoyed by them whether within or outside the territories of the State, immediately before the 15th August, 1947.

Article VI

The Dominion Government guarantees the succession, according to law and custom, to the gaddi of the State and to His Highness the Maharaja's personal rights, privileges, dignities, titles, authority over religious observances, customs, usages, rites and ceremonies and institutions in charge of the same in the State.

Article VII

No enquiry shall be made by or under the authority of the Government of India, and no proceedings shall lie in any Court in Manipur, against His Highness the Maharaja whether in a personal capacity or otherwise in respect of anything done or omitted to be done by him or under his authority during the period of his administration of that State.

Article VIII

(1) The Government of India hereby guarantees either the continuance in service of the permanent members of the Public Service of Manipur on conditions which will be not less advantageous than those on which they were serving before the date on which the administration of Manipur is made over to the Government of India or the payment of reasonable compensation.
(2) The Government of India further guarantees the continuance of pensions and leave salaries sanctioned by His Highness the Maharaja to servants of the State who have retired or proceeded on leave preparatory to retirement, before the date on which the Administration of Manipur is made over to the Government of India.
(3) The Government of India also undertake to make suitable provisions for the employment of Manipuris in the various branches of Public Services, and in every way encourage Manipuris to join them. They also undertake to preserve various laws, customs and conventions prevailing in the State pertaining to the social, economic and religious life of the people.

Article IX

Except with the previous sanction of the Government of India no proceedings, civil or criminal, shall be instituted against any person in respect of any act done or purporting to be done in the execution of his duties as a servant of the State before the day on which the administration is made over to the Government of India.

In confirmation whereof Mr. Vapal Pangunni Menon, Adviser to the Government of India in the Ministry of States, has appended his signature on behalf and with the authority of the Governor General of India and His Highness Maharaja Bodh Chandra Singh, Maharaja of Manipur has appended his signature on behalf of himself, his heirs and successors.

Bodh Chandra
Maharaja of Manipur

V.P. Menon
Adviser to the Government of India
Ministry of States

Shri Prakash
Governor of Assam

September 21, 1949
Shillong

ANNEXURE 2

Background to the National Liberation Struggle in Manipur
Kangleipak Communist Party

September 22, 2010

AN OPEN LETTER TO REVOLUTIONARY PARTIES OF SOUTH EAST ASIA

Manipur in Brief

Manipur, one of the occupied seven States in India's North Eastern Region, is in deep social and political turmoil. The national liberation struggle to restore Manipuri sovereign independence and the massive counter-insurgency measures by the Indian State forces have resulted in a disturbing situation of armed conflict. Thousands of innocent peoples have been killed, hundreds have disappeared from custody, and many women have been raped by the Indian State forces in the process of ruthless counter-insurgency operations. The entire state is filled with personal tragedies of families who lost their sons and daughters, and with young men de-capacitated, maimed and psychologically shattered without renewable capacity for rehabilitation. The impact of the armed conflict is severely felt by women and children.

The state's productive forces, particularly women, had been undermined resulting in deep urban and rural poverty, thereby adding to the cycle of violence. Under the so-called democratic system of

India, corruption in public life had reached unprecedented depths and the body polity is rent apart, the division between the haves and have-nots had widened, and family unity and family values had been shattered through severe economic strain.

The state which was self-sufficient in history is now reduced to a position of critical dependence on India's doles, and the State government of Manipur is unable to pay even the salaries for its employees regularly. Complete loss of initiative for economic growth keeping the State as a captive market for India had perpetuated a system of colonialism which is undermining the basic parameters for dignified living of its citizens. The people of Manipur want freedom and independence, and India wants to continue their colonial occupation. What is the cause for this conflict situation?

Manipur, the small but beautiful home to more than thirty fraternal ethnic groups, is a historical State having a recorded history of more than 2000 years. In her long history, Manipur never became a part of India. Manipur was a recognized Asiatic State when the British imperialists invaded and occupied it in 1891. The British Crown in its own wisdom, however, did not annex Manipur to their British Indian empire.

After 56 years, when the British government de-colonized the Indian subcontinent in 1947, Manipur also regained her sovereign independence on 14 August, 1947 despite the treaty relationship with the Dominion of India under the Instrument of Accession signed between the King and the Governor General of the British Indian government on 11 August, 1947.

Under the terms of this treaty India was to look after the Foreign Affairs, Defence and Communications for Manipur while the King retained the full sovereign right to reject or accept any future constitution of India. Meanwhile, the King had already promulgated the first democratic constitution of Manipur in July 1947 known as the Manipur Constitution Act, 1947. Under provisions of this constitution, the first ever democratic elections under universal franchise were held in Manipur in August 1948 to elect the first Manipur State Assembly having 54 members.

The State Assembly was inaugurated by the King on 18 October, 1948 thereby making the historic transition from absolute monarchy to democracy retaining the King as the customary and constitutional head of State. Thus Manipur became the first country in South Asia to establish democracy when India was yet to adopt her own constitution.

When Manipur was introducing democracy independently India was getting restless to discontinue the treaty relationship and annex Manipur within the Indian Union from strategic security considerations. So Manipur acquiring international personality as a sovereign democratic country was not palatable to India, particularly when the ruling alliance government of Manipur was openly opposed to the idea of Manipuri's merger with India.

To offset this development India hatched a conspiracy to make the King sign a treaty to merge Manipur with India. To this end they invited the King for consultation on some matter in September 1948. On arrival at the venue of the meeting the Indian representative asked the King to put his signature on the already drafted document for merger. The King, completely taken by surprise, felt betrayed and refused to sign the document on the ground that he no longer had the constitutional authority to do so as a Council of Ministers is already functioning in Manipur. He asked for some time to consult his Council of Minister and left the meeting. But when he returned he found his residence surrounded by Indian military personnel. He was told that he was under house-arrest and was not allowed to contact even his Council of Ministers.

After resisting for two days, the King signed the Manipur Merger Agreement on 21 September, 1949. Under terms of this agreement the Government of India announced the formal annexation of Manipur on 15 October, 1949. The Manipur State Assembly and the Council of Ministers were also abolished on the same day by an executive order of the Indian government.

The people of Manipur have never accepted the Indian annexation. Several public resolutions and a National Convention have declared the Manipur Merger Agreement null and void having no legal and constitutional legitimacy as it was done under duress and not ratified by the State Assembly. This is the crux of the problem and the very root cause of the present Manipur-India Politico-Military Conflict? Ever since day one, India has been using brute military force to suppress the legitimate aspirations of our people. Today Manipur is highly militarized with 50,000 plus Indian military and Para-military forces deployed against the indigenous population of just about 1.6 million. This amounts to one Indian soldier for every fifty locals.

The draconian law, Armed Forces Special Powers Act, 1958 has been in force in Manipur for over fifty years now. This Act empowers and gives immunity even to a Non-Commissioned Officer of the Indian military forces to arrest or shoot to kill anybody on mere suspicion and such acts cannot be challenged in a court of law. This Act has emboldened the Indian State forces to commit summary executions, enforced disappearances, rapes and killings in fake encounters with impunity. In short, this Act has legalized Indian State Terrorism. Even so, taking advantage of being the largest democracy in the world, India has manipulated to present the state of affairs in Manipur as simple law and order problem. But in reality, Manipur is now under Indian martial law.

So Kangleipak Communist Party (KCP) established in 1980 and its army wing Peoples Red Army to restore the sovereignty of Manipur and to establish a socialist Republic. We do not believe in empty theory.

Ideology

We are Marxists. We believe that the heritage of classical Marxism, in all its fundamental features, adequately reflects the social processes taking place in today's world. A correct approach to social phenomena is impossible without applying the method of historical materialism, the dialectic of the basis and the superstructure, the theory of proletarian revolution, proletarian internationalism.

The legitimate transformation and generalization of the Marxism of Marx and Engels was Marxism-Leninism which explained the transition of the capitalist nations to the stage of socialist nation.

As Maoists, we believe that the class struggle between the bourgeoisie and the proletariat continues to be waged under socialism and the principal arena of this struggle becomes the Communist Party leading the construction of socialism.

Problems of History

We believe that socialism which politically can be only the dictatorship of the working people under the leadership of proletariat is a necessary step towards a communist world—a world without inequality or dictatorship. We consider the Soviet Russia and the USSR under V.I. Lenin and J.V. Stalin (1917-1953) and China under Mao Zedong

(1949-1976) models of carrying of such political system in south east Asia.

Contemporary World

The world today appears to us divided into three groups of countries: (1) countries of the Metropolis (the USA, the Western European states, Japan, etc.); (2) comparatively rich and/or having a big military/ industrial potential countries which hold an intermediate position; (3) countries of the Third World, exploited by the former two groups of nations.

The revolutionary role of the proletariat in each of the above groups of countries is different.

In the countries of the Metropolis the working class is bought off with the super profits gained from the exploitation of the Third Worlds and cannot, at the present stage, be considered a revolutionary force. The national contradiction is to be considered the principal one in the given group of countries, while the principal revolutionary forces there are the oppressed minority of the working class usually not belonging to the historically dominant national groups and the revolutionary intelligentsia.

In the semi-imperialist countries the proletariat as a whole potentially is the main motive force of socialist revolution, while the principal contradiction at this stage is the class one. However, due to the ambivalent socio-economic position of these countries the proletariat here is infected with nationalist and chauvinist ideology, harbours reformist illusions. The main ally of the proletariat in its struggle against the bourgeoisie here is the revolutionary petty bourgeoisie.

In the Third World countries the struggle of the proletariat for its own rights is inseparable from the struggle of these nations for the true national independence. Here the natural allies of the proletariat are the petty bourgeoisie and the considerable part of the national bourgeoisie. The immediate task of the proletariat's struggle here in many cases is not a socialist, but a bourgeois-democratic revolution, and the main method of this struggle, the strategy of the People's War.

Strategy and Tactics

We believe that correct tactics flow from correct strategies, which flow from a correct ideological and political line. We believe that the fight against imperialism, capitalism and colonial ruler hand in hand with the fight against revisionism, chauvinism, and opportunism.

Our goal is carrying out a socialist revolution and going on to build communism—a society excluding any form of oppression of one social group by another: class oppression, national oppression, gender oppression.

The motive force of this revolution is the working class, while its conductor is an avant-garde disciplined revolutionary Communist Party, a Party with a system of democratic centralism. The latter system includes organization, leadership, discipline and hierarchy.

We believe that the ruling colonial, semi-colonial, imperialist and bourgeoisie will never give up its power without a fight. Putting an end to the bourgeois dictatorship is only possible by building public opinion to seize power through armed struggle. We believe, however, that any armed insurrection on the territory which we belongs will be inevitably crushed until an arising of objective conditions for its mass support of the potentially revolutionary strata of the population.

The building on the territory of South East Asia of an avant-garde disciplined revolutionary Communist party guided by the theory of Marxism-Leninism-Maoism is hindered by objective historical conditions resulting from the long years of rule of colonial Indian social-imperialist.

We believe our principal tactical task to be revolutionary agitation and propaganda of Marxism-Leninism-Maoism among the proletariat and the intelligentsia.

So we called all the revolutionary groups of the South East Asia.

We are eager to have your comment.

With Revolutionary Salute,

Comrade Malemnganba Meitei
Publicity and Propaganda
Kangleipak Communist Party
Manipur, Eastern Himalayan Region

Source: www. indianvanguard.wordpress.com, retrieved on 6 September 2013.

ANNEXURE 3

RPF Memorandum to De-colonisation Committee

[2nd Edition]

Memorandum submitted to the Secretary General United Nations and the chairman of the De-colonisation Committee (committee of 24) for de-colonisation of Manipur from Indian colonialism and alien racist regime, enlisting Manipur in the list of the non-self-governing-territories of the United Nations and, restoration of independence and sovereignty of Manipur.

REVOLUTIONARY PEOPLE'S FRONT

To

The Secretary General,
United Nations
And
The Chairman,
Decolonisation Committee (Committee of 24)
Geneva/New York Headquarters.

MEMORANDUM

Submitted on behalf of all the dependent and colonised people of Manipur representing the Meitei and the Meitei cognates, viz. the Nagas, the Kuki-Chins for granting and restoration of independence and de-colonisation of the State of Manipur from the present *colonial Administering Power of India, which has occupied Manipur since 15 October, 1949, till today.*

PRAYER

I. For supervising and examining historical materials/records relating to the illegal annexation and colonisation of Manipur by India;
II. For terminating the foreign and colonial regime of India over Manipur;
III. For international appraisal of the illegal and unjustified annexation of the Nation-State of Manipur in 1949 AD;
IV. For giving international recognition to the National Liberation Movement of Manipur, which continues since the time of annexation in 1949 till today, and allowing the people of Manipur to exercise their inalienable right to self-determination in conformity with the UN General Assembly Resolution 1514(XV) of 1960 and other subsequent resolutions;
V. For all necessary and elaborate steps, appropriate measures towards complete de-colonisation of Manipur and cessation of subjugation of her people to the earliest, and lastly, for holding emergent as well as periodic sessions of the De-colonisation Committee in Imphal city in 1999; and
VI. For enlisting Manipur in the list of the non-self-governing territories of the UN by enlarging the existing Mandate.

Respected Secretary General/Chairman

0.1. This is a factfully updated petition of the prayer submitted on 11 December, 1996 to the Chairman, UN De-colonisation Committee. We, the undersigned representatives of the Revolutionary People's Front (RPF), a front of **the national liberation movement** in the State of Manipur, which is currently a constituent State of the Republic of India, furnish the following facts, based on historical, political, socio-economic materials as well as legal and constitutional materials for your immediate consideration and urgent international supervision of the colonisation and dependence of the people of Manipur by the colonial power of India with the help of a colonial occupation army, which continues the ongoing repression, suppression, torture, extra-judicial murder and subjugation of the people of Manipur under a permanent colonial process and colonisation in different forms. Since time immemorial, Manipuris call Indians as **Mayangs**, i.e. foreigners.

0.2. We fully appreciate the de-colonisation process, adopted by the UN since 1960 and the emergence of a hundred independent sovereign states in conformity with the de-colonisation process. The de-colonisation process was initiated by the Special Committee on the Situation with regard to the Implementation of the Declaration on the Granting of Independence to Colonial Countries and Peoples (De-colonisation Committee hereafter) *vide* the UN General Assembly Resolution 1654 (XVI) of 27 November, 1961, the UN GA Resolutions 1810 (XVII) of 17 December, 1962, 2621 (XXV) of 12 October, 1970, 35/118 of 11 December, 1980, 40/56 of 2 December, 1985, 45/33 of 20 November, 1990, 46/181 of 19 December, 1991, and the UN GA Resolution 52/78 of 10 December, 1997.

0.3. It is pertinent that the UN GA Resolution 52/78 of 10 December, 1997 has mandated the Special Committee for "the Eradication of Colonialism in all Territories that have not yet exercised their right to self-determination, including independence", "to formulate proposals for the elimination of the remaining manifestations of colonialism" and "to recommend to the General Assembly the most suitable steps to be taken to enable the populations of those territories to exercise their right to self-determination and independence".

0.4. The Special Committee at its 1484th meeting, held on 6 February, 1998 has accepted to review the list of territories to which the Colonial Declaration of 1960 has applied. The Special Committee has continued its review of the list of Territories to which the Declaration is applicable and it also "intends to continue to review the list of Territories to which the Declaration is applicable".[1]

0.5. The non-self-governing territory of Manipur, illegally annexed and placed under military occupation since 15 October, 1949 deserves a legitimate place in the list of territories under the supervision of the Special Committee to enable the people of Manipur to exercise their inalienable right to self-determination, independence and sovereignty. The facts of colonisation and subjugation are furnished below under the relevant headings:

I. HISTORICAL EVIDENCE[2]

1.1. The State of Manipur[3], which lies in the latitude range of 23°83″ and 25°68″ (North) and in the longitude range of 93°03″ and 94°78″ (East), is one of the earliest States in the continent of Asia, including the Indian subcontinent. This ancient Asian State was known by different names to different countries that is—'Poirei Meitei Leipak' or 'Kangleipak' to the indigenous people of Manipur or Meiteis; 'Kathe' or 'Ponnas' to the Burmese; 'Hsiao Po-lo-mein' to the Chinese; 'Cassay' to the Shans; 'Moglai' to the Cacharis and Bengalis and 'Mekle' to the Assamese (as well as to the British in the 18th Century) in the pre-Christian period. Its location is identified with places within the jurisdiction of Tugma, Triglipton, Mareura and Kirrhadia as per the sources of Ptolemy. The Manipuris, themselves knew the State by as many as 22 names in different ages and at different times. The early state of Pragjyotishpur or, Kamrup or, present Indian state of Assam has been for millennia a buffer between State of Manipur and State of India known as Bharat for millennia. All the available maps available with India depict Manipur as an independent state till the *annexation* in 1949.

Genealogy of Manipur Kings

Sl. No.	*Name of King*	*Period (AD)*
1.	King Nongda Lairen Pakhangba	33 - 154
2.	King Khuiyoi Tompok	154 - 264
3.	King Taothingmang	264 - 364
4.	King Khui Ning-ngonba	364 - 379
5.	King Pengsiba	379 - 394
6.	King Kaokhangba	394 - 411
7.	King Naokhamba	411 - 428
8.	King Naophangba	428 - 518
9.	King Sareimang	518 - 568
10.	King Urakonthouba	568 - 658
11.	King Naothingkhong	663 - 763
12.	King Khongtekcha	763 - 773
13.	King Keirencha	784 - 799
14.	King Yaraba	799 - 821

(Contd.)

Sl. No.	*Name of King*	*Period (AD)*
15.	King Ayangba	821 - 910
16.	King Ningthoucheng	910 - 949
17.	King Chenglei Epan Lanthaba	949 - 969
18.	King Yanglou Keiphaba	969 - 984
19.	King Irengba	984 - 1074
20.	King Loiyumba	1074 - 1122
21.	King Loitongba	1122 - 1150
22.	King Atom Yoiremba	1150 - 1163
23.	King Iwanthaba	1163 - 1195
24.	King Thawanthaba	1195 - 1231
25.	King Chingthang Lanthaba	1231 - 1242
26.	King Thingbai Selhongba	1242 - 1247
27.	King Puranthaba	1247 - 1263
28.	King Khumomba	1263 - 1278
29.	King Moiramba	1278 - 1302
30.	King Thangbi Lanthaba	1302 - 1324
31.	King Kongyamba	1324 - 1335
32.	King Telheiba	1335 - 1355
33.	King Tonaba	1355 - 1359
34.	King Tabungba	1359 - 1394
35.	King Lairenba	1394 - 1399
36.	King Punsiba	1404 - 1432
37.	King Ningthoukhomba	1432 - 1469
38.	King Kyamba	1469 - 1508
39.	King Koiremba	1508 - 1512
40.	King Lamkyamba	1512 - 1523
41.	King Nong-en-faba	1523 - 1524
42.	King Kabomba	1524 - 1542
43.	King Tangjamba	1542 - 1545
44.	King Challamba	1545 - 1562
45.	King Mungyamba	1562 - 1597
46.	King Khagemba	1597 - 1652
47.	King Khunjaoba	1652 - 1666
48.	King Paikhomba	1666 - 1697
49.	King Charairongba	1697 - 1709

(*Contd.*)

Sl. No.	Name of King	Period (AD)
50.	King Garibaniwaz (Mayamba)	1709 - 1748
51.	King Chitsai	1748 - 1752
52.	King Bharatsai	1752 - 1753
53.	King Maramba	1753 - 1759
54.	King Chingthangkhomba	1759 - 1762
55.	King Maramba	1762 - 1763
56.	King Chingthangkhomba	1763 - 1798
57.	King Labyanachandra	1798 - 1801
58.	King Madhurjit	1801 - 1803
59.	King Chourjit	1803 - 1813
60.	King Marjit	1813 - 1819
61.	King Takuningthou (Heerachandra)	1819 -
62.	King Yumjaotaba	1820 -
63.	King Gambhir Singh	1821 -
64.	King Jay Singh	1822 -
65.	King Yadu Singh (Nongpok Chinglen Khomba)	1823 -
66.	King Raghav Singh	1823 - 1824
67.	King Nongchup Lamgaingamba (Badhra Singh)	1824 -
68.	King Gambhir Singh (Chinglen Nongdrenkhomba)	1825 - 1834
69.	King Chandrakirti (Ningthempishak)	1834 - 1844
70.	King Nara Singh	1844 - 1850
71.	King Debendra Singh	1850 -
72.	King Chandrakirti, KCSI	1850 - 1886
72.	King Surchandra	1886 - 1890
72.	King Kulachandra	1890 - 1891
73.	King Churachand Singh, KCSI	1891 - 1941
74.	King Bhodhachandra	1941 - 1955

Source: CHEITHAROL KUMBABA, the royal Chronicle of Manipur.

The international community would note that not a single Indian (Hindustani) king had ever ruled Manipur either directly or indirectly. The Indian history is of no concern to the people of Manipur till 1949. This is corroborated by the history of India positively and invariably.

1.2. The State formation was completed in the early Christian era, when as many as seven principalities amalgamated themselves to constitute the earliest Meitei State (Nagas, Kukis were Meitei Cognates), which territorially fluctuated but extended beyond the present territory. The earliest settlers were the ancient Meiteis of the present valley area, Meitei cognates re-named by British as the Nagas and Kuki-Chins. The Nagas[4] and Kuki-Chins are proto-Meiteis. The early Meitei State which is presently known as Manipur is a State of three major ethnic group of Mongolian race, namely, (i) the Meitei (valley Manipuri), Hill Manipuris re-christened by the colonial British as (ii) the Nagas and (iii) the Kuki-Chins. There was a centralised Constitutional Government since 429 AD, according to a renowned Meitei Scholar late Oinam Bhogeswar, whose works are found in plenty in Manipuri, i.e., Meitei language. The history of Manipur had been documented in a royal chronicle known as *"Cheitharol Kumbaba"* (33 AD to 1950 AD). The English translation is available in the Indian Office Library, London, and other Archives of the United Kingdom, which still preserve a large number of historical documents, treaties and other official records pertaining to the relation of the State of Manipur with the British Government since 1762 AD till 1949 AD. These materials, including local and native, may be closely examined as historical records by the De-colonisation Committee in order to form an objective and positive view of the people of the State of Manipur for at least three centuries so that the official and colonial perspectives of the Administrative Power of the Indian State alone may not form the sole basis for any objective appraisal. Early and medieval Indian history has never included present Manipur as its component till *India's illegal annexation* of Manipur in 1949. Even the Indian colonial historians admit this.

1.3. A centralised Constitutional Government had been functioning in the early State of Manipur invariably from 1100 AD, when the Meitei monarch Loiyumba had promulgated a political Constitution known as *"Loiyumba Shinyen"*, the translation of which is enclosed herewith as an Annexure (*Annexure No. I*). Several European states did not emerge as stable entities at that point of time.

1.4. The aforesaid constitutional Government continued from 1100 AD till the international conflict arose in between the Manipuris and the Burmese in the 18th and 19th centuries AD, when the Manipuri king Pamheiba alias Garibaniwaj invaded Burma in the 18th century several times with as many as 30,000 warriors. A large part of the Manipur territory was later ceded by the colonial power of India to

Burma (now Myanmar)—the Kabo (or Kabow) Valley, that had been a part of the Manipur Territory till the early part of the 19th century. The British gave annual revenue of Rs. 5000 to the Government of Manipur on behalf of the Burmese till Indian occupation of Manipur in 1949. The Government of India, which had annexed Manipur in 1949 unlawfully and unconstitutionally, ceded the Kabo valley to Burma (present Myanmar) after signing a secret Indo-Burma Treaty in 1953. The provision of the secret treaty are not yet made known to the people of Manipur as well as to the citizens of India. The colonial government of India holds up "Right to information" to the occupied territory and people of Manipur on this account. The colonial government operates like a Mafia on Kabo Valley.

1.5. After Burmese military occupation of Manipur for seven years in the period from 1819 to 1825, complete sovereignty was restored to Manipur following a bilateral treaty *Treaty of Yandaboo*, signed in 1826 in between the British Crown representative and the representative of the Burmese Government. By this treaty, the Burmese power in Asia and the imperial colonial power of the British Crown had accorded multilateral international recognition to the independent and sovereignty of the early State of Manipur. In 1835, the British set-up in Manipur a Political Agency, which was supposedly a Consulate in that period and it continued for a long time. The British power and the Manipur power had continued the friendly relationship by mutually opening Political Agency. The Manipur Power opened the Political Agency of Manipur in the British Territory at Lakhimpur (Cachar) as well as at Calcutta. The Anglo-Manipuri friendship was established for the first time in 1762[5], when a treaty had been signed between the representative of Maharajah Jay Singh (*alias*) Bhagyachandra of Manipur and Mr. Harry Verelst, Chief of the Chittagong Factory on behalf of the British Crown on the 14th September, 1762 (*Annexure No. II*). The treaty is a testimony to the independent, sovereign political Status of Manipur (known to British as Meckley). The basic parameters of an independent state, as stipulated by the Montevido Convention, 1933, viz., (a) territory, (b) population, (c) government and (d) capacity to maintain external relations, had been found in the State of Manipur. Manipur had, therefore, been recognised as sovereign state in as early as 1762 AD. The present Indian state did not exist in 1762.

1.6. There was mutually protective Anglo-Manipuri arrangement in between the Manipur Power when the British Viceroy had a summit meeting with Maharaja Chadrakirti of Manipur in August, 1874. By this arrangement in between the Manipur and the British powers, both the contracting parties had agreed to assist one another in the mutual and reciprocal interests of both the powers. The relationship broke down in 1891 March, when the aggressive British army had initially been defeated by the Manipuri army on 24.3.1891 and the Manipuri army had finally been defeated on 25 April, 1891. However, the British Queen did not annex Manipur to her empire[6] (*Annexure III*). At her worst situation, Manipur remained an international protectorate.

1.7. Subsequently, the British had military occupation in the State of Manipur till 1907 by totally disarming the Manipuris to the last man. However, the Queen did not annex the State of Manipur as part of the British Colony to the British territory for the several reasons (*Annexure No. III*). The British Parliamentary Proceedings on the subject would be found in the Hansards of U.K. in June and July 1891. Even after the defeat of Manipur, it had not been annexed to or colonised by the British although the British Crown considerably interfered in the local administration of Manipur by assuming the latter as an International Protectorate. Manipur was not a part of India in this period.

1.8. From the Manipuri perception, it was a political intervention in Manipur's political sovereignty. Manipur had been labelled as a Native State in the subcontinent of India from the British perspective. Thereafter, in fact, from the Manipur perspective, Manipur had never been a constituent of India, as this Asian State of Mongolian race and Mongolian population is completely different from the other so-called Native States of the Indian subcontinent, which are truly the realm of the Aryan and Dravidian races. Further, the leaders of the Indian freedom fighters and the Congress Party, led by Aryan leaders like M.K. Gandhi, J.L. Nehru and Sardar Patel had consistently defined the Native States of India as a blood-relation State, which means an Aryan or a Dravidian State. Since, Manipur is a Mongolian State, it had never been a part of Ancient State of the present British-created India. It is quite clear that no Mongolian State could ever be considered as a constituent State of the Aryan and Dravidian peoples, who are racially integrated. The Manipuris are alien race, subjugated, occupied and oppressed by the foreign Indian rulers. The colonial officials of India made attempts to dilute the independence of Manipur by citing her as one of the 560 native states.

II. The Manipur People—A People

2.01. The 2 million indigenous Manipur people comprising 31 population groups (clans) speaking Tibeto-Burman or, Sino-Tibetan language having their common pedigree from a common Mongolian ancestor constitutes a *People* or, nation absolutely distinguishable from the Indian or, the *Mayangs* as they are so known to the indigenous Manipur people—the Manipuri people in a composite-territorial sense.

2.02. The indigenous Manipur people being the first settlers or, autochthones in the present territorial state, presently occupied by the Indian colonial regime and her occupation army, had organised their own history and nation-state since 33 AD, independent of the historical experience of Indians.

2.03. No pre, proto-history, ancient and medieval history of India including broad-based works of history written by India's first Prime Minister Jawaharlal Nehru viz., Glimpses of World History, Discovery of India, Autobiography, have mentioned Manipur and her indigenous people even once. Even the history books, re-constructed with a view to incorporating India's recent illegal territorial acquisitions and pre-1949 Maps included in the text books do not include Manipur. This gives testimony to the self-evident fact of Manipur people being alien, dependent and foreign to the Indian People.

2.04. The royal chronicle of Manipur—*"Cheitharol Kumbaba*", which had recorded the genealogy of Manipur Kings since 33 AD and proto-history of Manipur as recorded in *"Kangbalol"*—which had noted the first proto-historical King Kangba of the then Manipur, had not been mentioned in any historical ties of Manipur with India. The historical records of neighbouring countries like Tibet or, Burma (Myanmar) have invariably corroborated the absence of Manipur-India historical ties, if any.

2.05. None of the Indian kings—Bharat, Ashoka, Chandragupta, Akbar to the last Indian emperor Bahadur Shah had any links with Manipur, let alone their temporary sway and administration. The British Crown who ruled India since 1858, in similar tradition, did not rule Manipur till the lapse of British intervention or Paramountcy in 1947. Manipur had remained an international protectorate of the British till 1947.

2.06. The native states of India save Manipur had been the successors to the Sikh, Hindu or, Maratha empires, notwithstanding the British consideration and treatment of Manipur like any other Indian states.

2.07. The status of the Manipur people as a 'PEOPLE' is decided by the following criteria: *Firstly,* the indigenous Manipur people being Mongolians are racially different from the Indian who are Aryan-Dravidians. Dr. Sunitikumar Chatterjee, the most renowned Indologist in his major work—'Kirata Jana Krti' admits this distinction. *Secondly,* Dr. Grierson in his most authoritative volumes of the Linguistic Survey of India, had recorded that the Manipur people are speakers of Tibeto-Burman language, unlike the Indians. *Thirdly,* as corroborated by all historical accounts of both Manipur and India, the people of these two countries had been distinctive, different and alien to each other in the last several centuries. *Fourthly,* Manipur state had remained independent of India till the latter had unlawfully and coercively annexed the former. *Fifthly,* the Manipur indigenous people have been subjugated, dominated and oppressed by an alien, foreign government of India.

2.08. Following the unlawful Indian *annexation* of Manipur, the demographic composition of Manipur has been dramatically altered during the half-a century old foreign, Indian occupation of Manipur. No better testimony could be addressed to this population grafting issue than by what the government of Manipur admitted in 1984 corroborated by the government of India's occasional statements on the subject. Subsequently, the predominantly Mongolian population of the state has been considerably altered.

2.09. The Manipur people as a 'PEOPLE' had not been consulted at the time of Indian annexation of Manipur in 1949 (*see* Annexation *infra*). This denial of popular consultation gives evidence of the Indian colonial behaviour.

2.10. The Manipur people, who had not exercised their inalienable right to *self-determination* in 1949 has not abdicated this right in any sense of the term. This right of a people has to be exercised as yet.

2.11. The government of India is run by the executive constituted by a President, a Union Cabinet of about 50 ministers, the Indian army led by hundreds of generals, an apex court—the Supreme Court of India and several creatures of the Constitution. No Manipur people had ever been inducted into these top echelons of power during the last half-a century. In a parliament of 793 Members of Parliament, only three members hail from Manipur. Besides, the local government and assembly have been held so as to masquerade a representative form of government at the local, state level. Similar elections have been held in East Timor also by Indonesian government. *Manipur is a de facto non-self-governing territory since the Indian annexation in 1949 and the Manipur indigenous people are non-self-governing people.*

2.12. However, the state-of-the-art colonial propaganda has successfully projected the non-self-governing people and territory of Manipur as one having a fully representative form of government and internal democracy, by stating that local elections are being held periodically, whereas, these farcical colonial elections, processed under the nose of the world's third largest army institutionalising large-scale corruption and bribery have not reflected the genuine wishes and aspirations of a people, let alone a plebiscite or referendum. 3,000 Indian dailies and powerful electronic multi-media cover-up the genuine aspirations of the non-self-governing indigenous people of Manipur. The Indian Colonial machinery has successfully divided Manipuri People into Meiteis, Nagas, Kukis so and so forth, thereby encouraging balkanisation of the 2000-year-old territorial integrity of Manipur[6a], whereas the boundary of Manipur can never be disturbed or altered to the prejudice of Manipur under *'UTI Possidetis Juris'* rule of International Law, that has been recurrently affirmed by the ICJ.

2.13. The colonial, non-self-governing status of Manipur people would remain unredressed as such, unless the UN includes Manipur in the mandate for de-colonisation by incorporating her in the list of non-self-governing people, through the good offices of the Special Committee on De-colonisation and the Fourth Committee of the UN General Assembly. The contemporary development of International Law has to take the publicists seriously. Jorri Duursman in his work —"Fragmentation and the international relations of Micro-States" observes—"Peoples who find themselves in similar circumstances as colonies will enjoy a complete right of self-determination even if they are not specifically mentioned in the list of Non-Self-Governing or Trust Territories." (Cambridge University Press, 1996 ISBN 0 521 56360 7, page 83).

2.14. The UN Declaration on Principles of International Law concerning Friendly Relations and Co-operation among state, 24 October, 1970 (UN GA Resolution 2625 para. 6) provides that

> "**6.** The territory of a colony or other Non-Self-Governing

> Territory has, under the Charter, a status separate and distinct status under the Charter shall exist until the people of the colony or Non-Self-Governing Territory have exercised their right of self-determination in accordance with the Charter, and particularly its purposes and principles."

The above-mentioned principle is applicable to Manipur, which is a *de facto* colony or, Non-Self-Governing territory of colonial power—India. *The UN and its members have the obligation to de-colonise Manipur either by enlarging or, modifying its mandate or, by way of appropriate intervention in order to eradicate colonialism in its wholeness.*

2.15. The UN shall be performing its Charter obligations, provided it sends a visiting or fact-finding mission to Manipur on a war-footing, before it takes a decision on this petition and a decision could be taken after *giving a full hearing to both the colonised people and the metropolitan colonising power—India.*

2.16. The government of India, on her own had accepted that the word "Peoples" applies to a large compact group, who made a conscious demand for the right of self-determination (see UN Doc. E/CN.4/SR. 2256 (1952) p.5). The 2 million-strong indigenous Manipur people in their compactness within the territory of Manipur, invariably constitute the 'People', as defined by India. *The government of India should, therefore, initiate the process of self-determination (both internal and external) for the indigenous Manipur People before 2000 AD.*

III. Military Siege and Illegal Annexation

3.01. Manipur King Maharajah Bodhachandra Singh had acceded only three subjects of *defence, external affairs* and *communications* to the then dominion of India as per the agreement or treaty signed on 11.8.1947. It was preceded by an earlier agreement, known as the Standstill Agreement. The agreement was signed by the Manipur Maharaja with a political entity—pre-independent India which did not have treaty-making power as on 11.8.1947 and as such the validity of the Accession Treaty is doubtful and questionable since India became legally independent and sovereign only on 15.8.1947, following the Indian Independence Act, 1947. Manipur became independent as per Section 7(1)(b) of the Indian Independence Act,

1947 (*Annexure No. IV*). By a proviso of Section 7(1)(b) and (c) of the aforesaid Act, whatever prejudicial relation Manipur had with the British Government before independence had been denounced and repudiated at the time, when Manipur adopted her own 1947 Constitution for installing a popular democratic government of the state with a constitutional monarch, as titular figurehead. The promulgation of the Manipur State Constitution Act, 1947 (*Annexure No. V*) and the Indian Independence Act, 1947, had washed out the obligation if any arising out of the *Instrument of Accession*[7]. Manipur state has not been bound by the agreement accordingly.

3.02. In a number of Privy Purse cases and similar other cases, the Supreme Court of India had closely examined the political status of the native States of India in the pre-1947, 1947 and post-1947 periods before their merger to India. It had consistently as well as categorically held and decided in its rulings given since 1954 till 1993 that *the Native State is fully independent and sovereign in 1947* during the relevant period (*Annexure No. VI*). Therefore, it is evidently clear and irrefutable that Manipur, which was considered as native State even from the British perspective, had become fully independent and sovereign on and from 15.8.1947. Further, its political status was an independent and sovereign ancient Asian State, which retained its independent and sovereign political status till 14.10.1949, although it did not join the United Nations. Being a land-locked, primitive state, the rulers lacked the information for seeking access to the UN.

3.03. As per the UN GA Resolution 2625 of 1970, the *Right to Self-determination* can be exercised by a people, who had reached a certain level of awareness and as such, the people of Manipur lacked the primary awareness—qualification to exercise their *right to Self-determination* in 1947-1949, at the time when Indian colonial power laid the trappings for military siege, occupation and *annexation* of Manipur in 1949. The signing of the *Instrument of Accession* by the King of Manipur and subsequent treacherous trappings had deprived the people of Manipur to exercise the right to self-determination in 1947-1949. But for the geographical and geo-political isolation, Manipur should not miss the opportunity of seeking UN membership in 1947. This basic right cannot be extinguished either as it had not been excercised in the past.

3.04. The independence and sovereignty of Manipur had been strengthened, when Manipur adopted her own political constitution, namely, the 'Manipur State Constitution Act, 1947' (*Annexure*

No. V). And an elected popular and responsible Government had been installed in the form of Manipur Legislative Assembly (*read as Parliament*), constituted by 53 members, duly elected by universal adult-franchise and a council of Ministers to aid and advise the Maharajah as the constitutional head had also been installed. As per the basic parameters of the Montevido Convention, 1933 that qualifies a state, Manipur constituted an independent State in 1947 till 1949.

3.05. The *illegal annexation* of Manipur by India on 15 October 1949 has been a carefully drawn-out plan, measured by stages.

Chronology of Illegal Annexation[8] of Manipur

		1947
1.	19 April	Nehru ultimatum to States—Threats with hostility.
2.	15 May	Manipur Draft Constitution ready.
3.	20 May	British Cabinet resolution—State to be fully independent.
3a.	2 June	Nehru-Mountbatten's Secret Revised Plan.
4.	3 June	Mountbatten's Negative attitude to the States.
5.	15 June	AICC stand: State's sovereignty lies with State people.
6.	17 June	Jinnah categorical: States to be independent, sovereign.
7.	25 June	Interim Cabinet accepts state department creation.
8.	1 July	Manipur King (Maharajah) becomes nominal figurehead.
9.	2 July	Assam-Manipur agreement: Indian agent to stay in Imphal.
10.	2 July	Secretary of State Listowell: States not subject to British Parliamentary legislation.

(*Contd.*)

11.	5 July	Patel on Blood theory, all knit by bond of blood possibly Aryan-Dravidian blood theory (?) of State.
12.	5 July	Gandhi to Mountbatten: States should not be independent. Gandhi possibly wants Indian empire (not British).
13.	10 July	Indian Independence Act, 1947: British suzerainty over States in Indian continent lapses.
14.	25 July	Mountbatten officially declares States' independence.
15.	26 July	Manipur Constitution adopted.
16.	28 July	Mountbatten reception to Rulers (Lunch on August 1): diplomatically pressurizes for Indian Dominion (His ambition to be India's Governor General).
17.	31 July	States Negotiating Committee approves 2 agreement drafts.
18.	8 August	Mountbatten reports to Listowell: States remain independent save three subjects—States not committed to Indian Constitution or, Government of India Act, 1935 etc.
19.	9 August	Listowell approves Mountbatten's 25 July proclamation.
20.	10 August	Manipur King directly takes over hill administration.
21.	11 August	King signs Standstill Agreement and Instrument of Accession: Under clauses 7 and 8, Manipur's independence retained in the escape clause (cf. 5 April 1946 meeting of Nikhil Manipur Mahasabha and MPM., Reso. 6 part II, Manipur to be independent—R.K. Bhubon in Chair).

(*Contd.*)

22.	14 August	King swears in the Interim Council: Manipur, proclaimed independent.
23.	15 August	King hoists PAKHANGBA FLAG in Council hall, Paramountcy, cleared in Manipur.
24.	28 August	King reiterates — Manipur is sovereign.
25.	6 November	Indian Congress agent Debeshwar Sharma admits that Manipur is Sovereign: Sovereignty lies with Manipur people (categorical).
		1948
26.	1st January	Deputy P.M. of India Sardar Patel visits Shillong for 3 days.
27.	2nd January	Manipur King attends Rulers' meeting at Shillong, attended by Sardar Patel and States Ministry—Later announced that Manipur becomes independent.
28.	28th February	Hijam Irabot attends Calcutta Communist Conference with Asian revolutionaries—Adopts militant Chinese revolutionary line (later on practised too).
29.	18th April	Rawal Amar Singh takes Dewan's charge.
30.	25th May	Congress Election Manifesto: To abide by Manipur Constitution (Congress members—majority in the Constitution drafting Committee).
31.	26th May	Assam Prime Minister Gopinath Bordoloi pleads Autonomy for Manipur State.
32.	11th June-27rd July	Manipur Assembly Election—popular Government.

(*Contd.*)

33.	23rd June-3rd July	Akbar Hydari's reconnaissance to annex Manipur.
34.	2nd August	Akbar Hydari's letter to the King: Dewan simply watches TREATY RELATIONS between two countries —Manipur and India. He is very categorical about the word Treaty like Katju.
35.	22nd August	Akbar Hydari abolishes Dominion agency.
36.	22nd August	P.C. Ghosh preaches Purbanchal theory meeting organised by Tompok Congress.
37.	18th September	Manipur Hills and Plains meeting opposes Ghosh proposal.
38.	20th September	Tomal Congress writes to Indian Constituent Assembly: Manipur independent unit of India (probably in the sense of continent).
39.	21st September	Manipur State Council declares Krishak Sabha and Praja Sangha unlawful organisations.
40.	21st September	Hijam Irabot goes underground.
41.	18th October	Manipur Legislative Assembly opened: popular sovereign government operates.
42.	26th November	Prajashanti-led government (non-Congress) sworn in; Insignificant Congress minority propagates for Indian annexation of Manipur: Annexation would nullify unlawfully the Manipur Constitution, they themselves drafted in the committee.
43.	29th November	Priyobarta holds C.M. post plus Dewanship.

(Contd.)

		1949
44.	10th March	Assembly Question Number 21 by L. Achou about Government's knowledge of the information about Manipur's Merger with India.
45.	22nd March	Assam Governor Shri Prakasa discusses with King about Manipur Communist insurgency: Rustomji Chatterjee at Imphal.
46.	14th April	Indian Government asks King to transfer all power to Dewan (an unconstitutional, parallel centre in power).
47.	16th April	King appoints Major General Amar Singh as Dewan.
48.	5th June	Manipur Socialist Party Meeting urges for referendum on Manipur-India relation.
49.	25th June	Prakasa secret Memo. to King—India does not recognise Manipur State Council and the elected assembly (popular sovereign).
50.	26th July	Congress bulletin 4: Indian Congress backs Manipur Congress—slogan to dethrone the Constitutional figurehead—King.
51.	27th July	Hill M.L.As oppose annexation of Manipur by India.
52.	29th July	Hill M.L.As Against annexation of Manipur by India.
53.	3rd August	Public meeting resolution to India's Prime Minister, Manipur cannot be merged with India.
54.	15th August	4,000 Congressmen celebrate Independence day and Student's Federation hoists black flag. Ex. Minister Dr. Leiren Hoists black flag.

(*Contd.*)

55.	25th August	Ruling Manipur M.L.As against annexation of Manipur, Meeting resolution to Deputy Prime Minister, India not to annex Manipur to his country.
56.	7th September	Shri Prakasa Telegrammes King to discuss 'affairs of State' at Shillong.
57.	8th September	Young Socialist League Meeting opposes annexation.
58.	13th September	Bhagyabati Patrica hints annexation.
59.	14th September	Speaker T.S. Tiang Kham on issue of annexation.
60.	15th September	Maharaja leaves Imphal for Shillong.
61.	17th September	King reaches Shillong.
62.	18th-19th September	King communicates to Indian agent at Shillong that he lacks capacity to enter into treaty, as all political powers have been lawfully transferred to people.
63.	18th September	Shri Prakasa telegrammes to Patel and V.P. Menon: Manipur Maharajah detained under regulation III and 'ANY OTHER MEANS' (code language of house arrest of King under military siege) — King as captive, mental torture and coercion by Indian forces.
64.	18th September	P.S. to King writes to Shillong S.P. to withdraw forces encircling Manipur King—siege continues—Maharajah's all communication lines, snapped. Literally, he was a captive and prisoner.
65.	20th September	Psychic oppression and siege continues on the King.
66.	21st September	King, coerced under duress to sign annexation treaty.

(*Contd.*)

67.	21st September	Bhagyabati Patrica—Manipur public opinion: Manipur cannot be subjugated and made subservient to a foreign nation (India).
68.	25th September	Maharajah leaves Shillong.
69.	15th October	Mr. Velody, State Ministry of India occupies Manipur; Congress celebrates the loss of their motherland. Major General Amar Singh takes over Manipur against peoples' will.
70.	15th Oct.	Gazette of India, Ministry of State, Notification No. 219 dated 15th October, 1949 order to dissolve popular Ministry and the elected Manipur Legislative Assembly. (suspended sovereignty).

3.06. The Manipur King Maharajah Bodhachandra Singh had been kept under *Regulation III and "any other means" which empowered military siege, arrest and captivity of Manipur King* by the Indian army at Shillong from the 17th to the 21st September, 1949. Sri Prakasa, Governor of Assam[9] sent the following Telegram to Sardar Patel, Deputy Prime Minister of India describing the abduction and captivity of Manipur King for coercing him to sign the Manipur Annexation agreement, 1949:

> "HH (*sic.* Manipur king) must not under any circumstances be allowed to return to Manipur with his advisors and I have accordingly instructed police to detain here his party if they attempt to return before signing of agreement (*sic.* 1949 Merger Agreement).
>
> Please telegraph immediately repeat immediately authority for detention of HH and advisers under Regulation III (*sic.* abduction and kidnapping of the king by foreign Indian security forces) or by whatever other means you consider might be appropriate.

Have already warned sub-area to be prepared for any eventuality (*sic.* covert military aggression and coup) in Manipur. Grateful for further instructions. Ends."

The further instructions as cited above are undoubtedly mandate for invasion in Manipur and coup of the power-centre of the sovereign state of Manipur. Orders of invasion and *aggression* are not yet made public. The appropriate committee of the UN should seek all the comprehensive documents of the invasion of Manipur by the Indian invading army. The Defence Ministry and the External Affairs Ministry of India classify the *aggression* as top secret.

3.07. The Manipur Maharajah in captivity of the enemy was physically and mentally forced to sign the *Manipur Merger Agreement* on 21.9.1949 under *duress* and *coercion* (*Annexure No. VII*). The Manipur Maharajah had formally communicated to the representative of the Government of India at Shillong that he was no longer functioning as a plenipotentiary of Manipur, since the political power had been totally transferred to the people of Manipur. The Maharajah being a constitutional monarch did not have any power under the Cabinet system of government to sign any effective and valid agreement or treaty with the foreign Government of India. In the past, the Government of India had interfered in the Manipur Administration by forcing the Manipur Maharajah to appoint one Major General Rawal Amar of the colonial Indian army as a Dewan of the State, which post had been manifestly extraneous and unconstitutional, as per the provisions of the Manipur State Constitution Act, 1947. These interventions are precursor to the Indian *aggression* in Manipur in 1949.

3.08. The Government of India had incited and instigated the so-called Manipur Congressmen the Aryan fifth columnists in Manipur, to persuade and press the Manipur Administration to merge the State of Manipur with India. However, the majority of the people's representatives of the 53 members Member Assembly (*read Parliament*) had opposed Indian annexation of Manipur, while only 13 Congress Deputies (members) who had been in the microscopic minority welcomed it. Besides, the people of Manipur in general had opposed the *annexation* by holding public meetings on 3.8.1949, 25.8.1949, 8.9.1949, 14.10.1996 and on several occasions till date. The forcible *annexation* of the sovereign State of Manipur by the foreign Indian administration has been null and void under both the customary International Law and the Vienna Convention of Treaties[10], 1969 *vide* its article nos. 49, 51 and 52 which render treaty reached by *fraud* and *coercion* as void. The Indian *annexation* of Manipur in 1949 is a blatant violation of article 2(4) of the UN Charter, the UN GA Resolution 2625 of 1970 and other norms of state practices of that period.

3.09. The popular resistance to India's *annexation* of Manipur State had been rendered by the militant guerillas even before Manipur was subsequently annexed. The Communist Party of Manipur in that period had maintained ties with the Communist Parties of Burma (now Myanmar) and also with her Indian counterpart. It had the militant upsurge against the Indian *colonialism* since 1949 onwards till 1950-51; however, the colossal Indian occupation army suppressed the movement by repressive means for half a century. Notwithstanding the gagging of the Indian media and ignorance of the world Christian media, *Manipur National Liberation Movements* had been proactive in 1950-51, 1963, 1964, 1969, 1978 onwards unremittingly decades before Western Sahara, East Timor, Northern Ireland, Kosovo sparked off.

IV. NATIONAL LIBERATION MOVEMENT—GENESIS[11]

4.01. Subsequently after the Manipuri armed struggle[12] in 1949 and 1950 against *Indian colonialism* and *occupation,* the Manipur Nationalist Party in the 1950s had demanded in public the revocation of the *Manipur Merger Agreement* with India. Several representatives of various parties including Shri Yangmaso Saiza, a Manipuri Tangkhul from Ukhrul district of Manipur, who later became Chief Minister of Manipur, resisted the annexation of Manipur. Even after the Indian *annexation* of Manipur, popular movements have ceaselessly continued. Although the methods of protests had been partly democratic and partly militant, *in the later 1960s, national liberation movement had turned out proactive in Manipur to free Manipur from Indian subjugation and colonisation. The Manipur National Liberation Movement* in 1960s had been a precursor of the world-wide de-colonisation movements that liberated a hundred independent States of the world. The UN took notice of European colonisation and ignored Indian colonisation.

4.02. In late 1960s, *National Liberation Movement* of Manipur and militant resistance had been started by the Meetei State Committee that militarily resisted the Indian forces. It was closely followed by the Revolutionary Government of Manipur (RGM). The nucleus of a sister liberation struggle had been seeded in 1964. After the dismantling and disbandment of the RGM, the Revolutionary People's Front (RPF, the political wing of the People's Liberation Army of Manipur) was formed on 25 February, 1979 and the PLA started operating for the liberation of Manipur from the Indian occupation army and Indian *colonialism* along with several sister organisations. In 1978, there had been PLA's full scale armed resistance all over the State against the Indian occupation army after sending publicity materials—*'DAWN'* to all embassies of the world. Since then, the Manipur freedom fighters unremittingly opposed militarily the Indian occupation army. Several hundreds of PLA freedom—fighters have laid down their lives to liberate their motherland.

4.03. Professor Emeritus V.V. Rao of the University of Gauhati in his books on the North-Eastern India, has recorded that the PLA has the broad vision encompassing the interest of all the colonised, subjugated people elsewhere, beyond the contours of Manipur. In spite of the PLA's best efforts to render the Manipur national question and national liberation, *an international agenda of the world community by enlightening all the embassies of the countries, which received series of volumes of—"DAWN" publication,* the members of the UN have failed to raise the issue of *Manipur National Liberation* on the floor of the General Assembly or, the Security Council of the United Nations. Eradication of *colonialism* by the UN by 2000 AD shall not be completed, therefore, without listing the *colonialism* of Manipur in the UN agenda, which has been due since the UN members individually took note of the issue from the "DAWN" in 1978. The UN should have listed East Timor and Manipur in the same slot of colonised states or, people before two decades. Several national daily papers of Indian *colonialism*, however, flashed the international attention, as sought by PLA through all the embassies. The *national liberation movement of Manipur* has been consistently opposing the colonial Government of India on political terms and had been struggling against the occupation army of India on military terms since the time of the Indian *annexation* of Manipur in 1949 till today. The PLA's armed resistance against the Indian occupation was contemporaries with FRETLIN's resistance in East Timor and POLISARIO's resistance in Western Sahara. The UN selectively took up similar cases by shelving de-colonisation of Manipur in the cold freeze. Ironically, the UN discriminates Indian colonialism against European *colonialism*.

4.04. Very few liberation movements in the world have been left outside the closest attention of the UN and her members except the half-century old *National Liberation Movement of Manipur.* The UN objective of eradicating *colonialism* by 2000 AD would remain a futility without de-colonising Manipur and her neighbourhood colonies of India like Assam, Nagaland and Tripura. The colonial government of India had permanently perpetuated *colonialism* of Manipur by proclaiming the *national liberation movements*[13] including the armed struggle triggered off by the PLA (RPF) since 1978 as unlawful organisation under the Prevention of Unlawful Activities Act, 1967 and suppressing the human rights[14] since 1958 by invoking the draconian, black Law the Armed Forces (Special) Powers Act, 1958 (amended in 1972), the Punjab Security of State Act, 1953, the Terrorists and Disruptive Activities Prevention Act, 1985 and the National Security Act, among other equally repressive laws. Absolutely in self-defence and self-preservation, the occupation army is resisted by the movement.

4.05. The colonial government of India has extrajudicially liquidated, tortured, molested, raped, maimed, injured thousands of Manipuris on the hills (Manipuri Tangkhuls, Mao, Kukis etc.) and Manipuri in the valley (Meiteis etc.) and destroyed properties worth crores annually. For adult population of 9 lakh Manipuris (in 19 lakh population), Indian security forces numbering about 90,000 are put into repressive service for colonial occupation. 30,000 Manipuri youths are drug/AIDS infected as a result of counter-insurgency approach of the *colonialism.*

V. SOCIO-ECONOMIC AND POLITICAL COLONISATION

5.01. The people of Manipur have been deprived of their inalienable birth-right to determine their political and socio-economic status on their own due to Indian colonial process, subjugation, alien and racist national oppression. They have been deprived of their inalienable right to exploit their natural resources as per their *self-determination* and this right has to be restored to them. Following the ICJ verdict, 1995 on Timor Gap Treaty, it is a criminal wrong for India to usurp the natural resources of Manipur. They have to exercise their inalienable right to *self-determination* for their permanent sovereignty over their natural resources, biomass, water-bodies, fauna and flora, among others.

5.02. The pre-dominantly Mongolian population of Manipur has been subjugated by the Indian racist and colonial regime which represents only the blue blood of the Aryan and Dravidian races (Annex No. VIII, Indian Party Representatives and Manipur Peoples, Photo). The administering power, i.e., the Indian colonial regime has never appointed any indigenous people of Manipur who are of Mongolian origin to any important position whatsoever in the Indian colonial regime. The people of Mongolian origin are treated as subjects and subjugated race only to be ruled by the occupation army. Since 1949 onwards till today, not a single day has ever passed in Manipur without the repressive measures taken by the Indian colonial army by torturing, insulting or extra-judicially murdering the indigenous people of Manipur. As cited above, a number of repressive laws or laws of legitimizing State Terrorism including the *Armed Forces (Special) Powers Act, 1958,* the Terrorist and Disruptive Activities (Prevention) Act, 1987 and several other draconian laws have been systematically introduced and enforced in the State of Manipur in order to subjugate the people of Manipur and incapacitate them from determining their own political destiny (Annexure No. IX). The UN Human Rights Committee and global NGOs have denounced them as incompatible with the International Bill of Rights, 1966 to which the colonial government of India has been a party. The government of India is accountable for enacting laws incompatible with the Covenants, ratified by her.

5.03. Under Section 4 of the *Armed Forces (Special) Powers Act, 1958*, the Armed Forces of the Union of India have been empowered to kill anybody on suspicion or out of hatred without any judicial process. Besides, this has enormously encouraged the Indian Armed Forces to precipitate and heighten their extra-judicial torture and execution of the Mongolian people bordering on genocide of the Mongolian races in Manipur. Even the Supreme Court of India, upheld the black law by its judgement given on 27 November, 1997. Not a single Manipuri has been appointed to the Supreme Court in the last half a century of *annexation.* These judges are racists and chauvinists like their political mentors.

5.04. It may be added that the Aryan and Dravidian racists in the Indian colonial regime have been guided by sacred religious scriptures like the *'Manusmrity'*[15]. In all its chapters, it authorised Aryan and

Dravidian racists, specially persons from high castes, to execute or torture women, infants and the races who are not of Dravidian or Aryan origin. The people of Manipur are not Hindu Sudras but Mongolians. From their in-built mental perspective, they cannot help but to conceive every people of Manipur as sub-Sudra, who is to be physically tortured and slaughtered. Hence, from the perspective of the Indian Colonial Army, whenever they physically execute any Mongolian people, they conscientiously assume that they have performed a sacred religious duty and rite to fulfil the scriptural mandate of their racist ancestors. It may be recalled that the *'Arthasastra'*[16] *of Kautilya* the equivalent of a military manual of colonial Blue books, gives religious sanctity to the suppression and wiping out of smaller nations and countries in order to establish Indian *imperialism* and *colonialism.* Therefore, the Indian Colonial Army and the Indian colonial political rulers have no alternative than cherishing a heritage of conquering smaller nations and physically executing people who are not of Aryan or Dravidian origin. The British Colonial Power, however, did not have such a transmitted mandate from their Bible. Indian Colonial regime and the Indian Colonial Army operated in such sophisticated and orchestrated way that the International community cannot easily understand or recognise the entire consequences of the overt and covert Indian *colonialism,* unless the UN despatches visiting missions to Manipur. The UN has not been successful to appoint a Special Human Rights Rapporteur for India, although one has been appointed for Myanmar.

5.05. The colonial development process and the colonial economy had not been helpful to the people of Manipur. Not a single major industry, much less an important establishment has ever been established in Manipur. Whereas several hundreds of crores of Rupees have been spent apparently on paper maintained for the record in order to refuel and recycle their colonial apparatus, quite a few families in Manipur are also used as colonial subsidiaries, the economic condition of the average people of Manipur specially those in the hill areas has not improved even up to the level of subsistence. People survive on grassroots in the Manipur hill areas because of colonial economic process. The Manipuri hillsmen and plainsmen are divided by the Presidential approval to a divisive law—the Manipur Land and Revenue Act, 1960 which debar plainsmen to seek access to Manipur hills. The apartheid has been created.

5.06. The colonial economy of Manipur[16a] has pushed down

68 per cent of Manipur people below the Poverty line. Centre for Monitoring Indian Economy in 1992-93 indicated that whereas Indian state of Punjab has reached index of 205, Manipur's index is 71. As per the Asian Development Bank Report, 11 May, 1997, Manipur rice production in kg/hectare is 1400 (against Indian average of 1740), Road in 100 sq. km. in Manipur is 32.64 km (against Indian average of 62.82 km), Banking credit in Manipur is Rs. 44/- (Indian is Rs. 1722.11), p.c.i. of Manipur is Rs. 5,326/- (against Indian average of Rs. 6,929/-), Annual budget of Rs. 400+ crore is literally for the maintenance of 90,000 colonial Indian army, innumerable mercenaries, police, espionage, supporting pro-colonial families and half the budget allocation is not available due to colonial fiscal policy.

5.07. We have living testimony of the socio-cultural colonisation of the indigenous people of Manipur by the casteist and racist socio-cultural apparatus of India. Firstly, the captive market is at the hands of Hindustanis; Secondly, no industry has been set-up for attaining industrial growth; Thirdly, all the natural resources have been exploited by the colonial regime; Fourthly, Manipur survives on subsistence economy. Details will be presented to the UN Visiting Mission. Not a single watch, electronic industry has been set up in Manipur, let alone major and heavy industries.

5.08. In sum, the *national liberation movements in Manipur* have strongly endorsed the view that Manipur has socio-economically and politically been exploited by the Indian colonial regime beside the political and military subjugation of the people of Manipur since 1949 till today. Majority of the colonised Manipuris have to learn Hindi and baptised in colonial religion.

5.09. Proxy elections are conducted by spending crores of Indian Rupees in order to perpetuate colonialism through quislings, puppet regimes and fifth columnists under the proxy election process by way of misleading the illiterate electorate. The Indian colonial regime can in no way justify the electoral process whatsoever, since the people of Manipur cannot exercise their *"independent political will" and resolve their destiny at the gunpoint of the massive, racist Indian colonial army and several thousands of mercenaries, subversives and spies.* The colonial elections held in the mighty presence of occupation army, mercenaries and pouring crores of rupees for bribery have debarred the people to exercise their free will and no plebiscite on de-colonisation had ever been held. Alcoholics, drugs, heroin, brown sugar and narcotics are freely distributed to the voters in the colonial elections.

VI. On Continuation of the Sovereign State of Manipur

6.01. The sovereign State of Manipur continues to exist since the Christian era, despite unlawful, political and military occupation by a foreign colonial power—India. Therefore, India and her intervention in Manipur is a political process. The nature of the sovereign State of Manipur is represented as follows:

6.02. Firstly, the sovereign status of Manipur state had been recognised bilaterally, when Manipur entered the Anglo-Manipuri Friendship Treaty in 1762 AD (*Annexure No. II*). The international recognition is vital, as Montevido Convention, 1933 defined independent state as one capable of entering treaty relations.

6.03. Secondly, the political sovereign independence of Manipur had been officially recognised by both the Burmese Government and the British Government as per the provisions of the Yandaboo treaty, 1826 *(Annexure No. X)*. The independent political status of Manipur has once again been re-affirmed in the 19th century.

6.04. Thirdly, after the military defeat of Manipur by the British army in 1891, the British Government did not annex Manipur to its empire (*Annexure No. III*); that itself gives testimony to the unremitting independence of Manipur. The debate on the independent political status of Manipur in the British Parliament for nearly one month in 1891 has been recorded in the Hansards[17]. In 1891, Churachand was Manipur King and British official Maxwell ruled the country. The British transferred the charge of administration to Manipur King on 17 May 1907. In 1916, the British official became the President of Manipur Darbar under the supervision of the King. In 1931, Manipur opened direct external relations with British India. In 1941, Maharajah Bodhachandra had succeeded Maharajah Churachand. Since 1942, Manipur unlike India has been the theatre of the Second World War. On 26 July, 1946, Manipur established her constitutional government thereby reducing the Maharajah to a titular head. These constitutional developments re-established the sovereign, independent status of Manipur and the official independence was declared on 14-15 August, 1947.

6.05. Fourthly, despite the British and Indian interference in Manipur affairs, Manipur became fully independent and sovereign on 15.8.1947 *vide* Indian Independence Act, 1947 (*Annexure No. IV*, and *Annexure No. VI* Indian Supreme Court rulings, 1954 to 1993). Manipur has fully regained her full sovereignty, which had been intervened by the British Paramountcy that retained the former as international protectorate.

6.06. Fifthly, although Manipur had entered into the treaty known as the *Instrument of Accession* on 11.8.1947, Manipur did not transfer more than 3 subjects to the Dominion of India. The *Instrument of Accession* was signed on 11.8.1947 (*Annexure No. XI*) in between Manipur and Dominion of India. It had clearly given prerogative right to Manipur to retain her sovereignty and independence and terminate the *Accession* treaty unilaterally, as the treaty did not incorporate a termination clause, as required by customary International Law, that has been codified by the Vienna Convention in 1969 and the subsequent convention.

6.07. Sixth, Manipur State Constitution Act, 1947 (*Annexure No. V*) was in operation at the time of signing the *Merger Agreement* between the Manipur Maharajah (King) who lacked the capacity and authority to enter into any treaty with any power or, the representative of the Government of India on 21.9.1949, since he was not the plenipotentiary of the independent and sovereign state of Manipur of which he was only the constitutional head. The cabinet government that Manipur installed in 1948 after holding elections to the Manipur Assembly (*read Parliament*) had neither authorised the king to sign the 1949 treaty nor ratified the same after 21.9.1949. It may be noted that a valid agreement or, treaty could be signed or, acceded by the plenipotentiary of Manipur as a High contracting party with the Indian government after fulfilling the following conditions:

I. Empowerment by the Manipur Cabinet;
II. Signature by the Chief Minister (read Prime Minister);
III. Constitutional endorsement;
IV. Ratification by the National Assembly (read Parliament);
V. Enactment of a municipal law on the accession of the treaty, as it is being done in Republic of India by now or, British Parliament;
VI. Final endorsement by a Popular referendum or, plebiscite in the event of altering the political status of the state.

The Merger Agreement of 1949 had been Reached in Blatant Violation of These Basic Rules and Therefore, It Had Been Void Ab Initio

6.08. Seventh, the people of Manipur had not deputed a genuine representative, duly elected by the people of Manipur to the then Constituent Assembly of India. Although from the Indian colonial perspective, a foreign national was considered as representative to the Constituent Assembly of India, who helped the illegal *annexation*. Any representation of Manipur people by a person of the colonial country professing to represent the people of Manipur is absolutely inconceivable, preposterous and accordingly null and void, as the foreign national lacked the capacity and jurisdiction. Hence, Manipur cannot be brought within the colonial constitutional framework of India, since it was not part of it. There has been no lawful representation of genuine representative of Manipuri people in the colonial Constitutional Assembly of India. Manipur people have not been a party to the Indian constitutional making process.

6.09. Eighth, no referendum or plebiscite of the people of Manipur had ever been held concerning the *annexation or merger* of Manipur to a foreign country the republic of India, whereas the *annexation* of Junagadh by imperial India in 1948-49 had been justified by three plebiscites held on the *annexation* of the former to the latter. Colonial rulers of India knew that Manipur people as a whole reject the merger with India.

6.10. Ninth, the installation of a colonial government on 15.10.1949 in the soil of Manipur did not repeal the Manipur State Constitution Act, 1947, although the colonial government without having any jurisdiction whatsoever had passed a colonial order under Notification no. 219-p. Gazette of India, Ministry of State, dated 15.10.1949. It illegally and unconstitutionally dissolved the popular Ministry as well as the popular Assembly (*read Parliament*) of Manipur, on the basis of an illegal Manipur Merger Agreement, 1949[18]. Indian proximity-*colonialism* has gobbled up independent Manipur and the UN helplessly remained silent by giving a free-hand to Indian occupation army till today.

6.11. Tenth, there is widespread popular awareness among the people of Manipur that the *Manipur Merger Agreement,* 1949, as stated above is null and void and unconstitutional from the point of view of the Manipur State Constitution Act, 1947. Moreover, it is in the backdrop of contemporary norms of the International Law that the National Convention on the Manipur Merger Issue was convened from the 28th to the 29th October, 1993 in the capital city, Imphal. *The Convention has unanimously resolved in plenum that the impugned Merger Agreement with India on 1949 is illegal* *and unconstitutional,* considering the entire process and circumstances that led to the Manipur Merger Agreement (*Annexure No. XII*).

6.12. Eleventh, the UN Security Council in similar circumstances had proclaimed similar *annexations* illegal, void, and untenable. The Security Council declared *annexation* of Goa by India as illegal (vide S/5033, SCOR, 988th meeting, 18 December 1961). But no liberation movement ensued in Goa. It acted against Iraq under Security Council Resolution No. 660-678 for *annexation* of Kuwait in 1991. The UN declared *annexation* of East Timor and Western Sahara illegal. The UN precedents, contemporary International Law, *Jus Cogens* and Vienna Convention of Law of Treaty would clearly regard *annexation* of Manipur by India in 1949 after two years of the independence of Indian independence unjustified and illegal. The official stance of the colonial government of India that the illegal *annexation* has assumed finality is not only absurd, null and void but also unacceptable to the people of Manipur, who are yet to exercise their *right to self-determination.* The colonial Government has failed to justify her *annexation* of Manipur, under International Law.

6.13. Twelfth, considering the historical materials and the records, documents and treaties which are enclosed herewith, the sovereign and independent political status of Manipur, which had been continuing for at least 2,000 years has been dislocated by the Indian Colonial Administration, and by the physical occupation of the Indian colonial army. The unlawful colonial occupation of Manipur shall have to be terminated by the Indian government at the earliest moment in adherence of the UN eradication of colonialism by 2000 AD. The UN is yet to oversee this process.

VII. RIGHT TO SELF–DETERMINATION

7.01. It is significant to reiterate the absolute commitment of the United Nations to eradicate colonialism in all its forms and manifestations by 2000 AD and to put in record the emergence of 135 independent states in conformity with the global de-colonisation process that sparked off since 1960s and 1970s. The official deadline for eradication of *colonialism* remaining unaltered, *colonialism* will be sustained in proximity-colonies of India like *Manipur, Nagaland, Assam, Tripura and Kashmir* and nearly fifty other territories, many of which are incorporated in the list of 48 unrepresented peoples of the UNPO—the Hague based Unrepresented Nations and Peoples Organisation. These colonies will survive the 2000 AD UN deadline, unless the UN and its main organs initiate proactive de-colonisation, as much as it did in 1960s and 1970s. The UN would not fulfil its objectives of total de-colonisation, in the event of sustaining the above colonies or, peoples who are yet to exercise their *right to self-determination.* India being a member of the UN De-colonisation Committee has to initiate de-colonisation of Manipur.

7.02. The Government of India has the treaty obligations to allow alien, dependent, subjugated and oppressed people like the Manipur people to exercise their inalienable *right to self-determination,* as the Government has rectified the ICCPR, 1966 and ICESCR, 1966, besides its being a regional power which facilitated national liberation and de-colonisation of several colonised peoples in the Third World. The UN Human Rights Committee in 1997, July has urged upon the Government of India to withdraw her reservation in respect of common article 1 of the ICCPR, 1966 and ICESCR, 1966. The government has to comply with this recommendation and report compliance by 2000 AD at the time of submitting the 4th periodic report to the UNHRC *vide* article 40 of the ICCPR, 1966.

7.03. Government of India's declaration in respect of her ratification of the ICCPR, 1966 on 10 April, 1979, is as follows:

ICCPR, Article 1

para 10. It has been the position of India ever since its independence that adherence to self-determination is co-existent with the principle of sovereign equality. The principle of domestic jurisdiction of state as enshrined in the United Nations Charter is to be equally respected.

para 11. In conformity with this position of principle on self-determination, India made the following declaration in 1979 at the time of its accession to the International Covenant on Civil and Political Rights:

> "With reference to article 1 of the International Covenant on Civil and Political Rights, the India, which was under British

imperialism. They might even argue that Manipur and Dominion of India became independent under a common Indian Independence Act, 1947. The absurdity of "historical ties" statement has been rejected by the ICJ in its advisory opinion on Western Sahara. It may be noted very carefully that Indonesia's argument in favour of her *annexation* of East Timor has been rejected by the ICJ judgement in Portugal *vs*. Australia in 1995 and innumerable Government of the Republic of India declares that the words 'the right to self-determination' appearing (in this article) apply to people under foreign domination."

7.04. The Manipuri people, who had never constituted a part of Hindustan or India or, British India had been placed under Indian foreign domination in the event of *the illegal annexation of Manipur in 1949*. The caveat to the declaration makes room for according the *right to self-determination* to the people of Manipur. The Vienna World Conference on Human Rights, 1993 and the UN Human Rights Committee in July, 1997 have mandated the government of India to remove even this narrow caveat and accord the right to deserving people including the Manipuri people who had been sovereign for two millennia before Indian *annexation*. India's present stance[19] prevents the world wide de-colonisation process and hence, she owes an explanation for her defence of *colonialism* of Manipur.

7.05. India's Declaration[20] stipulated that "Declaration contains enunciation of certain basic principles". Paragraph 1 declares, "The subjection of peoples to alien subjugation, domination and exploitation constitutes a denial of fundamental human rights." The people of Manipur obviously falls into the Indian enunciation of alien subjugation and domination. The colonial government of India has to prove that Manipuris are not alien to Indians.

7.06. The people of Manipur, who are colonised by alien Indian administering power are people of non-self-governing territories as much as the East Timorese after Indonesian *annexation* in 1975 constitute people of non-self-governing territories. Indonesian elections had been held in East Timor since 1977, yet East Timor is recognised as non-self-governing territory by the United Nations. Similarly, colonial elections have been held in occupied Manipur by the Indian administering power without any prejudice to the sovereign political status of Manipur.

7.07. The ICJ in Portugal *vs*. Australia, 1995 has decided that East-Timorese have their *right to self-determination erga omnes* (against the whole community). Similarly, the people of Manipur have their *right to self-determination erga omnes*, notwithstanding India's preposterous prevarication against the colonised Manipuris.

VIII. TERRITORIAL INTEGRITY

8.01. The Colonial Government of India defines in her 1950 Constitution, the territorial integrity of India in two places. Firstly, in the first schedule[21] serial No. 19, Manipur is defined as "The territory which immediately before the commencement of this constitution was being administered as if it were a Chief Commissioner's province under the name of Manipur."

8.02. The first schedule itself clearly and categorically records that the territorial State of Manipur preceded the Constitution of India. No other constitutional provision has more clearly given testimony to the **illegal annexation** of Manipur than this provision. Before Indian Commissioner had occupied Manipur, she remained independent till 1949.

8.03. Article 1 of the Constitution of India[22] defines the territory of India as follows: (1) India, that is Bharat, shall be a union of states. (2) [The states and the territories thereof shall be as specified in the first Schedule]. (3) The territory of India shall comprise— (a) the territories of states; (b) the union territories specified in the First Schedule; and (c) such other territories as may be acquired.

8.04. The Constitution of India, being a colonial and imperial instrument imposed upon the occupied people of Manipur after the *illegal annexation*, lacks legal and constitutional validity in regard to the annexed, occupied state of Manipur. East Timor has also been annexed as the 27th province of Indonesia and Kuwait in 1990 as the 9th province of Iraq. The United Nations has denounced these *illegal annexations,* let alone the validity of the colonial Constitution. The *territorial integrity* of India cannot lawfully incorporate colonial, occupied territory of Manipur. Nor can it impair the territorial integrity of Manipur as it existed in 1947 under the *uti Possidetis Juris rule*[23] of International Law.

8.05. The state sovereignty doctrine has been enunciated in articles 2(4) and 2(7) of the UN Charter as well as by the UN GA Resolution 2625, Declaration on Friendly Relations, 1970. The Union

Government of India pleads that her territorial integrity would be impaired if Manipur would be allowed to secede from the Indian Union. The argument may be further strengthened by citing the prevention of disruption of the "national unity and the territorial integrity" of India, as it is understood after the adoption of the 1950 Constitution (see para.6 of the UN GA Resolution 1514(XV) of 14 December, 1960). This argument is fallacious and ridiculous. State practices have denounced similar claims made by Indian colonial administration.

8.06. *The unity and territorial integrity as well as sovereignty of independent Manipur state has been impaired and terminated by the illegal Indian annexation of Manipur on 15 October, 1949.* The Government of India can never plead the illegally annexed territory of Manipur as her territorial integrity in the same way as the British failed to defend her 50 colonies as her territorial integrity. The para. 6 of the UN GA Resolution 1514(XV) of 14 December, 1960 should be understood in the genuine historical context of Manipur. The UN and the government of India are under obligation to accept Manipur as

> "Non-self-governing territory" in the same way as East Timor has been accepted. The union government of India should transmit information about Manipur to the UN under article 73(e) of the Charter. No judicious member of the UN should discriminate Manipur against East Timor.

IX. AGGRESSION

9.01. The captivity of Manipur Maharajah at Shillong on 18 September, 1949 by the Security forces of India and the Indian military intrusion in the soil of Manipur state with the active connivance of the fifth columnists and covert subversives, planted by the Government of India deep in the Manipur administration constitute Indian *aggression* in Manipur. At present, nearly every hill-top in the hilly state of Manipur has been occupied by battle-ready Indian army.

9.02. All the available documents and records give eloquent testimony to the parameters of Indian aggression in Manipur. On 19 April, 1947, Nehru sent threatening ultimatum to states. By an agreement reached on 2 July, 1947, Indian agency had been allowed to stay in Manipur. On 5 July, 1947, Hindu dictator M.K. Gandhi allegedly a pacifist communicated to Lord Mountbatten that state should not be given independence. Indian agent Akbar Hydari had abolished dominion agency in Manipur on 22 August, 1948. On 14 April, 1949, the colonial government of India asked the Manipur king to transfer all powers to an Indian Dewan under immense pressure and coercion; and the king was forced to appoint on 16 April, 1949 one Indian colonial Major General Amar Singh as Dewan of Manipur. Assam Governor Shri Prakasa sent a memo. on 25 June, 1949 that India de-recognised the Manipur State Council and elected Manipur Assembly (*read Parliament of Manipur*). All the political institutions and municipal administration had been subverted by India's Assam Governor Shri Prakasa who also initiated the covert Indian aggression in Manipur.

9.03. After the covert *aggression* had been triggered off by the colonial Governor of Assam, Shri Prakasa in Manipur, the second stage of his *aggression* is use of Indian security forces to keep Manipur king in captivity at Shillong by inviting him for professedly harmless negotiation. The Indians in their 2 millennia history had perfected the state-of-the-art treachery of inviting kings and annexing their territory and even their most respected theocratic leader M.K. Gandhi stood for conquest of states. (Read Arthasastra of Kautilya for these tactics). *On 18 September, 1949, Indian administration used force*[24] *to keep Manipur king as captive.* The private Secretary of the king wrote on the same day to withdraw the aggressive Indian forces, but they refused. The colonial government classifies the military details.

9.04. The United Nations should invite all the Government of India's records concerning Indian aggression in Manipur for the period 1947-1949 and can easily determine the facts in no time.

9.05. Manipur in 1949 had no obligations under the UN Charter, but the Indian Dominion, being a member of the UN since 1945 has Charter obligations not to use force against Manipur and also to honour the territorial integrity of independent Manipur. Article 2(4) of the Charter determines this responsibility:

> "All Members shall refrain in their international relations from the threat or use of force against the territorial integrity or political independence of any state, or in any manner inconsistent with the purposes of the United Nations."

9.06. The colonial government of India has further violated article 1 of the UN Charter by committing *aggression* and breach of peace. The *national liberation movement* is exercising its right to self-defence and self-preservation, without any prejudice to the genuine integrity of India.

9.07. The UN General Assembly in its Resolution 3314(1974) defines *aggression* in article 1: "Aggression is the use of armed force by a state (*read India here*) against the sovereignty, territorial integrity or political independence of another state, or in any other manner inconsistent with the Charter of the United Nations." Further, *Indian military occupation* and *annexation* of Manipur by use of Indian forces constitutes *aggression* under article 3 of the Resolution 3314(1974), regardless of declaration of war.

9.08. The UN GA Resolutions 2625(XXV), 1970 and 2734(1970) provide that no territorial acquisition resulting from the threat or use of force shall be recognised as legal. *Hence, India's military occupation of Manipur since 1949 till date is illegal and creates no legitimate claims of India over the sovereignty of Manipur.*

X. ILLEGAL ANNEXATION

10.01. As stated above in the context of *aggression*, Indian *annexation* of Manipur is illegal, null and void and unenforceable, notwithstanding the ongoing colonial occupation. (Please see para. 5.07 *supra*). The ICJ evolved the principle of non-annexation in South-West Africa case (1950, ICJ Reports, p. 132).

10.02. In the event of integrating Manipur to India, the freely expressed wishes of the people of Manipur should have been ascertained either by holding a referendum or plebiscite at the time of *annexation*. That did not happen at all in 1949 and the right of the Manipur people to *self-determination* had not been exercised in 1949 or, thereafter. This right has not been extinguished.

10.03. The principle IX of the UN GA Resolution 1514(XV) of 1960 provides that:

(a) The integrating territory should have an advanced stage of self-government with free political institutions, so that its peoples would have the capacity to make a responsible choice through informed and democratic processes.

(b) The integration should be the result of the freely expressed wishes of the Territory's peoples acting with full knowledge of the change in their status, their wishes having been expressed through informed and democratic processes impartially conducted and based on universal adult suffrage. The United Nations could, when it deems it necessary, supervise these processes.

10.04. Manipur did not have an advanced stage of self-government and the "freely expressed wishes" of the people of Manipur had not been ascertained by the colonial government of India at the time of *annexation. Therefore, Indian annexation lacked legality*. (Annexure No. XIII).

10.05. The colonial government of India and their advocates would occasionally trace historical argument by advancing a fallacious statement that Manipur while remaining under British paramountcy till 1947 had certain historical nexus with British the UN General Assembly resolutions and resolutions of the Security Council since 1975. The UN and De-colonisation Committee have to apply the same standard to East Timor and Manipur on equal terms.

10.06. In 1976-77, the General Assembly of the United Nations by its Resolutions 31/53 and 32/34 rejected the Indonesian *annexation* of East Timor. The UN Security Council by Resolutions 384 (1975) and 389 (1976) while demanding the respect for the *territorial integrity* of East Timor categorically affirmed the right of the East Timorese to *self-determination*. Of late, the Special Committee on De-colonisation at its 1474th to 1477th meetings on 16 and 17 June, 1997 re-affirmed the earlier UN positions. The same principle is applicable in the case of *Indian annexation* of independent Manipur. The Security Council by its Resolutions 660-678 (1991) had rendered Iraqi *annexation* of Kuwait null and void. The same norms is applicable to Manipur.

XI. POST-OCCUPATION GROSS HUMAN RIGHTS VIOLATIONS AND HUMANITARIAN LAW

11.01. During India's repressive, colonial regime in Manipur, human rights violations have been massive, colossal, brutally de-humanizing and absolutely barbarian[25]. Indian military occupation, compounded by the invocation of the world's most barbaric laws including the *Armed Forces (Special) Powers Act, 1958* for half a century in both the hills and plains of Manipur and shielding the entire genocidal progroms from the glaze of independent international media by prohibiting any foreigner to step into Manipur under the *Restrictive Areas Permit Act* without the closest scrutiny of the Home Ministry of India, resulted to unprecedented state terrorism, repression and barbaric human rights violations. Ironically, execution of five Catholics in Northern Ireland is a news—even in the headlines of the global media, but daily execution by the state of India, of several dozens of civilians or freedom fighters in Manipur has not been accepted as newsworthy. Manipur had been shielded like Gulag Archipelago from the outside world for half a century and therefore, the United Nations took action in favour of 8 lakh Christian East Timorese since 1975 but closed its eyes to 20 lakh non-Christian Manipuris' cause since 1949 till today. Even the super-powers had maintained double standards.

11.02. The Government of India and her defence forces which are under obligations after government of India's *accession* to the Four Geneva Conventions, 1949 and subsequent enactment of the Geneva Conventions Act, 1961 by the Indian Parliament, to fully comply with the humanitarian laws, had consistently breached the humanitarian laws by way of committing relentless state repression on the unarmed civilians of Manipur and captured combatants or *horse de combat* of the *Manipur National Liberation Movement*. Even the ICRC has not been allowed to visit Manipur, since the Home Ministry refused to lid off the Auschwitz iron curtain of Manipur. No force-commander nor even a single military General has ever been punished for the breach of the Geneva Conventions, 1949 or, the Geneva Conventions Act, 1961 passed by the Indian Parliament. No other testimony could be more appropriate than citing the Government of India's refusal to sign, accede and ratify the two "Protocols Additional to the Geneva Conventions of 12 August 1947", 1977[26] and the Rome International Criminal Court (ICC) treaty, July 17, 1998. The leaders and cabinet of the *Gandhian state of India, who led the Non-Aligned Movement and the global de-colonisation Movement had been deliberately committing "war crimes", "crimes against Humanity", "Genocide", and "Aggression" in Manipur for half a century,* while the international community chose to remain a silent spectator for half a century.

11.03. From the year 1978, the People's Liberation Army had relentlessly fought and resisted against the occupation Indian army without any rest in order to defend the Manipur People against Indian *colonialism* and Indian military occupation. Several hundreds of PLA freedom fighters sacrificed their lives for the sake of their motherland. Nearly every top, middle-ranking PLA leader died or killed while fighting the occupation army in quick succession, thereby pushing forward the *national liberation* movement, which is more extensive and mass-based after more than two decades of unremitting armed resistance to the occupation forces and regime.

11.04. Article 1(4) of the First Additional Protocol, 1977 provides legal protection to peoples, who are "fighting against colonial Domination and alien occupation and against racist regimes in the exercise of their right to self-determination", but the occupation army of India has been ceaselessly torturing by using 3rd degree methods, arrested POW guerillas of the *National Liberation Movement.* The RPF—*Revolutionary People's Front of Manipur and its military wing PLA—People's Liberation Army has signed common article 3 of the Four Geneva Conventions in 1997* and has been strictly complying with the International Humanitarian Laws, but the Indian occupation forces[27], their mercenaries who love to wear civilian dresses while committing heinous crimes[28] against mankind in the midst of the civilian populace have routinely committed grave breach of the Geneva Conventions. These common criminals are awarded and rewarded profusely and ostentatiously by the President of India (*read Union Cabinet*) in public annually for committing heinous crimes against mankind in Manipur. The 10 channels of the official television—DD, 3000 Indian racialist dailies, 300 Radio stations daily project Manipuri freedom fighters as criminals and terrorists. This hatred campaign helps the genocide with impunity.

11.05. The anti-*National Liberation Movement* networks of the colonial government has degraded the lives of 30,000 Manipuri youths and students into drug-addicts and HIV/AIDS patients in order to distract them from joining the *National Liberation Movements*. It is noted by the government that a Cabinet Minister late Mr. Ngurdingleng has been leading the Heroin-HIV/AIDS trade some years back, till he was executed in a church in southern part of Manipur. Dailies publish news of several army personnels, and police-men, who have been caught red-handed with narcotic drugs while transporting them for trade. Nearly all of them have been released scot-free, if not rewarded with national medals and honours. No massive Heroin trade could have been possible in the thick of army, mercenaries and spies without the connivance of the colonial government.

11.06. The United Nations and its appropriate agencies, the ICRC, NAM, ASEAN, SAARC, among others, refrained from making a close watch on monitoring and deterring the de-humanizing human rights violations, committed by the Indian state terrorism and the occupation Indian army. Consequently, peace and stability in this part of the world have been a permanent casualty and would remain so until the colonial army is withdrawn as it has been done in Kosovo.

XII. PETITION

12.01. The Revolutionary People's Front (RPF) wholeheartedly acclaims the UN action in the de-colonisation process and the UN's efforts to eradicate colonialism by 2000 AD. The Revolutionary People's Front (RPF), therefore, draws your kind immediate attention to the above-mentioned facts and the evidence of *colonialism*, thrust upon the people of Manipur by the Indian colonial power and its occupation forces by despatching a *"VISITING MISSION"* to Manipur on a war-footing and for hearing the *National Liberation Movement* in the appropriate forums of the UN De-colonisation Committee and the Fourth Committee, among others, of the UN General Assembly.

12.02. The Revolutionary People's Front (RPF) holds the opinion that the UN's endeavour to eradicate *colonialism* shall be materially achieved only after de-colonising proximity or, neighbourhood *colonialism* in Asia-Pacific, beyond the scope of the classical European Salt-water *colonialism*. In this sacred UN Mission, the UN cannot leave the world half-decolonised and half-recolonised. Indonesia and India, which are considered to be world-leaders in neutrality movement or, in some contexts, had non-self-governing territories or, colonies like East Timor in Indonesia and Manipur in post-1949 India.

12.03. The Revolutionary People's Front (RPF) strongly urges upon the UN Secretary-General, UN agencies, Fourth Committee of the UN GA and the "open-ended Bureau" of the UN Special

Committee on De-colonisation to kindly enlist "Manipur" in the list of NON-SELF-GOVERNING TERRITORIES of the UN and initiate all necessary action *towards eradicating Indian colonialism and hostile military occupation of Manipur.*

12.04. The Revolutionary People's Front (RPF) beseechs and petitions all the appropriate UN authorities to allow the indigenous Manipur people to exercise their inalienable *right to self-determination, independence and sovereignty.*

Signatories

sd/-
Irengbam Chaoren
President

sd/-
Manohar Mayum Ngouba
Vice-President

sd/-
Sanasam Gunen
Secretary-General

sd/-
Yangambam Guni
Secretary, External Affairs

sd/-
Wangkhem Ibohal
Secretary, Finance

sd/-
Gurumayum Jame
Executive Committee Member

sd/-
Ahanthem Mema
Executive Committee Member

Dated this 21st Day of September 1999

FOOTNOTES

Acknowledgements and References

1. UN General Assembly A/53/23 (Part I), 53rd Session 24 September 1998 (English) para. 83, 89, p. 16. See GA A/53/23 (Part II), 17 December 1998, p. 3 recommendations.
2. For historical documents and Treaties, see N. Sanajaoba, Manipur Treaties and Documents (1110-1971 AD), Vol. I, 1996, Mittal Publications, New Delhi. All the secret documents regarding annexation of Manipur are found in the National Archives, New Delhi. Foreign Ministry has classified them as top secret.
3. See N. Sanajaoba, ed, Manipur Past and Present, Volume I, II, III, IV (up), Mittal Publications, New Delhi. The independent political history of Manipur has been recorded in the Royal Chronicle—"Cheitharol Kumbaba", Manipuri Sahitya Parishad, 1991 (33 AD to 1950s).

See also Gangmumei Kabui, *History of Manipur, 1991*, Vol-I (early period).

Note: All the British reports corroborate the independent history of Manipur viz., Dr. R. Brown, P.R. Pemberton, Johnstone, Dun, W. McCulloh, T.C. Hodson, G.H. Damant, E.A. Gail, Mrs. E. Grimwood, Sir W.W. Hunter, Sir C. Lyall. These British reports are easily available in any of the library of the world.

4. The Tangkhul Naga folk-tradition accepts this ethnogenesis. See, *Manipur Past and Present*, Volume III, Introduction.
5. September 14, 1762 Agreement and 1773 Protocol, Manipur Past and Present, Volume I, 1988.
6. Official letter of Secretary Durand, 1891, See *Manipur Past and Present*, Volume I, 1988.

6a. See N. Sanajaoba, Why India can not disturb Manipur Boundary of 1947? UTI POSSEDETIS JURIS, in the Souvenir of the All Manipur Students' Union (AMSU), pp. 19-25, 19 July 1999, Imphal.

7. Consensus of Manipur Seminar on the Instrument of Accession held on 13 January, 1996 in Imphal City by MSSA, MURC, FINS, and CLK at the State level.
8. Countdown—Annexation of Manipur, in Professor N. Sanajaoba, Manipur Puwaari Kunshuba Chahicha, 1997, Imphal, pp. 160-164.
9. Telegram in Appendix II-A, N. Sanajaoba, *Manipur Past and Present*, Volume I, 1988, p. 354.
10. Article 52 of Vienna Convention on the Law of Treaties, 1969 provides: "A treaty is void if its conclusion has been procured by the threat or use of force in violation of the principles of international law embodied in the Charter of the United Nations". The Manipur Merger Agreement, 1949 is therefore void.
11. See articles on Insurgency by Professor Gangmumei Kabui, Professor N. Joykumar, Professor Lal Dena, History Department, Manipur University and also Professor N. Sanajaoba, "Genesis of Insurgency" in *Manipur Past and Present*, Volume I, 1988.

    cf. Professor Emeritus V.V. Rao, Gauhati University, a Century of Politics, Manipur, Chapter on Insurgency (now banned), 1990—The leftists in Manipur launched armed struggle to re-establish a sovereign independent Manipur, after Indian annexation in 1949.

    Ph. Tarapot, Insurgency in the North-East, 1993.
12. Soyam Chattradhari, Hijam Irabot, 1996, Imphal.
13. In March, 1999 - the RPF (PLA), the UNLF and the PREPAK of Manipur have been consolidated under the banner of 'MPLF'—Manipur People's Liberation Front. The 'MPLF' extensively continues the armed resistance against the Indian colonial army. They concertedly

resist the occupation force of India. The RPF has signed the Common article 3 to the Four Geneva Conventions, 1949, while strictly complying with the Laws of Armed Conflict under the International Humanitarian Law, whereas the Indian Army Generals routinely breach the Geneva Conventions by liquidating and abducting unarmed civilian populace and no - Army General has been prosecuted under the Geneva Conventions Act, 1961, enacted by Colonial Indian Parliament. They start throwing bombs recurrently on the Manipuris since early 1998—see local dailies.

14. See proceedings of UN Human Rights Committee Session in 1991 and July 1997 on Human Rights Violations, Amnesty International Reports on India for decades.
15. See Manusmriti, Penguin Publication for details and Arthasastra, Penguin, 1992.
15a. Professor H. Nabakishore, Manipur University, Economy, in Eikhoigi Yaol (Manipuri Monthly), June 1999, pp. 6-10;
16. N. Sanajaoba, Manipur Past and Present, Volume I, 1988, op. up.
17. See supra f.n. 10.
18. India's Third Periodic Report to the UN Human Rights Committee, CCPR/C/76/Add. 6, 17 June 1996 India 1/29 November, 1995.
19. *Ibid.* para. 29.

    The National Liberation Movement in Manipur has demanded right to self-determination. See Revolutionary People's Front (RPF), a Brief Account for Demanding Sovereignty of Manipur, 25 February, 1995 and also RPF Memorandum Submitted to the UN De-colonisation Committee, Dated 11 December 1996 - 72 pages.
20. Constitution of India, First Schedule, Serial 19.
21. *Ibid.* Article 1.
22. See N. Sanajaoba, "Why India cannot disturb Manipur boundary of 1947", in the Souvenir of the All Manipur Students' Union (AMSU), p. 19-25, 19 July 1999, Imphal, see also his book Manipur Puwaari, NRC, Imphal, 1997, pp. 36-55 and Dr. L. Chandramani Singh, The Boundaries of Manipur, PANMYL, 7 May, 1970, pp. 1-63, Imphal.
23. See f.n. 1 supra.
24. ICJ Advisory opinion on Western Sahara (1975) ICJ, 12.
25. See, COHR, Imphal, (i) Right to Life, 13 February, 1997 (ii) Alternative Report to 3rd India's Periodic Report, 1997, (iii) The Killings Continued, January 14, 1998,

    Also Where Peace-Keepers Declare War, New Delhi, 1997 (Full report of Indian army's massive liquidation of thousands of lives); SAHRDC Report, 1997; and Amnesty International reports till 1999 on Manipur and North-Eastern states. International media black out these large-scale violations to please Indian rulers and win them towards Western strategic goals.

26. ICRC, Protocols additional to the Geneva Conventions, 1977.
27. The Chief Secretary of Manipur, by his order dated 7 June, 1999 invokes Unlawful Activities (Prevention) Act, 1987 in these words: "Whereas there has been unprecedented increase in the commission of crimes, such as killings of police, military and paramilitary personnel by insurgent outfits (read National Liberation Movements) and also violations of the provisions of the Unlawful Activities (Preventions), 1987 together with SECESSIONIST ACTIVITIES by unlawful elements in the entire areas of the State of Manipur".

    "Now, therefore in exercise of the Power Conferred by Section 3 of the Armed Forces (Special) Powers Act, 1958, the Governor of Manipur (read Colonial Governor from India) hereby declares the entire areas of the State of Manipur to be disturbed area for a period of 6 (six) months with effect from 1.6.1999".

    "SCHEDULE: Whole of the entire Areas of the State of Manipur".

    Note: A] Indian armed forces empowered by licence to kill any Manipuri to death *vide* Section 4 of the 1958 Act at pleasure and the colonial executioner is given impunity under Section 6 of the same Act. For decades, the colonial army in uniform or civilian dress have been liquidating alien Manipuris with complete impunity.

    B] The Supreme Court of India has upheld this black colonial Law as excellent law on 27 November, 1997.

    C] The colonial Governor of India at present is Sri. Srivastava, a high official of the India's IB Intelligence Bureau comparable to CIA or, Mossad or, FBI of India. Earlier, the Governor of Manipur was a Major General of the Indian army.
28. The National Human Rights Commission and the State Human Rights Commission have no jurisdiction over crimes, committed by colonial security forces. See Sec. 19 of the Protection of Human Rights Act, 1993-1994. The Commonwealth Human Rights Initiative denounced this section in August, 1998.

Index